THE POWER

of

GEOGRAPHY

Ten Maps That Reveal the
Future of Our World

Tim Marshall

SCRIBNER

New York   London   Toronto   Sydney   New Delhi

Scribner
An Imprint of Simon & Schuster, Inc.
1230 Avenue of the Americas
New York, NY 10020

First Scribner hardcover edition November 2021

SCRIBNER and design are registered trademarks of The Gale Group, Inc., used under license by Simon & Schuster, Inc., the publisher of this work.

For information about special discounts for bulk purchases, please contact Simon & Schuster Special Sales at 1-866-506-1949 or business@simonandschuster.com.

The Simon & Schuster Speakers Bureau can bring authors to your live event. For more information or to book an event, contact the Simon & Schuster Speakers Bureau at 1-866-248-3049 or visit our website at www.simonspeakers.com.

Interior design by Wendy Blum

Manufactured in the United States of America

1   3   5   7   9   10   8   6   4   2

Library of Congress Cataloging-in-Publication Data has been applied for.

ISBN 978-1-9821-7862-8
ISBN 978-1-9821-7864-2 (ebook)

Sources for maps: p. 13: Australian Bureau of Statistics; p. 52: Geopolitical Futures; p. 128: BBC / UNCHR; p. 143: Encyclopedia Britannica; p. 152: Geopolitcal Futures / BAU DEGS; p. 173: acleddata.com; p. 249: U.S. Army Acquisitions Support Center; p. 251: Wikipedia.

Maps: JP Map Graphics Ltd

To the youth of Generation Covid who did their bit.
Now is your time!

CONTENTS

INTRODUCTION

The falcon cannot hear the falconer;
Things fall apart; the centre cannot hold

—William Butler Yeats, "The Second Coming"

In the Middle East, the vast fortress of Iran and its nemesis, Saudi Arabia, face off across the Persian Gulf. South of the Pacific, Australia finds itself caught between the two most powerful nations of our time: the United States of America and China. In the Mediterranean, Greece and Turkey are in a contest that has roots going back to antiquity but could flare into violence tomorrow.

Welcome to the 2020s. The Cold War era, in which the US and the Soviet Union dominated the entire world, is becoming a distant memory. We are entering a new age of great-power rivalry in which numerous actors, even minor players, are jostling to take center stage. The geopolitical drama is even spilling out of our earthly realm, as countries stake their claims above our atmosphere, to the Moon and beyond.

When what was the established order for several generations turns out to be temporary, it is easy to become anxious. But it has happened before, it is happening now, and it will happen again. For some time we have been moving toward a "multipolar" world. Following the Second World War, we saw a new order: a bipolar era with an American-led capitalist system on one side, and on the other the Communist system operated by what was in effect the Russian Empire and China. This lasted anything from about fifty to eighty years, depending on where you draw your lines. In the 1990s we saw what some analysts call the "unipolar" decade, when American power went almost completely unchallenged. But it is clear that we are now moving back to what was the norm for most of human history—an age of multiple-power rivalries.

It's hard to pin down when this began to happen; there is no single event that sparked a change. But there are moments when you catch a glimpse of

1

something, and the opaque world of international politics becomes clearer. I had one such experience on a humid summer's night in 1999 in Pristina, the ramshackle capital of Kosovo. The breakup of Yugoslavia in 1991 had led to years of war and bloodshed. Now, NATO's planes had bombed the Serbian forces out of Kosovo and its ground troops were waiting to enter the province from the south. During the day we heard rumors that a Russian military column had set off from Bosnia to make sure Russia maintained its traditional influence in Serbian affairs.

For a decade the Russian bear had been out of the game, impoverished, uncertain, and a shadow of its former self. It had watched haplessly as NATO "advanced" on its western borders, as time and again the peoples of the nations it had subjugated voted in governments committed to joining NATO and/or the European Union; and in Latin America and the Middle East its influence had waned. In 1999 Moscow had reached a decision vis-à-vis the Western powers—this far and no farther. Kosovo was a line in the sand. President Boris Yeltsin ordered the Russian column to intervene (although it's thought the upcoming hard-line nationalist politician Vladimir Putin had a role in the decision).

I was in Pristina as the Russian armored column rumbled down the main street in the early hours of the morning, heading for Kosovo's airport on the outskirts of town. I'm told President Bill Clinton heard of their arrival, ahead of NATO's troops, via the TV report I filed, "The Russians Rolled into Town, and Back onto the World Stage." It was hardly Pulitzer Prize material, but as a first draft of history it did the job. The Russians had staked their claim to play a role in the biggest event of the year and announced that the tide of history, which had been running against them, would now be challenged. In the late 1990s the US was apparently unrivaled, the West seemingly triumphant in global affairs. But the pushback had started. Russia was no longer the fearsome power it had once been—now it was one among many—but the Russians would fight to assert themselves where they could. They would go on to prove it in Georgia, Ukraine, Syria, and elsewhere.

Four years later I was in the Iraqi city of Karbala, one of the most holy places in Shia Islam. Saddam Hussein had been overthrown by the American- and British-led coalition, but the insurgency was getting under way. Under Saddam (a Sunni Muslim), many of the Shia ways of worship had been banned, including ritual self-flagellation. On a scorching-hot day I watched as more than a million Shia poured into Karbala from across the country. Many of the men were whipping their backs and cutting their foreheads until their whole bodies were covered in blood, which dripped down onto the streets, turning the dust red. I knew that across the border to the east, Iran, the major Shia power, would now play every trick in the book to help engineer a Shia-dominated Iraqi government and use it to project Tehran's power with even greater force westward across the Middle East, connecting to Iran's allies in Syria and Lebanon. Geography and politics made it almost inevitable. My take that day was along the lines of "This looks religious, but it's also political, and the waves from this fervor will ripple out as far as the Mediterranean." The political balance had changed, and the increasing reach of Iranian power would challenge US dominance in the region. Karbala provided the backdrop to begin to paint the picture. Sadly, one color would dominate—blood-red.

These were just two seminal moments that helped to shape the complicated world in which we find ourselves, as myriad forces push, pull, and sometimes clash in what in previous times was called "the great game." Both gave me a glimpse of the direction in which we were headed. It started to become even clearer as events unfolded in Egypt, Libya, and Syria in the 2010s. Egyptian president Hosni Mubarak was deposed in a coup d'état by the military using violent street theater to hide their hand; in Libya, Colonel Muammar Qaddafi was overthrown and then murdered; and in Syria, President Bashar al-Assad hung on by his fingertips until the Russians and Iranians saved him. In all three cases the Americans signaled they would not save the dictators they had done business with for decades. The US slowly withdrew from the international scene during the eight years of the Obama presidency, a move continued under Donald Trump for four years. Meanwhile, other countries such as India, China, and Brazil began to emerge as new world powers, with rapidly growing economies, looking to expand their own global influence.

Many people dislike the idea that America played the role of "world policeman" in the post–Second World War era. You can make a case for both the positives and negatives of its actions. But, either way, in the absence of a policeman, various factions will seek to police their own neighborhood. If you get competing factions, the risk of instability increases.

Empires rise, and they fall. Alliances are forged, and then they crumble. The post–Napoleonic Wars settlement in Europe lasted about sixty years; the

Thousand-Year Reich lasted for just over a decade. It is impossible to know precisely how the balance of power will shift during the coming years. There are undoubtedly economic and geopolitical giants that continue to have huge sway in global affairs: the US and China, of course, as well as Russia, the collective nations of Europe in the EU, the fast-growing economic power of India. But the smaller nations matter too. Geopolitics involves alliances, and with the world order currently in a state of flux, this is a time when the big powers need small powers on their side as well as vice versa. It gives these countries, such as Turkey, Saudi Arabia, and the United Kingdom, an opportunity to strategically position themselves for future power. For the moment, the kaleidoscope is still being shaken and the pieces have not yet settled.

It is likely that by the end of the century we will again be in a bipolar era, this time between China and the US. It will not be the same as the previous one, nor will it be the same "Cold War," but as shorthand terms, they are useful to frame where we are heading.

In this new version, the term "Western" will be outdated. This time the competition will be between an American-led informal coalition of industrialized democracies and a loose alliance of authoritarian states dominated by China. It was not a coincidence that when the UK hosted the G7 summit in the summer of 2021 it invited South Korea, India, and Australia to attend. Together the Democratic 10 populations compose 85 percent of people living in advanced democracies. The invitations dovetailed with the slowly emerging Biden Doctrine, which hopes to reenergize democracy and offer a global economic alternative to China's Belt and Road Initiative.

In 2015, I wrote a book called *Prisoners of Geography*, in which I aimed to show how geography affects global politics and shapes the decisions that nations and their leaders are able to make. I wrote about the geopolitics of Russia; China; the US; Europe; the Middle East; Africa; India and Pakistan; Japan and Korea; Latin America; and the Arctic. I wanted to focus on the biggest players, the great geopolitical blocs or regions, to give a global overview. But there is more to say. Although the US remains the only country capable of projecting serious naval power into two oceans simultaneously, the Himalayas still separate India and China, and Russia is still vulnerable in the flatlands to its west, new geopolitical realities are emerging all the time, and there are other players worthy of our attention, with the power to shape our future.

INTRODUCTION

Like *Prisoners of Geography*, *The Power of Geography* looks at mountains, rivers, seas, and concrete to understand geopolitical realities. Geography is a key factor shaping what humanity can and cannot do. Yes, politicians are important, but geography is more so. The choices people make, now and in the future, are never separate from their physical context. The starting point of any country's story is its location in relation to neighbors, sea routes, and natural resources. Live on a windswept island on the periphery of the Atlantic Ocean? You're well placed to harness wind and waves. Live in a country where the sun shines 365 days a year? Solar panels are the way ahead. Live in a region where cobalt is mined? That could be a blessing and a curse.

There remains among some people a disdain for this starting point as it is deemed deterministic. There has been talk of a "flat world" in which financial transactions and communications through cyberspace have collapsed distance, and landscape has become meaningless. However, that is a world inhabited only by a tiny fraction of people who may well speak via videoconference, and then fly over mountains and seas to speak in person; but it is not the experience of most of the other 8 billion people on Earth. Egyptian farmers still rely on Ethiopia for water. The mountains to the north of Athens still hinder its trade with Europe. Geography is not fate—humans get a vote in what happens—but it matters.

There are many factors that have contributed to what will be an uncertain and divided decade as we progress toward a new era. Globalization, antiglobalization, Covid-19, technology, and climate change have all had an impact, and all feature in this book. *The Power of Geography* looks at some of the events and conflicts that have emerged in the twenty-first century with the potential for far-reaching consequences in a multipolar world.

Iran, for example, is shaping the future of the Middle East. A pariah state with a nuclear agenda, it must keep its Shia "corridor" to the Mediterranean open via Baghdad, Damascus, and Beirut to maintain influence. Its regional rival Saudi Arabia, a country built on oil and sand, has always counted America as an ally. But as demand for oil declines and the US becomes more energy independent, its interest in the Middle East will slowly wane.

Elsewhere it is not oil but water that is causing turmoil. As the so-called water tower of Africa, Ethiopia holds a crucial advantage over its neighbors, particularly Egypt. This is one of the key sites for potential "water wars" this century, but also shows the power of technology as Ethiopia uses hydroelectricity to change its fortunes.

That is not an option in many parts of Africa, such as the Sahel, the vast scrubland at the southern edge of the Sahara, a war-torn region that straddles ancient geographical and cultural divisions, and where in parts Al-Qaeda and ISIS now hold sway. Many people will flee, some heading north toward Europe. What is already a major humanitarian crisis may worsen.

As the gateway to Europe, Greece is one of the first countries to feel the effects of new waves of migration. Its geography has also placed it at the heart of one of the geopolitical flashpoints of the coming years: the eastern Mediterranean, where newly discovered gas fields are bringing this EU member to the brink of conflict with an increasingly aggressive Turkey. But while Turkey is flexing its muscles in the eastern Med, it has much wider ambitions. Its "neo-Ottoman" agenda derives from its imperial history and position at the crossroads of east and west. Turkey aims to fulfill its ambition to emerge as a major global power.

Another nation that lost its empire, the UK, a group of chilly islands at the western end of the north European plain, is still looking for its role. After Brexit, it may find one as a middle-ranking European power forging political and economic ties around the world. But the challenges it faces are internal as well as external, as it grapples with the prospect of an independent Scotland.

To the south, Spain, one of Europe's oldest nations, also faces the threat of breakup from regional nationalism. The EU cannot offer support to the Catalonian independence struggle; but rejection of a fledgling state could leave the door open to Russian and Chinese influence within Europe. Spain's struggles epitomize the fragility of some nation-states, and of supranational alliances, in the twenty-first century.

However, perhaps the most fascinating development of current times is that our geopolitical power struggles are now breaking free of our earthly restraints and being projected into space. Who owns space? How do you decide? There's never really a "final frontier," but this is as close as it gets, and frontiers tend to be wild, lawless places. Above a certain height there's no sovereign territory; if I want to place my laser-armed satellite directly over your country, by what law do you say I can't? With multiple countries racing to be the preeminent power in space, and private companies entering the fray, the stage is set for a dangerous cutting-edge arms race, unless we can learn from past mistakes and accept the many benefits of international cooperation.

But we begin down on Earth, in a place that for centuries was considered isolated and unknown, but now, finding itself between China and the US with the power to shape events in the Indo-Pacific region, it is a key player in our story: the island continent, Australia.

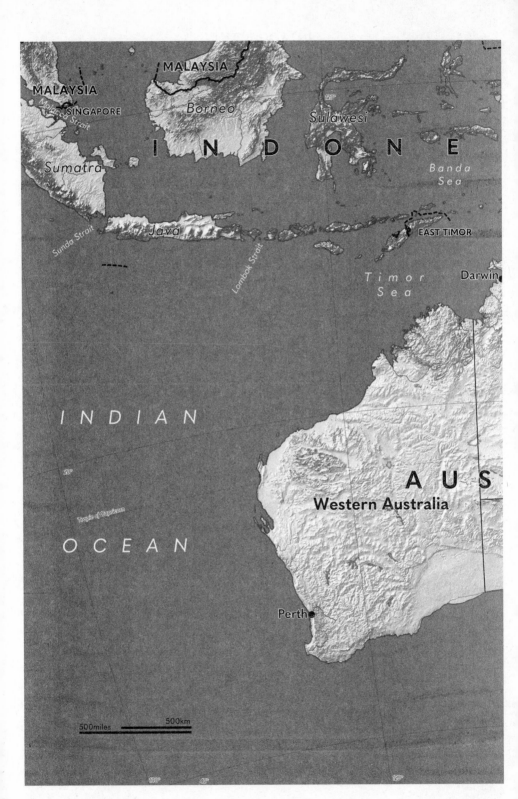

PACIFIC OCEAN
Equator
SIA
New Guinea
PAPUA NEW GUINEA
Arafura Sea
SOLOMON ISLANDS
Coral Sea
Northern Territory
Queensland
TRALIA
South Australia
Brisbane
New South Wales
Sydney
Adelaide
Australian Capital Territory
CANBERRA
Victoria
Melbourne
Tasman Sea
Tasmania

AUSTRALIA

Play it tough, all the way. Grind them into the dust.

—Don Bradman, cricketer

Australia was in the middle of nowhere, became a very big somewhere, and is now center stage. How did that happen?

The land "down under" is an island, but an island like no other. It's massive—so massive that it's also a continent encompassing lush subtropical rain forest, baking-hot desert, rolling savannah, and snow-covered mountains. Driving from Brisbane to Perth you cross one country, but a similar distance would be from London to Beirut via France, Belgium, Germany, Austria, Hungary, Serbia, Bulgaria, Turkey, and Syria.

As for being in the middle of nowhere, well, from Brisbane looking northeast across the Pacific Ocean it is 7,000 miles to the United States, and South America is due east 7,500 miles distant; west from Perth across the Indian Ocean it's 5,000 miles to Africa. Even Australia's "neighbor," New Zealand, is 2,600 miles to the southeast and from there down to Antarctica is another 3,000 miles of water. Only when we look north do we see Australia's true position in a geopolitical sense. There it sits, a territorially huge, Western-oriented, advanced democracy, and there above it is the world's most economically and militarily powerful dictatorship—China. Put it all together and you see a national state/continent positioned right in the middle of the Indo-Pacific—the economic powerhouse of the twenty-first century.

The story begins when the British decided to deport their convicts, wanted them as far away as possible, and then wanted nothing to do with them. Where better than the bottom of the world, a place from which they could never return? They were locked up and the key was thrown away. And yet eventually, as the faraway world changed, the prison bars of geography were bent, and Australia found itself a player on the stage of global politics. For a long time it was one hell of a hellish journey.

In the quote at the start of this chapter, Don Bradman may have been referring to playing England at cricket but his words are rooted in an Australian psyche that has been forged by the country's geography. The popular concept of the egalitarian, straight-talking, no-nonsense, indomitable Aussie spirit may be a cliché, but it is also real. It has emerged from a vast, scorchingly hot land, much of which cannot be inhabited, out of which has sprung a flourishing modern society that has shifted from being virtually monocultural to one of the most multicultural in the world.

Now Australia looks around at its neighborhood and wonders what role it should play, and whom it should play it with.

When it comes to foreign policy and defense, a country's starting point is not what it intends to do but what it is capable of, and that is often limited by geography. Australia's size and location are both a strength and a weakness. They protect it from invasion but also held back its political development. They make it necessary to have extensive long-distance trade links, which in turn requires a strong navy to ensure the sea lanes are kept open. And Australia is isolated by distance from its key allies.

Australia became an island only about 35 million years ago, after it broke off from Antarctica and drifted northward. It is currently on a collision course with Indonesia, but inhabitants of both countries should not be too alarmed as it's moving at three inches a year and they have several hundred million years to brace for impact.

Comprising 3 million square miles, Australia is the world's sixth-largest country. The bulk of modern Australia consists of six states; the largest is Western Australia, which accounts for a third of the continent and is bigger than all of Western Europe. Then, in terms of size, come Queensland, South Australia, New South Wales, Victoria, and the island of Tasmania. There are two main territories, the Northern Territory and Australian Capital Territory, and numerous minor territories, including the Cocos Islands and Christmas Island.

Life in Australia presents many challenges. For starters, between becoming an island and the arrival of humans (about 60,000 years ago), there was ample time for the singularity of Australia's animal life to develop. Given that so much of it appears to want to bite, sting, peck, or poison you, it's a wonder that humans spread out across the whole continent within 30,000 years of showing up.

More challenging to avoid are the land and climate. Much of the terrain consists of vast, flat, arid plains, and only 6 percent of it is above 2,000 feet in elevation. As a continent it experiences extreme diversity in its climate and topography, from deserts to tropical forests to snowcapped mountains. But the majority of it is taken up by what is known as the Outback, covering about 70 percent of Australia, much of it uninhabitable. The great plains and deserts of the interior, where summer temperatures commonly reach 100°F and there is little water to be found, stretch out over vast distances with no relief and no one to come to your aid if you get into trouble.

In 1848 an attempt to cross the entire continent from east to west, begin-ning inland from Brisbane across to Perth, ended in failure when the expedition leader, Ludwig Leichhardt, and his team—a party of seven men, including two Aboriginal guides, fifty bullocks, twenty mules, seven horses, and a mountain of equipment—simply vanished. The great Outback holds many secrets, among them Leichhardt's fate. They are still looking for him to this day.

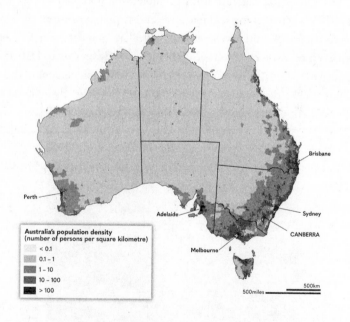

Much of the Australian Outback is uninhabitable; the majority of Australia's population is located in the southeast of the country along the coastline.

Over millennia this geography has dictated where human activity has taken place. While Aboriginals conducted the ritual walkabout in the Outback,

European settlers tended to cling to the shoreline, a practice continued today. There's a crescent-shaped belt of populated areas starting in Brisbane halfway up the east coast; it wraps itself around the coastline, running through Sydney, Canberra, Melbourne, and down to Adelaide on the south coast. Along the crescent heading west are the suburbs and satellite towns, which extend inland for about 250 miles before petering out once you are over the mountains and heading into the extreme remote regions. Right across on the west coast is Perth, and way up north is Darwin, but here also the populations are tied to the coastal areas. It's likely to stay that way.

A century ago, the founder of geography at the University of Sydney, Griffith Taylor, caused outrage when he argued that due to Australia's topography its population would be restricted to about 20 million people by the year 2000. He dared to state that the Australian desert was "almost useless" for permanent settlement, a sentiment considered unpatriotic. "Jeremiah!" howled the press, "Environmental determinism!" grumbled the politicians, who preferred an American "sea to shining sea" narrative of constant expansion. He was right; they were wrong. A hundred years on Australia's population is still only 26 million. Even now you can fly the 2,000 miles from Sydney up to Darwin (or all the way across to Perth) without seeing a town. Almost 50 percent of the people live in just three cities—Sydney, Melbourne, and Brisbane. By no coincidence, they are adjacent to the location of the Murray–Darling River Basin.

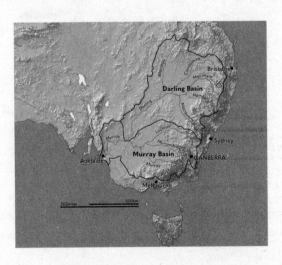

The Murray–Darling River Basin supported the early European settlements in southeast Australia.

Most of the country's rivers are seasonal in their flow, so water links were never a major part of its development. The annual discharge of all the rivers on the continent amounts to less than half of that just from the Yangtze in China. If we exclude Tasmania, the only Australian rivers that have a permanent flow are in the eastern and southwestern regions. The two biggest are the Murray River and its tributary the Darling River. Fed by melting snows in the Australian Alps, the Murray has enough volume to run uninterrupted for 1,600 miles to the southern coast. Parts of it are navigable and it is the jewel in the crown of the Murray–Darling Basin. However, shipping cannot enter from the sea, which limits the river's ability to move goods. It was used in the nineteenth century to support upriver trade, but even these smaller vessels had problems with the lack of rainfall, and some would become stuck upstream on dried-out tributaries. Nevertheless, the Murray–Darling system contains the fertile lands that have fed and watered generations of Australians. Without it the first settlers would barely have got off the beach.

It's worth contrasting the history of Australia with that of another colonial experiment—the US. America also grew from settlements on a fertile east coast and then pushed inland. But, once over the Appalachian Mountains, the fledgling nation expanded into the greatest river system in the world, situated in some of the most fertile land anywhere—the Mississippi River Basin. In Australia a similar-sized region contained next to nothing to sustain transport, farming, or permanent settlement, and was far more isolated from the international trading system than was America: it was 12,000 miles back to the UK, whereas the thirteen colonies that became the US were only 5,000 miles away from Europe.

It's a common misconception that Britain's Captain James Cook "discovered" the continent in 1770. Leaving to one side the problematic term "discovered," the first recorded landing was in 1606, when Willem Janszoon and the crew of the Dutch sailing ship *Duyfken* went ashore in northern Australia. Janszoon thought he was on the island of New Guinea and, after a hostile encounter with locals, soon departed. Several more European expeditions came and went, but no one bothered to explore inland.

By the time Cook showed up it was clear that the fabled *terra australis incognita* had been found. The term, meaning "unknown southern land," originates from the ruminations of the Greek mapmaker Claudius Ptolemy in about 150 CE. He reasoned that if the world was a sphere, and on the top of it was the land he knew of, it followed that to prevent it from toppling over there had to be land underneath. Some of this was spot-on. Australia is still thought of as down under in Europe.

Cook's maps were of course more up-to-date than those of Ptolemy. He became the first European to make land on the eastern coast. He went ashore in Botany Bay, now part of Sydney, and stayed for seven days. At the time his crew's first encounters with the people who lived there must have seemed like minor incidents; in hindsight they were momentous and a harbinger of what would follow. Writing in his *Journal of the Right Hon. Sir Joseph Banks During Captain Cook's First Voyage in HMS* Endeavour *in 1768–71*, Cook's chief scientific officer ruminated on this clash of civilizations and the differences between them: "Thus live these, I had almost said happy, people, content with little, nay almost nothing; far enough removed from the anxieties attending upon riches, or even the possession of what we Europeans call necessaries. . . . From them appear how small are the real wants of human nature, which we Europeans have increased to an excess which would certainly appear incredible to these people could they be told it."

This encounter was not enough to prevent Banks from later recommending that Botany Bay should be the location for Britain to establish a penal colony, the idea being both to alleviate appalling prison overcrowding in the UK and to send the felons to a place from which they might never return. The strategic implications of planting the British flag 12,000 miles from the center of the empire were also considered.

Ships were readied, convicts assembled, supplies loaded, and the so-called First Fleet set sail from Portsmouth, England, on May 13, 1787, reaching Botany Bay on January 24, 1788. The eleven ships carried about 1,500 souls, 730 convicts (570 men and 160 women) and the rest free persons, mostly navy personnel.

After two weeks the man in charge, Governor Arthur Phillip, decided the location was totally unsuitable for settlement and moved lock, stock, and convict a few miles north to what became Sydney Harbour. On the beach of this new location, in this land now claimed for the British crown, he gave a speech in which, as recorded by a naval surgeon, George Worgan, "the Governor gave strict orders that the natives should not be offended or molested on any account . . . they were to be treated with friendship." It didn't turn out that way. Governor Phillip was dealing with the Eora and Darug peoples in the region around Sydney. After first contact the early interactions were based on trade, but what the Eora and Darug didn't know was that these new, strange people in their midst had come not for trade but for their land.

Although many generations thought of the Aboriginals as a single people, there are numerous diverse groups and languages throughout the country—for example, the Murri from Queensland, the Nunga from the south of South Australia, and the Palawa from Tasmania—all of which can be broken into subgroups. In 1788 the populations are thought to have totaled between 250,000 and 500,000, although a few estimates go higher. In the following decades it's estimated that at least tens of thousands of these Aboriginals died in what became a frontier war lasting into the twentieth century.

As the settlements around Sydney expanded, and others grew in Melbourne, Brisbane, and Tasmania, so did the Frontier Wars, as they became known. Historians argue over the levels of violence, but it's estimated that about two thousand colonists and many times that number of Aboriginals were killed, the latter suffering numerous massacres. It is a sorry tale of one side seeing the other as having no rights; indeed, many colonists regarded the Aboriginals as barely human.

As early as 1856, the devastation of cultures was articulated in a searing article by the journalist Edward Wilson in Melbourne's *Argus* newspaper:

> In less than twenty years we have nearly swept them off the face of the Earth. We have shot them down like dogs . . . and consigned whole tribes to the agonies of an excruciating death. We have made them drunkards, and infected them with diseases which have rotted the bones of their adults, and made such few children as are born amongst them a sorrow and a torture from the very instant of their birth. We have made them outcasts on their own land, and are rapidly consigning them to entire annihilation.

The bleakness of their existence continued right through the nineteenth and twentieth centuries, long after the killing stopped. Starting in 1910, Aboriginal children from the surviving nations were taken from their families and raised either in the homes of white families or in state institutions; in both cases the idea was to force assimilation. The practice was only halted in 1970, by which time the "stolen generation" numbered more than 100,000. The right to vote in national elections had been given them only in 1962, and it took until 1967 for the Aboriginal people to be formally acknowledged as part of the Australian population. A referendum changed the constitution to allow them to be counted in the census and thereby gain greater access to state resources. As the civil rights activist Faith Bandler put it in 1965, "Australians have to register their dogs and cattle, but we don't know how many Aborigines there are."

The referendum was passed with a 90 percent majority on a 93 percent turnout. The vote is regarded by many as a turning point, even if the short-term practical effects were limited. It revealed a desire to extend equality, although there was a long way to go in a battle that is still being fought today. Aboriginal men and women are graduating from universities, entering the middle class, and populating all aspects of modern Australia; however, their life expectancy is lower than the national average and incidents of chronic illnesses are higher, as are infant mortality rates and imprisonment. Unemployment, alcoholism, and illness are rife among some communities, together with psychological problems partially brought on by a sense of alienation, accentuated by the drift from rural areas to the towns and cities beginning in the 1970s.

A gradual change in attitudes toward the peoples of the First Nations can be charted partially by symbolic moves. In the 1990s the name of the massive rust-colored desert monolith known as Ayers Rock was changed to Ayers Rock/ Uluru to acknowledge its original name in the language of the Anangu people, for whom it is a sacred site, and in 2002 was switched to Uluru/Ayers Rock. In 2008, recognizing the ongoing responsibility for more than two hundred years of devastation, repression, and negligence, Prime Minister Kevin Rudd issued a formal apology to the Aboriginal peoples for the abuses they had suffered.

Despite all the deprivations, the population grew during the twentieth century. Estimates in the 1920s put it as low as 60,000, whereas now there are about 800,000 Aboriginal and Torres Strait Islander people (who are ethnically different from Aboriginals), centered mainly in Queensland, New South Wales, Western Australia, and the Northern Territory. Most of the hundreds of languages are lost, and of those that survive there are perhaps 50,000 people who can speak at least one.

The drive across the continent by the settlers who caused this havoc was slow but relentless. As more shiploads of people, mostly convicts, arrived from the UK the white population increased by several thousand each year. By 1825 explorers had already breached what was considered an impassable barrier—the Blue Mountains to the west of Sydney—and discovered that beyond them lay the great Outback. The population then was 50,000; by 1851 it had grown to about 450,000, by which time penal transportation had dropped significantly as many of the newcomers were immigrants seeking a new life in a new world.

They'd arrived in time for the first Australian gold rush, located north of

Melbourne, which began to transform Australian society as hundreds of thousands of people came from abroad to try their luck. Most of them were from Britain, but they also arrived from China, North America, Italy, Germany, Poland, and a smattering of other countries. Thanks to this "gold generation," Australia's population not only rocketed to 1.7 million in the early 1870s, but gradually started to become more ethnically and culturally diverse.

The madness of the early gold rush meant that the first few waves crashing onto Melbourne's shores consisted mostly of young single men. They gave rise to a Wild West atmosphere, but prosperity slowly led to a change in the nature of immigration, attracting skilled craftsmen, traders, and professionals such as accountants and lawyers who began to arrive with their families.

They all contributed to the emerging Australian character, but there is a theory that the diggers, as the prospectors were called, forged the resourcefulness, can-do attitude and friendliness for which Australians are known. The Old World social niceties meant little up in the rugged, muddy prospecting regions, and the independent, yet simultaneously collegiate spirit of the diggers contributed to an identity with less respect for British colonial authority than before.

As it approached the twentieth century, Australia was becoming a modern country, albeit comprised of colonies that were almost like separate countries; they had few formal relations with one another and were often preoccupied with their own economic and political systems. The distances between the settlements had proved a challenge. The rivers, as we've seen, were not suited to trade and transport, and so initially, in order to move anything by land humans usually had to drag it themselves over rough tracks, since there were few beasts of burden available. The early transport systems concentrated on each individual port sending goods inland, or back out to the mother country, the UK. Because each region was a separate colony, connecting them along the coastline was not a priority; so these early roads led inland but not, at least for significant distances, along the coast. With such limited options, each colony continued to develop as a separate entity.

In the second half of the nineteenth century, a fledgling railway system began to emerge, some of which linked the coastal towns and paved the way for a connected economy. As the transport and communications systems developed, so did the idea of the different regions coming together as a federation. A referendum was held in 1899 and passed but with significant opposition, and on July 5, 1900, the British Parliament passed the Commonwealth of Australia Constitution Act 1900, which was signed by Queen Victoria four days later; on January 1, 1901, the six British colonies united to form the Commonwealth of Australia. Half a million people lined the streets of Sydney to celebrate. Australia had not become a sovereign state, only a "self-governing colony" (despite becoming a UN member in 1945, it wasn't until 1986 that full independence was achieved by the Australia Act), but a great leap forward in self-determination had been achieved.

By this time the population was past the 4 million mark and Australia had started to become an urban society, with Sydney and Melbourne each boasting populations of just under 500,000. The majority of immigrants arriving were still from the UK, but wherever they came from almost all were white. One of the first laws the new government passed was the Immigration Restriction Act, which became known as the White Australia policy. The wording of the act is not explicit on the page but is clearly racist in intent, barring "any person who when asked to do so by an officer fails to write out at dictation and sign in the presence of the officer a passage of fifty words in length in an European language directed by the officer."

In the extraordinary circumstance that, say, a would-be immigrant from China could write out fifty words dictated in Portuguese, he or she could always be asked to do the test again, this time in, let's say, Flemish. As stated, the language was chosen "by the officer," and the application of the test was usually to put a legal stamp on a decision already made. Most people refused entry were nonwhite, but the act could also be used to deport immigrants who were not naturalized if they were jailed for a violent crime. None of this fit with the words of the popular song "Advance Australia Fair," played at the inauguration ceremony for the new commonwealth and later to become the national anthem:

> We've boundless plains to share;
> With courage let us all combine
> To advance Australia fair.

The overwhelming political and popular opinion was that the boundless plains should be shared only with white people, preferably British white people. The new law was aimed mostly at Chinese, Japanese, Indonesians, and anyone else from the wider neighborhood who might not only come and undercut wages but also dilute the racial "purity" of Australia. The White Australia policy continued up into the 1970s. At all times it was viewed extremely negatively by Australia's Asian neighbors, especially those emerging from the colonial era.

The post–Second World War period saw the so-called Ten Pound Poms arrive in droves. Australia still needed to grow its workforce, and so for just £10 Britons could sail to Australia to start a new life. The full fare was about £120, almost six months' wages for many working-class people, and the offer was one that many in drab, postwar, class-bound Britain could not refuse. Between 1947 and 1982 more than 1.5 million set out for down under, opportunity, sunshine, and at first—frequently—hardship. My aunt, uncle, and four cousins were among them. Ann was a nurse and Dennis worked in a shoe shop. Sailing from Southampton docks in 1972, they swapped Leeds for Melbourne and (after moving from a hostel) relatively low wages for a significantly higher standard of living. They and the others were poms, shortened from pomegranate, sometimes spelled pommygrant, which was close enough to the word "immigrant" to be incorporated into Aussie slang.

During this period, Brits were still the main source of labor, but gradually the demographic of the country began to change as world events drove increasing numbers of Europeans to Australia, opening the floodgates and gradually relaxing the White Australia policy. Italians, Germans, and Greeks arrived to join the communities established after the Second World War. Following were many Hungarians who had escaped after the 1956 revolution, then Czechs after the Soviet occupation in 1968. Gradually people from South America and the Middle East came, many fleeing persecution. In the 1970s thousands of boat people from Vietnam were allowed in, and in the 1990s refugees from the Yugoslav wars.

This resulted in a pronounced cultural shift from what was essentially a British, or perhaps Anglo-Celtic, society to a multicultural country. It was a remarkably rapid conversion into what we see now in modern Australia— a nation of people whose heritage can be traced back to 190 countries. In the 2016 census, the proportion of the population born abroad was 26 percent, but exactly where they come from shows the changes in policy, attitudes, and global economics since the start of the twentieth century. Of the foreign-born, the British were still the most numerous, but in the top ten were New Zealanders (8.4 percent), Chinese (8.3 percent), Indians (7.4 percent), Filipinos (3.8 percent), and Vietnamese (3.6 percent); five of the top ten nationalities are Asian.

This is a long way from 1901, even further from 1788, and not just in terms of time. As in every other country racism and inequality still exist, but the change was summed up in a speech by Kevin Rudd in 2019: "Our definition of

Australia's national identity must be grounded in the ideals, institutions, and conventions of our democratic society, not in its racial composition."

The country remains an attractive destination for outsiders, including migrant workers and refugees. It is so popular, and people are so desperate to get there by any means, that successive governments this century have enacted tough laws against those who seek to enter illegally.

In 2001 the Australian navy began intercepting boatloads of refugees and migrants. The boats are either forced to turn round or taken to a third country; if people are taken on board the navy ship, they are then transferred to the tiny nation-state of Nauru or the remote Papua New Guinea island of Manus. The policy was halted in 2008 but resumed in 2012. Since then, well over 3,000 people have been detained. Some have returned to their own countries, while several hundred have been granted refugee status in the US. In 2020 about 290 remained in what Australia calls "processing centers" on the islands, where they have been subjected to violent attacks by local people.

The policy has been vilified as inhuman and illegal by human rights activists, but it is still popular enough with the Australian electorate for it to remain in place. The number of boats arriving has declined, and the number of people arriving by air who then claim asylum has increased.

They come because to a great extent modern Australia remains the "lucky country." The phrase comes from a 1964 book of the same name by Donald Horne. He meant it somewhat sarcastically, but it has stuck as a positive description and with reason. The land down under is among the richest in the world and looks destined to remain that way. It has abundant natural resources, including many that are perfectly suited for selling around the world. Its wool, lamb, beef, wheat, and wine industries remain world leaders; it holds a quarter of the world's uranium reserves, the largest zinc and lead deposits, and is a major producer of tungsten and gold, as well as having healthy deposits of silver; and it is a key supplier of liquefied natural gas while also still producing large quantities of coal. And there we see how the country is caught between an Ayers Rock and a hard place.

Australia is acutely aware that fossil fuels are driving climate change. Global warming was a significant factor in the devastating wildfires of 2019–20, which were exacerbated by record temperatures and water shortages. The human fatality toll was in the dozens, but thousands of koalas, one of the symbols of the country, were killed along with hundreds of thousands of other creatures. The flames did not reach the urban areas, but clouds of acrid smoke hung over Canberra, causing the capital's air quality temporarily to sink to one of the lowest in the world. Flakes of white ash moved across the land like warm snow and traveled on as far as New Zealand. On January 4, 2020, Sydney was one of the hottest places in the world—the temperature was measured at 48.9°C (120.02°F).

Who can live in such conditions? At the moment the answer is about 26 million people, but if the Australian Bureau of Statistics' medium-growth prediction is correct then in 2060 the answer will be about 40 million.

If the climate-change modeling is on target Australia will continue to suffer record-shattering heat waves, droughts, and forest fires, creating a scorched, uninhabitable landscape. The more the suburbs of the great cities sprawl out into the countryside, the greater the number of people at risk. This means Australians are likely to continue to cling to the coastline, creating ever more densely packed urban areas, even as sea levels may be rising. The country could require a slow retreat from some areas and a long-term building plan for locations designated as lower risk.

Australia has an abundance of one potential energy source, sunshine, but a lack of another—water. Hydroelectric power generation is restricted because of the mostly flat topography of the regions through which its rivers flow, and because of their variable volume of water. The exception is Tasmania, where the terrain and climate have already allowed a hydroelectric industry to flourish. Water scarcity, already an issue, may become a top priority, and the nation will have to have a frank discussion about sustainability.

That will include talking about coal. Given that all the states have coal mines, and that the AU$69.6-billion industry employs tens of thousands of people, that won't be easy. Before he became prime minister, Scott Morrison caused an uproar in Parliament when he brandished a large lump of coal and exhorted the House of Representatives: "Don't be afraid, don't be scared, it won't hurt you. It's coal." Australia could close down its industry tomorrow and not significantly reduce global pollution—it is part of a problem that will not be resolved without each country working to reduce its carbon footprint—but it would have a profound effect on the Australian economy. As such, coal is likely to remain king for years to come, even as the country looks to alternative sources of energy.

Access to energy is a major concern for Australia—and, given Australia's geography and location, it's unavoidably linked with security issues.

Economically, modern Australia is increasingly tied into its location. Its politicians declare it is part of the Asia-Pacific community, but tend to shy away from the debate about whether that community considers it is part of them.

In its "near abroad," for example the South Pacific island nations, this former colony and ally of the West is the main power and is respected, but not loved; in the wider region it is one of several major powers and a potential ally or enemy.

Strategically, most of Australia's focus is to its north and east. As a first line of defense, it looks up to the South China Sea area; below that it views the Philippines and the Indonesian archipelago, and then the seas between it and Papua New Guinea. To its east it focuses on the islands of the South Pacific such as Fiji and Vanuatu.

Australia does have some advantages: it would be difficult to invade—not impossible, but difficult. The bulk of any invasion force would have to conduct amphibious assaults, and because of the islands to Australia's east and north the probable lines of attack are narrow. Once enemy troops were ashore, it would not be feasible to occupy the whole continent, and places of value would be fiercely contested. If these forces landed in the Northern Territory they would still be 2,000 miles from Sydney, the supply lines would be a nightmare, and getting there would be difficult.

However, Australia is vulnerable to blockade. Most of its imports and exports flow through a series of narrow passageways to the north—including the Malacca, Sunda, and Lombok Straits—and many of those could be closed in times of conflict. The Malacca Strait is the shortest route from the Indian Ocean to the Pacific. Just this one passageway sees eighty thousand vessels pass through it each year, carrying about a third of the world's traded goods, including 80 percent of the oil heading for northeast Asia. If these straits were closed, then alternative routes would have to be found; for example, the oil tankers feeding Japan could try to sail farther south, cut across the north of Australia, past Papua New Guinea, and out into the Pacific. This would add hugely to transport costs but would keep Japan and Australia open for business.

In the event of a successful blockade, Australia would quickly be in a state of energy crisis. It holds about two months' oil supply in its strategic reserves onshore, and at any one time there's another three weeks' worth or so making its way there on tankers. Canberra took advantage of the oil price crash in 2020 to top up with a few extra days' supply, but stored it in America's Strategic Petroleum Reserve stockpiles and so might not be able to access it.

Australian defense strategy is partially focused on this scenario. It has ships and submarines that could be used to protect convoys, and planes capable of long-range maritime patrols. It has six air force bases north of the 26th Parallel, three fully staffed and three mothballed for emergencies. The 26th Parallel is the line dividing the north and south of the continent. It begins just over 100 miles north of Brisbane and runs across the continent to Shark Bay on the Indian Ocean. Only 10 percent of Australia's population lives above the line and there are theories, never acknowledged, that, in the event of invasion from the north, they would be abandoned as the military concentrated on defending the main population centers. But that is a theoretical last-ditch scenario, one the government seeks to avoid by having what it hopes is a robust "forward defense" posture in the shape of the air bases and the navy. The Royal Australian Air Force is now investing in F-35A fighter jets, which are useful for defending the shores of the country but appear several years behind being able to meet the emerging threat of long-range and hypersonic-speed missiles. As part of its response, the air force has been tasked with creating a Space Division.

However, given the size of the country, its population, and its middle-ranking wealth, Australia cannot operate a navy capable of protecting all of the sea approaches to its shores. Simply patrolling the seas closest to Australia is a challenge. The mainland has 22,000 miles of coastline and there's an additional 15,000 miles of island coastline to keep an eye on.

To deter any of the above scenarios from taking place, as well as investing heavily in its navy, Australia has concentrated on diplomacy, choosing its allies carefully. Canberra has always had an eye on who is the dominant sea power. When it was Great Britain, the old imperial power was the most important ally, but when it became the US it was obvious whom to choose as the new number one political, military, and strategic priority.

When the First World War broke out, Australians rallied to the cause in huge numbers. But the Second World War was the turning point in the military relationship between Australia and the UK. It was obvious the British could not defend Australia, and, as the tide of war turned, it became ever clearer who the world's dominant power would be in the aftermath.

As early as December 1941, following Pearl Harbor, Prime Minister John Curtin spelled it out in an article titled "The Task Ahead": "The Australian Government, therefore, regards the Pacific struggle as primarily one in which the United States and Australia must have the fullest say in the direction of the democracies' fighting plan. Without any inhibitions of any kind, I make it quite clear that Australia looks to America, free of any pangs as to our traditional links or kinship with the United Kingdom." With characteristic Aussie bluntness he laid out the realpolitik of the message: "We know too that Australia can go and Britain can still hold on."

It was a watershed moment—the Yanks were coming. The advance parties were already on the ground, and by mid-1943 150,000 US military personnel were in Australia, the bulk of them in Queensland, where General Douglas MacArthur established his headquarters. Ships from the US Navy were anchored in Sydney and Perth, and "made in America" put down roots. Coca-Cola, hamburgers, pizza, hot dogs, Hollywood films, and American consumer goods began to displace the more conservative British-based imports of previous decades.

The war also came to Australia. On February 19, 1942, the Japanese air force unleashed a devastating attack on the Allied military port of Darwin, using the same aircraft carrier group that had attacked Pearl Harbor ten weeks earlier. In January, the Japanese had already launched an invasion of New Guinea, and they quickly took over the north of the massive island. The landmass is the second-largest island in the world and it is directly north of Australia. Had it fallen, it could have been used either as the launchpad for an invasion of Australia or to blockade it. However, a planned amphibious landing at Port Moresby was thwarted by the Battle of the Coral Sea. The Japanese plan was turned against them and New Guinea was used as the springboard for General MacArthur's retaking of the Philippines as part of the island campaign leading to the defeat of Japan.

Since then, Australia's relationship with America has been similar to the one it had with the British. Australia contributes parts of its military (especially its well-trained special forces), while the US Navy keeps international sea lanes open and holds a nuclear umbrella above the Australians. Canberra sent troops to fight in the Korean War (1950–1953), the Vietnam War (1955–1975), the first Gulf War (1990–1991), and the invasion of Iraq (2003), just as it had during both world wars. The Americans meanwhile remain resolute in their determination to maintain their control as the greatest sea power. They have established a major base in Darwin. It hosts 2,500 US marines, not enough to keep the Chinese military awake at night, perhaps, but more than enough to send the signal that the Americans are in town, and willing to defend Australia. For now . . .

And there's the dilemma for Australia. With the rise of China, the US is having to make choices in the west Pacific region. It can resist China's push to control what Beijing sees as its backyard, it can attempt to create an understanding of regional spheres of influence, or it can make a long, slow retreat, pulling in its horns all the way back to California. After all, between there and the Chinese coast is 7,000 miles of ocean. American military and diplomatic officials assure Australia that the alliance is rock solid, but President Trump made Australia nervous, often giving the appearance that he preferred authoritarian strongmen from tin-pot dictatorships such as North Korea to long-standing democratic allies. The change in president brought a change in tone. Joe Biden's victory in November 2020 was followed a month later by a stark warning from the chiefs of the US Navy, Marine Corps, and Coast Guard that, of all the world powers, China represents the most "comprehensive, long-term" threat to America and its allies. More alarm bells had begun to ring earlier in 2020 as the Chinese started to scope out Papua New Guinea's Daru Island following an agreement to build a huge fisheries complex there. The island is just 125 miles from the Australian mainland, and while the seas around it are not renowned for their commercial fishing potential, Chinese trawlers are known to be frequently used as spy ships. Perhaps this is a simple commercial enterprise; then again, perhaps the port will be built to accommodate Chinese warships. It's an example of the constant vigilance Australia must now keep when it comes to China's activities in the region, and why it must also constantly assess the American commitment to joint security.

Australia knows it is probable that by the mid-twenty-first century the US will no longer outspend China on defense. The difference between the Cold War and now is stark: a declining Soviet Union fell massively behind the US in economic terms and eventually could not compete in the arms race. China is a rising power expected to exceed America's GDP by midcentury, if not sooner. America's decisions on these issues will impact Australia's "China choice."

We tend to think of China and Australia as being relatively close to each other, which is probably for two reasons. Australia is so far from any other major landmass east, west, or south that we tend to look north on the map, see China, and mentally associate the two. But the classic map most of us use, the Mercator, distorts our view as it portrays a curved distance on a flat surface. If you want to see how much Mercator influences our idea of where things are, take a look at the Waterman maps, which take a little getting used to but offer another perspective. We never think of China as being geographically close to Poland, but Beijing is as close to Warsaw as it is to Canberra. This is why China has a constant 360-degree view of the map, while Australia looks mostly north. Put simply, China has more choices than Australia.

When it comes to China, Australia must walk a difficult line between economic interests, defense strategy, and diplomacy. China is by far its biggest trading partner, although levels of investment fluctuate sometimes in line with those of diplomatic warmth. In recent years, about 1.4 million Chinese arrived annually for holidays, and Chinese students made up 30 percent of people from abroad studying in the country. China buys almost a third of Australia's exported farm produce, including 18 percent of its beef exports and half its barley. It is also a major market for Australia's iron ore, gas, coal, and gold. But China's wider interests in the region, its attempts to expand its territorial claims and influence, don't always align with Australia's.

The region off China's coastline is a complicated place. China claims geographical and historical rights over 80 percent of the South China Sea. A quick look at the map suggests that might not be entirely fair, as Vietnam, the Philippines, Taiwan, Malaysia, and Brunei are always ready to point out. These nations hold different geographical and historical views, which explain their often overlapping territorial claims. But Beijing is still busy pouring concrete onto small rocks sticking out of the water more than 1,000 miles from its mainland, calling them islands, and then constructing runways, radar stations, and missile batteries on them.

Much of the rapid military progress shown by the Chinese People's Liberation Army suggests a medium-term ambition to extend the range of its "area-denial capability"—a concept meaning the ability to prevent enemy forces from coming into, staying in, or even crossing a defined geographical area. In recent years that has meant developing weapons which could, in case of war, try to push the Americans, or others, out of the South and East China Seas and past the first island chain, the string of islands stretching from Japan down to the Philippines. Australia now worries that China hopes eventually to project the area-denial region even farther—south of Indonesia and the Philippines. If so, this would take it into the Banda Sea and the shores of Papua New Guinea. In Australia, memories of the Japanese invasion of New Guinea remain strong. There are minor concerns about the slim possibility of an Islamist takeover of Indonesia, but what worries the military strategists more is the Chinese moving down toward them.

One scenario to deter this is the rapid movement of Australian forces. But where to base most of them? Putting them in the north of the country means that further northward movement goes through various choke points where an enemy can lie in wait. Putting them in the south means that it takes longer to transport them, although they can head out into open seas.

Southward expansion by China might be considered as stretching territorial sovereignty to its breaking point; exactly where this elasticity would snap is for the international lawyers, but it's certainly north of the Coral Sea. There China cannot make territorial claims, nor, without provoking conflict, can it go in for island building and military construction. What it can do, though, is use its economic muscle to try to gain a foothold, but that's where it runs into the region's only major power. Australia can't feasibly prevent China from dominating the South China Sea, but it can try to ensure Beijing has limited influence when it comes to the South Pacific.

Battle has commenced. Australia is the largest aid donor to the Pacific islands, but China has been increasing financial aid and loans and, as it did elsewhere, it was quick to move in when the Covid-19 virus struck. In April 2020 a Royal Australian Air Force plane carrying aid to the island of Vanuatu was approaching Port Vila airport when it spotted a Chinese plane on the single runway, which had arrived carrying PPE and other Covid-19–related equipment. Despite being cleared to land, it turned around and flew the 1,200 miles back home. Everyone argues about whether it was, or was not, safe to land, but the point remained—the Chinese were on the ground.

What's in it for them? Influence equals access, and China wants access to fishing zones, ports for its fleets, possible mining of seabeds, and something else that is often overlooked: votes at the United Nations and other world bodies. The Chinese have successfully picked off many African countries and persuaded them not to recognize Taiwan, and they are now attempting the same in the Pacific. In 2019, despite intense American and Australian lobbying, Kiribati and the Solomon Islands severed ties with Taiwan and established diplomatic relations with China.

Canberra has been engaging in what is dubbed the Pacific step-up policy, but has to move carefully. The Pacific islanders are keenly aware of Australia's colonial history and take a dim view of anything that might hint at paternalism. It helps to refer to places such as Vanuatu not as "small island nations" but "large ocean states," as the islands now prefer, based on their large, exclusive maritime zones. Depending on how you define the region, the islands, including maritime zones, make up about 15 percent of the world's surface.

In 2018 Australia beat off a challenge from China to fund the main military base in Fiji, signed a bilateral security treaty with Vanuatu, and donated twenty-one new military patrol boats to several of the islands. It also used its aid budget to build an underwater high-speed communications network, called the Coral Sea Cable System, linking Australia, the Solomon Islands, and Papua New Guinea. Despite this and many other measures, China is making inroads especially in Fiji, the Cook Islands, and Tonga, but given its own problems back home it often insists on Chinese-sourced materials for infrastructure projects and, as it does in Africa, brings in its own workers, causing local resentment. So far Australia remains the major player, but it will have to concentrate hard to stay that way.

China's technology and power exceed Australia's. The range of Beijing's ballistic missiles has also made the water-filled moat around Australia less useful, as have cyberweapons, because it is no longer necessary to send large pieces of metal to targets in order to blow them up. Any country could be horribly damaged by a cyberattack on its critical infrastructure—the electricity grid, water, food supply chains, transport system, etc. Australia is still a long way from anyone who might come to its physical assistance but technologically the world has moved closer.

Covid-19 made Australia more aware of the limitations of the "just in time" economic system and, like many countries, has hardened its attitude toward being China dependent and allowing China into critical infrastructure projects. For example, Australia has frozen China's Huawei company out from its 5G network—a bold move. The relationship can be fragile. In the summer of 2020, when Prime Minister Morrison called for an international inquiry into the origins of the Covid-19 virus, this was seen in Beijing as an attack on China. Within days Chinese customs officials noticed "issues" with the labeling on some imported Australian beef products and imposed a ban on supplies. As Canberra stood firm, Beijing began muttering about barley and iron imports and made a thinly disguised threat via its English-language mouthpiece the *Global Times*. The newspaper wrote that the economic measures "don't necessarily represent China's economic punishment for Australia, though they may serve as a wake-up call for Australia to reflect on its economic links with China." The diplomatic "don't necessarily represent," when translated into plain English, appeared to be "do represent." In early 2021 the figures for Chinese imports of Australian copper concentrates were released. They had dropped from 100,000 metric tons in December 2019 to zero in December 2020.

Six months prior to that, Australia had suffered a sustained cyberattack on government, education, health, and other critical infrastructure sites. Prime Minister Morrison didn't identify the attacker but said, "There are not a large number of state-based actors that can engage in this type of activity." It was clear who he meant.

Managing the relationship will be difficult: handle it wrong and you risk being part of an Indo-Pacific cold war; being too weak risks allowing a People's Liberation Army base in your backyard. The Covid-19 crisis magnified and accelerated existing trends. The Indians, Japanese, Taiwanese, Malaysians, Australians, and others all saw their underlying anxieties about China come into sharp focus. While they were busy battling Covid-19, China embarked on a series of provocative moves, including sailing their aircraft carrier fleet in a full circle around Taiwan. The timing was interesting: one of the US carrier fleets normally in the area was in dock for repairs, the other was in dock with hundreds of its crew stricken with the virus. A Vietnamese fishing vessel was rammed and sunk by the Chinese coast guard, and a Malaysian oil-drilling survey ship was harassed. Beijing's increasingly assertive stance over Hong Kong also concentrated minds.

So far Australia is sticking close to its best friends in America. Its diplomats work overtime on Capitol Hill, at the Pentagon, and CIA headquarters in Langley to maintain the ties forged over eighty years. Australia is also an enthusiastic member of what is probably the world's most efficient intelligence-gathering network—the so-called Five Eyes—along with the US, the UK, New Zealand, and Canada. It hosts the Pine Gap military base near Alice Springs, which is among the most important US intelligence-gathering facilities in the world. It is the ground station for CIA satellites that hoover up intelligence communications, it provides battlefield intelligence for American troops operating in places such as Afghanistan, it detects ballistic missile launches, it supports the US and Japanese missile defense systems, and it increasingly plays a role in the newly formed US Space Force. This is not a piece of real estate the Americans want to leave and is among the bargaining chips Canberra has as it measures the US commitment to the Pacific.

The world now is very different from when Five Eyes and other defense structures were set up. Then the American commitment was considered rock solid, Japan had been defeated, and China was incapable of mounting a threat. The center of the Cold War was a world away, and Australia's defense posture assumed there would be a ten-year horizon for anticipating a regional threat. Now the advance notice of probable conflict has shrunk, and China is a major player. So while Canberra is investing heavily in its relationship with Washington, it is also making a few side bets, although they are not substantial and some are merely prudent.

Australia and Japan are developing a military relationship that includes joint air and sea combat exercises and a "visiting forces agreement." Both are acutely aware of their lack of self-sufficiency in energy supplies and the consequent dangers of supply routes being blocked. Japan imports 85 percent of its crude oil from the Middle East and South Korea imports over 60 percent from the same source. Both countries have well-developed refining industries and they sell Australia almost half of the refined petroleum it imports. As we have seen, if the routes from the Middle East into the South and East China Seas and across to Japan are blocked, Australia would run out of energy and grind to a halt within weeks.

All the countries in the wider Indo-Pacific region agree that the international sea lanes must be kept open. To do that means pushing back every time China lays claim to the South China Sea as its sovereign territory, or says that the islands it has constructed in the area are as much a part of China as is Sichuan. Beijing is busy buying friends and influencing people, and the only way in which the other major players (apart from the US) can compete is to stick close to each other.

Both Japan and Australia also cooperate with the Indian navy within the Quad, or Quadrilateral Security Dialogue, which includes the US, in order to prevent such a scenario. The Quad is not quite an alliance, it's more a strategic framework for the navies of the four countries to collaborate in the Pacific. It is not openly stated, but the rationale is to work together to ensure sea lanes remain open and to curb Chinese influence. It was given a boost in 2020 during the Covid-19 crisis, when countries became more concerned about Chinese belligerence and after some brutal hand-to-hand fighting between Chinese and Indian troops on their border. As its naval power has grown, India is buying into the idea that the Indo-Pacific region needs to be thought of as one space within which Australia plays a key role. There's now talk of extending to a "Quad Plus," drawing in New Zealand, South Korea, and Vietnam, although the latter two are treading carefully due to their proximity to China.

The Australians have never waited for their hand to be held and have always attempted to have a military capable of at least mounting a solo defense of the country, preferably as far away from its shores as possible. Realistically, that means trying to ensure that the islands to its north and east are not aggressive and/or dominated by a superior power.

Australia faces tough choices, a careful balancing act in which a misstep could have serious and lasting consequences in a region now considered to be the most economically important in the world. Some analysts define the Indo-Pacific as stretching from the east coast of Africa across to the west coast of the US. It's an old-fashioned view that is coming back into fashion as the world has turned. An early advocate in the modern era was Shinzo Abe, Japan's former prime minister, who in 2007 quoted a book written by a Mughal prince named Dara Shikoh, *The Confluence of the Two Seas* (1655). In his speech to the Indian parliament, Abe said: "The Pacific and the Indian Oceans are now bringing about a dynamic coupling as seas of freedom and prosperity" and then spoke about ensuring that they would be "open and transparent to all."

Sitting between the two great bodies of water is Australia, with the Indian Ocean to its west, the Pacific to its east, and to the north, China. For now, Canberra will attempt both to forge a constructive dialogue with Beijing, with one eye on the economy, and to maintain defense and other ties with the US, and it'll "play it tough, all the way."

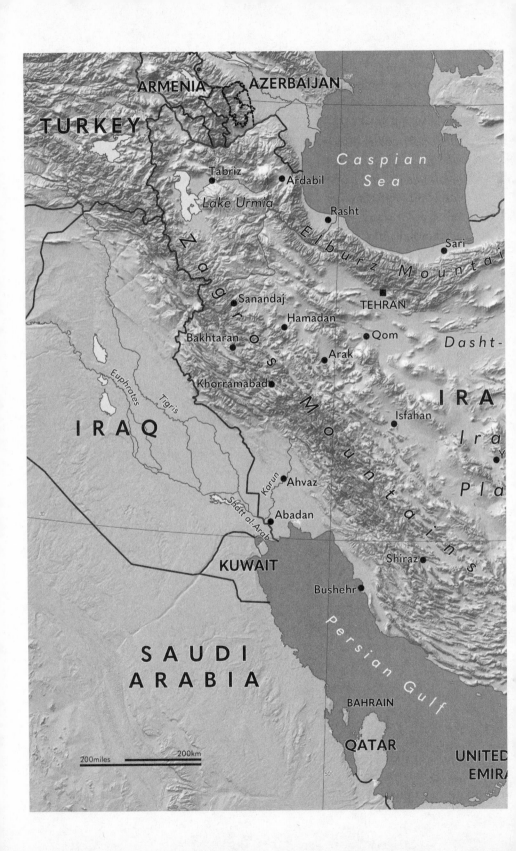

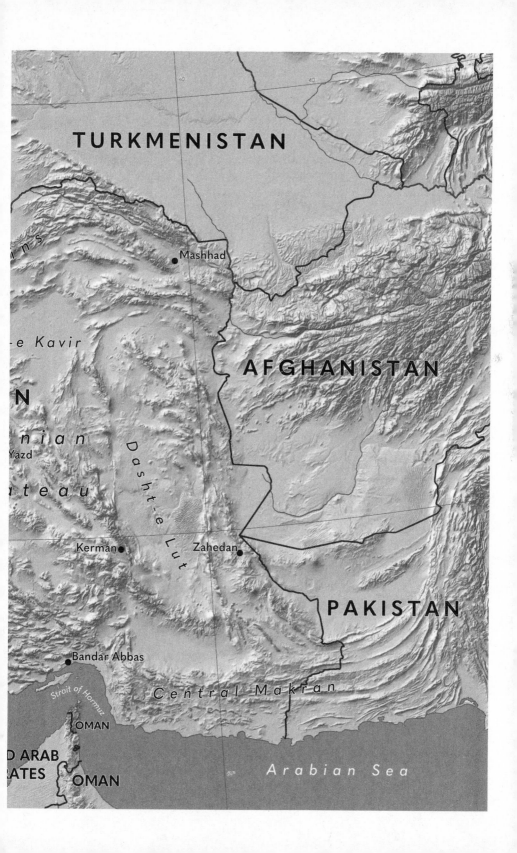

2

IRAN

Islam is political, or it is nothing.

—Ayatollah Khomeini, Supreme Leader of the Islamic Republic of Iran

The Iranians make a variety of wonderful breads; one of the best known is the crispy, wheat-based *naan-e-barbari*, which contains sea salt, is sprinkled with sesame and poppy seeds and eaten at breakfast. It is usually formed into a long, roughly oval shape with a crust and a few interior parallel lines cut across the top. Inadvertently, its appearance often resembles the country in which it is made.

Iran is defined by two geographic features: its mountains, which form a ring of crust on most of its borders, and the mostly flat salt deserts of the interior, along which run lower-range hills roughly parallel to one another. The mountains make Iran a fortress. Approaching it from most angles, you soon bump up against rising high ground that in many places is impassable. The mountains encircle the desolate interior wastelands of the Dasht-e Kavir and Dasht-e Lut.

The Dasht-e Kavir is known as the Great Salt Desert. It's approximately 500 miles long and 200 miles wide—about the size of the Netherlands and Belgium combined. I've driven through parts; there's not much to see other than dull, flat scrubland. But it's not necessarily wise to try to find something to see. In some parts layers of salt on the surface conceal mud deep enough to drown in—and drowning in a desert seems a particularly stupid way to die. The other main desert may sound more attractive, until you learn that the Dasht-e Lut is known as the Plain of Desolation.

This is why, even if you are of a warlike nature, you really don't want to invade Iran, especially in the modern era of large, professional armies controlled by strong states. The country is rarely out of the news: it's a key Middle East power, a repressive regime linked to terror and bloodshed across the region, and a potential nuclear state in a tense standoff with Israel; and it regularly seems to be close to blows with the US. And yet the Americans—and everyone else—are loath to send in the troops. Some of the hawks in the George W. Bush administration of the early 2000s pushed the president to attack Iran, but wiser heads prevailed. Secretary of State Colin Powell, a former chairman of the Joint Chiefs of Staff, argued that airpower alone would have limited success and the ensuing war might require "boots on the ground"; he fell back on the old adage "We do deserts, we don't do mountains." The US and Iran have history, but Iranian history is littered with foreign soldiers dying in large numbers in the country's mountains.

For most of that history, the land was known as Persia. It was renamed Iran only in 1935 in an attempt to represent the country's non-Persian minorities, which constitute about 40 percent of the population. Its borders have shifted around through the centuries but the shape of the *naan-e-barbari* remains the basic geographic frame.

To follow this, it's useful to go clockwise from the 1,000-mile-long Zagros Mountains, beginning on the coast along the Strait of Hormuz. The mountains run north along the parts of Iran that face Qatar and Saudi Arabia across the Persian Gulf, then head farther north along the Shatt al-Arab waterway, up the land borders with Iraq and Turkey, before swinging northeast along the frontier with Armenia. This is the wall that faces any enemy west of Iran almost as soon as it crosses the border. The exception is the Shatt al-Arab waterway, where, on the Iraqi side of the border, the Tigris and Euphrates Rivers meet. But even this is not necessarily a weak spot for Iran. It is the main gate out of Iran, leading to anywhere valuable for its leaders. A gate can be opened in either direction, and so the Persians have always sought to advance out of it, close it, or create a buffer zone between the gate and potential enemies. On the Iranian side of the border much of the terrain is swampland, giving the defender a natural advantage; and even if an aggressor made it off the soft, low ground they would soon run into the Zagros Mountains a few miles inland.

Where the Zagros end, the Elburz Mountains begin. Again, moving clockwise, the Elburz run briefly along the Armenian border and then Azerbaijan before taking a sharp turn south, where they overlook the Caspian Sea. The coastline is 400 miles long and the 10,000-foot-high mountains are never more than 70 miles from it, usually much less. As in the west of the country, any hostile invading force cannot get far before hitting the mountain wall. The mountains then curve again, running along the Turkmenistan and Afghanistan borders. Lower mountains taper down almost to the Gulf of Oman before meeting the Central Makran Range, which takes us back to the Strait of Hormuz. This means that if you want to invade and occupy Iran, you have to fight on marshland, over mountains, and across deserts, or make an amphibious landing and do the same.

Overall, this terrain is a formidable obstacle for a would-be invader and occupier; the price to pay for breaking through the mountain wall is considerable, and the occupier ends up going home. However, this geography has not deterred all hostile forces during Persia/Iran's long history. Alexander the Great made headway, but within a few years of his death in 323 BCE Persia again controlled its own affairs. In the 1200s and 1300s the Mongols, and Tamerlane, arrived from across the vast Central Asian steppe, wrecked the place and slaughtered hundreds of thousands of people, but didn't stay long enough to significantly influence Persian culture. The Ottomans ventured into the Zagros several times starting in the 1500s, but only skirted the periphery of the country. The Russians did the same, then the British arrived and decided the best bet was to co-opt some of the minority groups and buy their way to influence.

Conversely, this geography also restrains Iranian power. In the past millennia, the Persian Empire came down from the mountains and pushed outward; but for most of its history it has been contained within the territory described above. On rare occasions it has dominated the plains to its west, but usually other powers—Greek, Roman, Byzantine, Ottoman, British, and most recently American—have been the controlling influence there, and some have used the territory to try to manipulate what happens inside Iran. This is one reason that Tehran is on constant guard against interference from outside.

Internally, the desolate and unforgiving landscape is why almost all Iranians live in the mountains. Because they are difficult to traverse, populated mountain regions tend to develop distinct cultures. Ethnic groups cling to their identities and resist absorption, making it harder for the modern state to foster a sense of national unity. Because of its mountains, Iran's main centers of population are widely dispersed and, until recently, poorly connected. Even now, only half of the country's roads are paved. So although the population are all Iranians, they are from many different ethnic groups.

Persian (Farsi) is spoken as a first tongue by about 60 percent of Iranians and is the official language of the Islamic Republic. However, Kurds, Balochis, Turkmen, Azerbaijanis (Azeris), and Armenians all use their own languages, as do a host of smaller groups, such as Arabs, Circassians, and the seminomadic Lur tribes. There are even a few villages in which Georgian is spoken. The tiny community of Jews (around eight thousand people) can be traced all the way back to the Babylonian Exile in the sixth century BCE.

This diversity, especially among the larger groups such as the Kurds and Azeris, means that the country's rulers have always attempted to have a strong, centralized, and often repressive government in order to keep its minorities under control and ensure that no region can break away or assist outside powers. This is as true of the ayatollahs as it was of their predecessors.

The Kurds are one of the best examples of a mountain people retaining their culture in the face of the state's aggressive assimilation policies. Exact population numbers are difficult to pin down, as the government prefers not to disclose statistics on ethnicity; but most sources suggest that the Kurds form about 10 percent of the population—perhaps 8.5 million people. They are the second-largest minority after the Azeris (16 percent). Most Iranian Kurds live in the Zagros Mountains adjacent to the Kurds in Iraq and Turkey, with whom many share a dream of an independent Kurdish state. Their ethnicity, language, independent spirit, and the fact that most are Sunni Muslims in a Shia-dominated country have brought them into conflict with the central authorities for centuries. Amid the confusion at the end of the Second World War, a small Kurdish region declared independence but survived less than a year once the central government had stabilized the country. Their most recent uprising, which followed the Islamic Revolution of 1979, took the Iranian military three years to crush.

The Azeris are concentrated in the northern border regions near Azerbaijan and Armenia; the Turkmen live close to the Turkish border, and the Arabs, of whom there are about 1.6 million, are clustered near the Shatt al-Arab waterway across from Iraq and on small islands in the Gulf.

Most Iranians live in urban areas, many of which are built on mountain slopes, concentrated in just one-third of the country. If you draw a line from the Caspian Sea, running south through Tehran and then southeast down to the Shatt al-Arab, the majority of people live to the west of it. Elsewhere, urban centers are few and far between. Tehran sits below the Elburz Mountains. It is a feature of Iranian towns that, due to their lack of water, many are at the feet of hills and get their water supply from tunnels dug on the mountain slopes that feed small canals running down into the urban areas. I fell into one once while being chased by the Tehran police—more on which later.

This lack of water is one of several factors that has held Iran back economically. About one-tenth of the land is cultivated, a mere third of which is irrigated. There are only three large rivers, and the Kārūn alone is navigable and able to transport cargo. Air travel has enhanced internal and foreign trade, and there are now international airports in Tehran, Bandar Abbas, Shiraz, Abadan, and Esfahān. In a country larger than the UK, France, and Germany combined, air travel is the only way to connect quickly with the dispersed urban areas.

Given that Iran holds the world's fourth-largest reserves of oil and second-largest of gas, it should be a rich country; but the Iran-Iraq War (1980–1988) saw the refining facilities in Abadan destroyed, and only recently has production recovered to preconflict levels. The country's fossil-fuel industries are notoriously inefficient, a situation exacerbated by international sanctions that make modern equipment difficult to access. The pool of foreign experts willing to work in Iran is limited, as is the number of countries willing to buy Iranian fuel.

Energy is Iran's most important export. Its oil fields are in the regions facing Saudi Arabia, Kuwait, and Iraq, with a smaller field inland near Qom. The gas fields are mostly in the Elburz Mountains and the Persian Gulf. One of the main export routes is into the Gulf of Oman via the Strait of Hormuz. This is Iran's only way out to the open ocean lanes and at its narrowest the strait is just twenty-one miles across. The width of the shipping lane in either direction is about two miles, with a two-mile buffer zone between them to avoid accidents. For Iran this is a double-edged sword. One of the reasons it has never been a sea power is that it can easily be prevented from reaching the ocean. However, the width of the strait means that Tehran can threaten to close it to everyone else. Given that one-fifth of global oil supplies pass through it, closure would mean a world of pain. Closure would hurt Iran as well and probably mean war; but it's a card it can play, and the regime has invested in means by which to try to make it a trump card.

Iranian forces frequently practice "swarming" large vessels, using dozens of fast attack boats, some armed with antiship missiles. In the event of a full-scale conflict, Iran might also use suicide squads, as it did during the Iran-Iraq War. Its conventional naval forces, including a handful of submarines, would probably be quickly found and easily disabled, but a combination of shore-to-ship missiles, special forces operations to mine oil tankers, and the swarming tactics could be enough to both temporarily close the strait and bleed an enemy to the point of retreat. It would also cause massive disruption to oil and gas shipments from Iraq, Kuwait, Saudi Arabia, and the UAE, leading to a huge rise in energy prices and potentially a global recession. When Tehran feels under pressure, especially when its oil exports are threatened, it uses a variation of a warning issued in 2018: "We will make the enemy understand that either everyone can use the Strait of Hormuz or no one."

It is not known if it would go that far, but that's the nature of gambling at this level. To hedge against it, the Americans have advanced plans to try to wipe out as much of Iran's offensive capabilities as they can within hours of a major conflict breaking out, and the Gulf states have been building pipelines to take oil and gas to the Red Sea, from where tankers can access the Indian Ocean—hopefully, without being targeted by the missiles Iran has given to its Houthi allies in Yemen.

Modern Iran is a troubled nation, but one with a great history. The Persian Empire was a leading civilization in the ancient world. Iranian history has a similarly glorious, magnificent, and murderous sweep to that of Greece, so it's no surprise the two civilizations collided, nor that Persia went on to clash with Rome. First, though, there was a little "local difficulty."

Persian origins begin about four thousand years ago, with the migration of tribes from Central Asia. They settled in the southern Zagros Mountains adjacent to the Medes peoples, with whom they shared ethnic roots. It's a lot easier to come down the mountain and attack the plain than it is to climb up from the plain and attack the mountain, and in 550 BCE the Persian leader Cyrus II took over the Medes kingdom, merged it with the Persian Empire, and announced the arrival of the Achaemenid Persian Empire on the world stage.

Cyrus created the greatest empire the world had known, reaching all the way across Mesopotamia (modern Iraq and Syria) and on to Greece, before coming to a sticky end in 529 BCE at the hands of a sort of Xena: Warrior Princess figure named Tomyris. She was queen of a region in Central Asia to which Cyrus had taken a fancy and was most put out when he captured her son. She warned him: "Restore my son to me and get thee from the land. . . . Refuse, and I swear by the sun . . . I will give thee thy fill of blood." In a subsequent battle most of Cyrus's army was slaughtered, and he suffered the indignity of not only being killed but having his head dunked in a skin filled with human blood. She did tell him.

Cyrus was succeeded by his son, who added Egypt and parts of what is now Libya to the empire before Darius I took over in 522 BCE and pushed the empire's borders into parts of what is now Pakistan and northern India, and up into the Danube Valley in Europe. He authorized the Jews in Israel to rebuild the Temple in Jerusalem and encouraged the religious beliefs of Zoroastrianism.

The world's first postal service was created via a network of relay horses, and he undertook a huge construction project that included paved roads running for thousands of miles.

Darius didn't have it all his own way. Irritated with some of the Greek city-states for not showing enough respect (or paying him protection money), he invaded mainland Greece. It went a bit wrong at the Battle of Marathon in 490 BCE, a runaway victory for the Greeks. Darius died four years later and was succeeded by his son Xerxes, who also lost to the Greeks, marking the beginning of the end of the first Persian empire. Cyrus and Darius named themselves "the Great," but their empire was destroyed by an even bigger name from history—Alexander the Great of Macedonia. In 331 BCE he smashed the Persian army and then burnt its capital, Persepolis.

It took almost a hundred years before the next Persian empire rose. The Parthians fought the Roman Empire for control of Mesopotamia and to prevent it entering Persia from the north in modern-day Turkey and Armenia. This culminated in a victory—and a horrific ending to a career made famous by Laurence Olivier. In the film *Spartacus* (1960), General Crassus of the Roman Empire (Olivier) demands to know which man in the defeated slave army is Spartacus. He then crucifies everyone. What goes around comes around. In 53 BCE Crassus took on the Parthians, lost, and because the Persians thought he was greedy, they poured molten gold down his throat.

Some 250 years later, the Parthians were overthrown from within by the Sasanians. They continued to fight Rome, and then the Byzantine Empire, leaving them exhausted and open to the next challenge, which arose from the west—the Arabs, and Islam. The seventh-century Sasanian defeat was the result of unprecedented political weakness and being vanquished by an enemy with the light of God in their eyes. Persia lost its buffer zone in Mesopotamia, and then most of its heartland. However, it took the Arabs twenty years to capture the urban areas; they never fully controlled the mountains, and there were frequent uprisings.

Eventually the Arabs lost, but Islam won. Zoroastrianism was suppressed, its priests murdered, and Islam became the dominant religion. Persia was incorporated into the Caliphate, but the sheer size of the country, and the strength of its cultures, meant that the people never assimilated and always thought in terms of the borders between them and the outsiders. This would be amplified several centuries later, when Persia converted to Shi'ism.

Before this, we see waves of migration by Turkic and Mongol warriors. Again, invasion came after central power had collapsed and Persia was divided into small kingdoms. It was only after the Safavids (1501–1722) united the country that it regained the strength to govern itself and defend its borders.

The Safavids are a key turning point in history. In 1501 King Ismail announced that Shia Islam was the official religion. The origins of the Sunni-Shia split within Islam go back to the dispute over who should succeed the Prophet Muhammad following his death in 632 CE and the Battle of Karbala in 680. Many historians argue that King Ismail's motivation was mostly political. Just as Henry VIII needed to define his kingdom in opposition to Rome and created the Church of England, as we'll see in chapter 4, so Ismail needed the Safavids to be defined in opposition to their archrival—the Sunni Ottoman Empire.

The Safavid Empire's conversion to Shi'ism created deep hostility toward Persia, which in turn helped Persia form a nationalist identity, a strong central government, and a suspicion of minorities that has been passed down through the centuries. It also helped Iran become the country it is and contributes to the tensions in Lebanon and the wars in Yemen and Syria, and it has been a factor in the clash between Iran and Saudi Arabia since the Iranian Revolution of 1979. This is not to say that political state rivalries can be dismissed in these events, but the religious split was fundamental in forming identities, and Iranian religious identity goes back to the Safavids.

You may have seen footage of processions of shirtless Muslim men beating themselves on their chests and whipping their backs to draw blood. This is during the festival of Ashura, and they are feeling the pain of the martyred Hussein, the grandson of the Prophet Muhammad, killed at the Battle of Karbala. The remembrance of Karbala goes deep in Iranian culture: you see it in poetry, music, and plays, and it is intrinsic to the people and their flag. In the center of the flag there is a red tulip—a symbol of martyrdom. When Hussein was killed, it is said, a tulip sprang from his blood.

The Safavids were overthrown in 1722 by clerics on the grounds that only a learned religious man should rule, and they in turn were removed by an Afghan warlord who said that religion could control religion but that "politicians" had the power of taxation and lawmaking. This division of power between secular and religious institutions remains an issue in modern Iran, as many people believe the clerics again wield far too much power in the political arena.

After the Safavids lost power, the next couple of centuries saw the cycle of internal weakness and foreign threats return. Persia's declaration of neutrality in the First World War didn't prevent British, German, Russian, and Turkish forces using it as a battleground. In the aftermath, the Russians were preoccupied by their revolution and the Germans and Ottomans were defeated, and that left the British.

Oil had been discovered before the war, so now the British ensured that they won the exclusive rights to get the stuff out of the ground and sell it. As Winston Churchill wrote later, "Fortune brought us a prize from fairyland beyond our wildest dreams." The Anglo-Persian Oil Company (later British Petroleum) had been formed in 1909, and the British bought the controlling share. After the war London fully intended to make Persia a protectorate, but an officer from the Persian Cossacks Brigade had other ideas. In 1921 Reza Khan marched into Tehran at the head of 1,200 soldiers and effectively seized power. In 1925 the Iranian parliament, the Majlis, voted to depose the then shah, and Reza Khan was appointed Reza Shah Pahlavi.

The country was on its knees. Centuries of weak misrule had left it on the verge of disintegration and so when this military man arrived in the capital, talking about restoring Persian power, people listened. His mission for the newly renamed Iran was to drag it into the twentieth century, and he embarked on a building program that included a cross-country rail network connecting some of the major cities. However, what Reza Shah Pahlavi did not do was take control of the Anglo-Persian Oil Company, and as long as the British controlled that they still had a huge say in Persian affairs. The British had built the world's biggest refinery at the port of Abadan, and from it flowed cheap oil for the British Empire.

In the Second World War, the country again attempted to be neutral, but once more fell victim to outside powers. On a pretext about the shah's pro-Nazi sentiments, the British and Soviets invaded and, after forcing him to abdicate, achieved their aim of securing the oil fields, constructing a supply line to Russia. He'd built the railway system; they wanted to play with it.

The shah was replaced by his twenty-one-year-old son, Mohammad Reza Pahlavi. In 1946, with foreign troops gone, the young man set about trying to continue economic reforms, but in foreign policy threw his lot in with the British and Americans to establish Iran as an ally in the developing Cold War.

But these were new times. The winds of anticolonialism were blowing and turned into a storm over what was now called the Anglo-Iranian Oil Company. Demands for it to be nationalized grew, and in 1951 a vehement supporter of nationalization, Mohammad Mossadegh, became prime minister. A bill was soon passed as a result of the promise that money from Iranian oil would now go only to Iran.

The reaction was swift. Iranian assets in British banks were frozen, goods destined for Iran were held back, and technicians at the Abadan refinery were withdrawn. To no avail: the Iranians held firm. In 1953 London and Washington sent in MI6 and the CIA to help organize a military coup, the trigger for which came when Mossadegh dissolved parliament, intending to rule by decree and effectively stripping the shah of power. It's often said that the British and Americans overthrew Iranian democracy; it is fairer to say that they helped Iranian factions overthrow a democratically elected government. American motives were driven by fears that the chaos in Iran could lead to a Communist takeover; British profits from Iranian oil were not high on their list of priorities. The shah, who had run away to Italy, returned, and all was right with the world. Except it wasn't.

To some the coup seemed a success, but it threw a long shadow. Iran's emerging democracy was halted in its tracks as the shah spun into a spiral of increasing repression. He soon faced opposition from all quarters. Conservative religious groups were enraged when he granted non-Muslims the vote; the Moscow-sponsored Communists worked to undermine him; the liberal intelligentsia wanted democracy; and the nationalists felt humiliated. The coup had reminded people of what happened when the country was subject to outside influence. The result of the nationalization of oil meant more revenue for the state, but little of it trickled down to the masses. The coup was a fork in the road of Iranian history, and the country accelerated toward the revolution of 1979.

The current regime likes to tell a tale about masses of fervently religious people taking to the streets desperate for a new age when the ayatollahs would rule the land. It wasn't quite like that. The demonstrations in the lead-up to the shah's overthrow involved secular groups, the Communists, trade unions, and the religious establishment centered on Ayatollah Khomeini. The latter quickly murdered thousands of the former, and thus got to tell the story.

Khomeini was a well-known figure. In 1964 he'd accused the shah of reducing "the Iranian people to a level lower than that of an American dog." For his troubles he was banished, living first in Iraq and then in France. By 1978 there were massive demonstrations across the country. The shah reacted with savagery, and the SAVAK (the secret police) became a byword for torture and murder. At year's end, after hundreds of demonstrators had been killed, martial law was declared. The demonstrators kept coming and in January 1979 Mohammad Reza Pahlavi fled the country. He was the last of the shahs, and the last Iranian leader influenced by the Americans. They quickly switched their support to Iraq.

Khomeini had been busy during exile. Broadcasts on the BBC's Persian Service meant his voice was familiar to many, and thousands of his cassette tapes had been smuggled into Iran to be played in mosques. Two weeks after the shah fled, the ayatollah arrived to a rapturous welcome as more than a million people lined the streets to greet him. What most did not know was that they had exchanged the crown for the turban.

Those who did not understand revolutionary Islam assumed the elderly ayatollah would be a hands-off figurehead helping to guide the country toward a less repressive future. They were soon put right. The radical Egyptian intellectual Sayyid Qutb, who was executed in Cairo in 1966, may have been a Sunni Muslim but his writings influenced the religious Shia revolutionaries in Iran. His seminal work, *Milestones*, had been translated into Farsi and fed into the idea that the answer to the problems in the Muslim world was Islam. Qutb had more influence in Arab countries, where the systems of royalty, nationalism, socialism, and secular dictatorship had failed to better people's lives, but when Khomeini declared that "Islam is political, or it is nothing," he was saying what Qutb's followers in the Muslim Brotherhood had been promulgating for more than a decade. Qutb believed in violent jihad to defeat "Crusaders and Zionists"; this, fused with the strain of martyrdom in Iranian Shia culture, was central to the fanaticism that gripped the religious masses during and after the revolution.

The secular intellectuals, dazzled by the somberly charismatic figure of Khomeini, had put aside their disdain for the religious establishment and joined forces to oust the shah. As so often in revolutions, the liberals failed to understand that what the true believers said, they meant. On the day he landed in Tehran, Ayatollah Khomeini informed the people: "From now on it is I who will name the government." Almost before anyone could say "Who voted for you?" the terror began.

Ten days after the crowds welcomed Khomeini, the military declared neutrality. The prime minister went into hiding before making his way to France, where he was assassinated in 1991. Minor religious groups and the Communists were swept aside amid waves of torture, executions, and disappearances. To ensure that there was no counterrevolution, Khomeini set up the Islamic Revolutionary Guard Corps (IRGC). This thuggish militia excelled at intimidating opponents. It has become the country's most formidable military force, while its senior personnel have grown wealthy since it branched into construction and other businesses.

Desperate to reverse freedoms for women, the new regime banned coeducational schools, protections within marriage were reduced, and gangs of Komitehs (committees) roamed the streets enforcing the wearing of hijab. Religious freedoms for minorities such as Jews and Christians were maintained in law but came to an end in spirit, and people of the Baha'i faith were subjected to particularly harsh persecution.

Those in the liberal middle class who could afford to leave did so in a hurry, followed by hundreds of thousands of others in a massive brain drain. Among them were about sixty thousand of the country's Jewish population after the Islamic Republic became Israel's most virulent, and usually deeply antisemitic, critic.

The new leaders were not keen to win friends, but they did influence people to regard Iran as a pariah state. As well as the repression at home, there were terror attacks abroad, and an infamous fatwa was placed on the British author Salman Rushdie over his book *The Satanic Verses*.

Justification lay in Khomeini's concept of *velayat-e faqih*—guardianship of the religious jurist. The idea, embedded within Shia belief, is that the most learned religious man should have political and religious control. So Khomeini became Supreme Leader, a position enshrined in the constitution. Subsequent leaders would be selected by an Assembly of Experts made up of senior clerics. In a way, the system of choosing the top figure is not dissimilar to the way in which the Roman Catholic pope is elected, but the pope doesn't get to be commander in chief of a country's armed forces, nor does he have the power to declare war—a task the ayatollah had to undertake a year after he came to power.

In Iraq, the secular dictatorship of Saddam Hussein saw the creation of a Shia Islamic republic next door as both a threat and an opportunity. Saddam was alarmed by Khomeini's call for Islamic revolutions in Arab countries and cracked down on Iraq's already embattled Shia majority. He then tried to invade Iran—which, as we saw at the beginning of this chapter, is not a good idea.

Saddam hoped to use the chaos of the revolution to make a land grab of the east bank of the Shatt al-Arab waterway and the oil-producing, ethnically Arab province of Khuzestan. What he didn't want was an eight-year bloodbath ending with each side where they started. Declassified recordings of Saddam and his advisers on the eve of war show that he felt he could get away with a brief conflict and hoped the Iranians "do not go further than what we want, dragging both of us into a situation that neither we nor they possibly wants." Instead he wanted "to bombard military targets, twisting their arm until they accept the legal facts. . . . However, if it becomes a full-scale war, then we will land wherever we need to."

It was carnage. Saddam expected a quick victory, a disastrous miscalculation contributing to more than 1 million deaths. The Iraqi army advanced along a 400-mile front and made early gains, including the city of Khorramshahr, where they used mustard gas against the defenders. But they failed to capture the oil port of Abadan, and the assault ground to a halt within weeks. Nowhere were the Iraqis able to penetrate farther than about 60 miles before they ran into the Zagros Mountains and out of morale. Within a few months a counteroffensive drove the Iraqi forces back across the border. Both capital cities were hit with air raids as the Iranians pushed on into Iraq in a bid to capture Shia strongholds such as Karbala. In 1988 Iraqi counteroffensives reversed Iranian gains and Khomeini, realizing his country was exhausted, accepted UN-brokered cease-fire terms. The two sides withdrew to their prewar positions.

The Supreme Leader died the following year, and the position passed to Ayatollah Ali Khamenei. Limited economic progress was made, but the clerics retained an iron grip on society as they determined to bring the revolution into every aspect of people's lives. The political system was rigged. To run for the Majlis, you must be approved by a twelve-member Council of Guardians, half of whom are chosen by the Supreme Leader. A list of some of the parties represented in the Majlis gives a clue as to how to get on the ticket; they include the Militant Clerics Society and the Society of Pathseekers of the Islamic Revolution. With that lot in front of them, you can see how the Pervasive Coalition of Reformists would have trouble finding their way. When the Majlis passes legislation, it must be approved by a majority of the Council of Guardians.

So in 1997 the hard-liners were shocked when a relatively moderate religious scholar, Mohammad Khatami, won the presidency in a landslide. During his term the clerics vetoed more than one-third of the bills proposed, most of them liberal measures that Khatami and his supporters had been elected to introduce. The ultraconservatives also continued their campaign of terror to destroy "counterrevolutionaries." Liberal media outlets were closed down and journalists jailed. Reform-minded intellectuals were murdered, and when students protested they were beaten off the streets, chased into their dormitories, and beaten again.

Over the next decade the economy still struggled, the religious thugs still enforced their beliefs on society, and Iran's confrontational attitude on the international front ensured isolation. In 2005 Khatami lost power to the former Revolutionary Guard Mahmoud Ahmadinejad, but in the 2009 election campaign another reformist emerged: Mir Hossein Mousavi, a former prime minister. After a record turnout, and amid concerns over voting irregularity by the authorities, Mousavi made the first move and said he'd been informed by the Interior Ministry that he'd won. Almost immediately there was an announcement on state media channels contradicting him. Ahmadinejad was declared the victor. The streets erupted in violence.

I'd managed to get a rare journalist visa to report on the election and the following day was on the streets of the capital with an Iranian colleague. As we walked down a boulevard, I noticed several people murmuring something under their breath as they passed. "What's going on?" I inquired. My colleague explained that people were saying the name of a particular street, and a time of day. At that time of day, on that particular street, I watched as dozens of people began to gather, then hundreds. As they gained confidence, antigovernment chanting broke out, and within a few minutes thousands of people had arrived. So did the riot police and thugs from the Basij militia. Scuffles turned into fights, bottles and stones began to be thrown by both sides, and battle lines were drawn.

The riot police had adopted a successful tactic of riding two to a motorbike with the passenger carrying a large club. When a group of these accelerated into a crowd, it quickly scattered. As I phoned in live reports, I found myself between the lines as several motorbikes readied for another charge. As they came down the road I stepped up onto the pavement, only to find one of the bikes mounting it and heading straight for me. There was no escape. As an officer lifted his baton in the air, I raised my hands in the surrender pose. Just as he began to swing for my head, he stopped—I can only assume because he saw a foreigner who perhaps had been caught in the chaos. I've never been so grateful for having freckles. The bike sped past, the officer whacking other less fortunate people with fewer freckles, before roaring back to the police lines.

I dived into the crowd for cover as they began attacking symbols of the regime, including a Bank of Iran building, which had its windows smashed. Again, I found myself at the front of the crowd as another police charge began. As I turned to run, a large rock, thrown by the security forces, hit me in the back with enough force to send me tumbling into one of the narrow water canals that run through the city, scraping the skin off the entire length of my leg as I went down. A group of protesters dragged me out and I staggered into a side street before deciding that was quite enough live reporting for one day. That's the last time I'm turning my back on a policeman, I thought. Five years later I received very minor injuries when shot with bird pellet in the back in Cairo. By a policeman. But that's another story.

The demonstrations continued for several days, during which dozens of people were killed; but the regime's grip was easily strong enough to ensure that Ahmadinejad served a second term. However, the fault lines had not gone away; indeed, they are magnified each year as the population grows younger, and enough of the youth grow up wanting change. This was reflected in the 2013 election, when a moderate cleric, Hassan Rouhani, won power by a margin the establishment realized was too big to change.

This was not entirely because everyone longed for a liberal Iran, although that was a major factor. "It's the economy, stupid" translates into many languages, including Farsi, and the 2013 vote was also a rebuke to the wasted years under Ahmadinejad, who had increased the country's international isolation and witnessed the economy shrink yet further.

Rouhani won again in 2017, but then for the election of 2021 the fix was in months before the vote. The Council of Guardians flexed its robes and disqualified almost six thousand candidates from running, among them ninety sitting members of the Majlis. Millions of Iranians asked themselves "What's the point?" and on election day stayed home. The lowest turnout since 1979 resulted in a landslide for the conservative hard-liners in the shape of the cleric, and former head of the judiciary, Ebrahim Raisi. The message was clear: one way or another, the ayatollahs and the Revolutionary Guard were staying in charge.

Which brings us to the present. Its leadership sees Iran as an isolated country beset by enemies. They're not wrong. Some of the ideologues talk about a "Sunni circle" surrounding Iran, with countries such as Saudi Arabia, encouraged by the Americans, actively working to undermine the Islamic Republic from within and without. This also has some validity, which is why the ayatollahs and Revolutionary Guard commanders could scarcely believe their luck when the Americans unknowingly delivered the historic Persian dream and secured their western flank by invading Iraq in 2003.

The US removed the Sunni-dominated regime that had invaded Iran, so once again the flat land of Mesopotamia became a buffer in front of Iran deterring potentially hostile forces and acting as a space within which force can be projected. The Bush administration's naïve belief that democracy would flourish resulted in the leaders of Iraq's majority-Shia population manipulating the system to ensure they dominated the country. They were helped every step of the way by Iran, which drove out foreign forces by backing a variety of Shia militias in the civil war following the invasion. The roadside bombs that killed so many US and British troops were often made in Iran, and the militias were financed, armed, and trained by Tehran. Iraq is not an Iranian poodle, but now its leadership often looks sympathetically toward its neighbor to the east.

It was a major step in Iran's ongoing battle with many of the Arab states. The ebb and flow of history has left many Arab countries with large Shia minorities—notably, Saudi Arabia, Lebanon, and Yemen, although there are also sizable communities in Syria, Kuwait, and the UAE. Often, they are less well off than the majority-Sunni populations and many feel discriminated against. Iran has sought to use this to gain influence throughout the region. In Yemen's civil war, for example, it sided with the Shia Houthi faction against Saudi-backed Sunni forces. And Tehran has spent twenty years creating and holding a corridor to the Mediterranean, giving it access to the sea and allowing it to supply its proxy—Hezbollah. In Baghdad it now finds a Shia-dominated government; in Damascus it dominates President Assad, who is from the Alawite minority, an offshoot of Shia Islam. Iran came to his rescue in the Syrian civil war to keep this corridor open. From there it is a short hop to the Lebanese capital, Beirut, where the strongest military force is not the Lebanese army but the Iranian-financed Hezbollah militia. Hezbollah controls the Bekaa Valley, south Beirut, and most of southern Lebanon, all the way to the Israeli border. This is the Islamic Republic's way of projecting its force in Mesopotamia and the Levant, just as its predecessors in previous centuries had done.

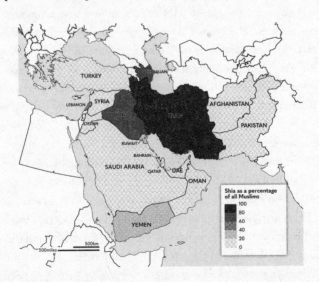

Most of the Muslim-majority countries surrounding Iran have Sunni majorities; however, Iran is sometimes able to look for allies within the Shia minorities in these countries.

While Iran clashes with the Sunni-led states, the country it despises most is Israel. Prior to the 1979 revolution Iran had a cordial relationship with Israel and was not noted for its antisemitism. Since then it has engaged in an over forty-year campaign of hate against not just the state of Israel but Jews in general. There is a steady stream of antisemitic rhetoric in which the hand of the "Zionists" is seen everywhere, and the mainstream Iranian media routinely publishes cartoons featuring the sort of stereotypical caricatures used by Nazi Germany. World leaders are frequently depicted with a Star of David on their sleeves, suggesting they are operating on behalf of their Jewish masters. Tehran has sent death squads to Argentina, Bulgaria, Thailand, India, Kenya, and many other countries to kill Jews, the worst attack being the murder of eighty-seven Argentinians in a Jewish community center in 1994.

It is useful for the Islamic Republic's leaders to blame Israel and Jews for the world's woes in order to deflect from their own shortcomings, but it seems likely their hatred runs deeper than politics. As early as the 1960s, Ayatollah Khomeini demonized Jews, calling them "impure creatures" and saying that they "have faces that manifest debasement, poverty, indigence, beggarliness, hunger, and wretchedness. . . . This is nothing but their inner poverty and spiritual abasement." He also enjoyed suggesting to the Iranian people that the shah was a Jew. His successor as Supreme Leader, Ayatollah Khamenei, has said, "Israel is a malignant cancer gland that needs to be uprooted." These rantings suggest a pathological loathing, one rooted in religion, and dangerous not just because they are made by people in power but because despite being led by Shia, the Iranian Revolution has inspired people with similar views in the Sunni Arab world to believe that they too can achieve power through religious violence.

In the minds, and indeed voices, of the Iranian leadership, the US is almost always linked with Israel and is even portrayed as a puppet of Israel. Iran's hard-liners believe the American role in their region is to keep its decadent Satanic jackboot on the heart of the Muslim world in order to steal its wealth and protect the evil Zionists, who are behind every dastardly plot against them. However, they do sometimes get a bit mixed up, since America is known as the "Great Satan" and Israel as "Little Satan." In 2001 President Bush engaged in his own labeling, describing Iran as part of an "axis of evil" and claiming that its nuclear energy facilities were a cover for building a nuclear weapons arsenal. Tehran already had missiles capable of reaching targets more than 3,000 miles away, so the idea that these might be nuclear tipped alarmed everyone within range.

In 2002 an Iranian dissident group revealed that Tehran was building a uranium-enrichment complex and a heavy-water facility, both of which can be used to make nuclear weapons. The government insisted its nuclear activity was only for peaceful purposes. Few in the international community were convinced, especially after an International Atomic Energy Agency report said that the enrichment process suggested Iran was seeking weapons-grade material. UN, EU, and US sanctions followed, limiting Iran's ability to produce and sell oil or gas.

Rouhani did make efforts to establish an international agreement on Iran's nuclear program, leading to a deal with global leaders in 2015. He even had contact with President Obama—the first direct dialogue between the countries' political leaders in almost forty years. This was not well received by the hardliners of the Islamic Revolution. Diplomatic relations between Iran and the US were cut in 1980 following the taking of hostages at the American embassy in Tehran, the event which set the course of the relationship. A mob attacked the embassy in November 1979 and took more than fifty Americans hostage. The 444-day crisis haunted President Jimmy Carter and helped usher in the presidency of Ronald Reagan.

Tensions between Iran and the US have been a constant, but there was a temporary "cease-fire" of sorts during the rise of ISIS in Iraq and Syria that was linked to the nuclear deal of 2015. Tehran realized that the more powerful ISIS became in the region, the greater the risk of Iranian influence being blocked. If ISIS defeated either the Iraqi Shia government or the Assad regime in Syria, its corridor to the Mediterranean would be cut off. The Americans, exhausted by their losses, could get Iran to do some of the fighting against ISIS in Iraq. Tehran knew that agreeing to the nuclear deal would open the door to discreet cooperation with the Americans; Barack Obama desperately wanted a foreign-policy success—and the nuclear deal could provide it. So Iran agreed to give up 98 percent of its highly enriched uranium. It was an example of how a marriage of convenience to solve a short-term problem can override deeper differences—temporarily.

ISIS was on the back foot, but tensions quickly returned, especially after Donald Trump came to power amid fears of war. He took the US out of the nuclear deal, reimposed sanctions, and bullied European companies so that they were too wary to do deals with Iran. There followed a series of incidents that raised the temperature. Two oil tankers near the Strait of Hormuz were mined and suspicion quickly fell on Tehran. There was no solid proof of who was responsible, however, and the Iranians had what diplomats call "plausible deniability." Nobody wanted a shooting match in the strait, so no action was taken. It was the same when missiles hit a Saudi oil refinery; the Houthis in Yemen said they fired them, but the evidence suggested the most likely finger on the trigger was Iranian. It looked as if the Iranians were probing America's tolerance levels. In 2019 they almost went too far. A US spy drone was shot down and the American air force was readied for air strikes, which were called off at the last minute. When Trump came into office, some analysts made a number of interesting claims, among them that he'd never wanted to be president, that he'd resign within months, that he'd be impeached and out of office within two years, and that he would start wars. They were all something of a stretch, but the idea that in 2019, with a year to go before the presidential election, he actively wanted a war that could trigger a global recession was beyond elastic.

And that's not the only reason a war was unlikely. US losses in Iraq and Afghanistan are among the factors reducing the American public's tolerance of military adventures. Iran knows this and so can gamble on pushing back against what it sees as unwarranted American aggression to a certain, but unknown, level. Tehran knows that if tensions boil over Iran might suffer air strikes, but the Americans are neither coming to the Zagros Mountains from Iraq, nor going ashore in force from their ships in the Gulf. Iran's military may be poorly equipped, but it can draw on millions of men who have been through conscription and 600,000 active personnel, including 190,000 in the IRGC.

However, none of this alters the effects of sanctions on Iran. The economy nose-dived, unemployment and inflation rose, and as winter approached in late 2019 the Iranian government raised fuel prices, triggering more huge nationwide demonstrations. The establishment had been surprised by previous protests; now they were shocked and nervous.

What particularly worried them was that the bulk of protesters were often no longer students and the liberal classes: now the working class, the backbone of the 1979 revolution, was coming out against them. Chants of "Death to Khamenei" were heard, and in a rebuke to Iran's foreign policy, crowds shouted, "Not Gaza, not Lebanon, my life for Iran," and "Get out of Syria." People were signaling that they were sick of their young men being sacrificed in Arab civil wars. It was also noted that when the authorities painted huge American flags on roads and squares, demonstrators went out of their way not to tread on them and so disrespect the US.

There was a respite after the US assassinated Qasem Soleimani, commander of the elite Revolutionary Guard's Quds Force, in early 2020 as he arrived in Baghdad to meet a militia leader. He was a nationally known figure who had orchestrated Iran's involvement in Syria. A few days later, Iran retaliated by firing missiles at Iraqi military bases hosting US troops; but on the same night, while on high alert for US air strikes, it accidentally shot down a civilian passenger jet leaving Tehran airport, killing all 176 people on board. After denying involvement the government eventually accepted responsibility, sparking another wave of protests. It had squandered any political capital it might have made in uniting the country over Soleimani's killing.

Then came Covid-19, and respect for the government took another blow. President Rouhani's administration consistently played down the threat of the virus and, when it spread, covered up the number of cases and botched public-health messages. The Revolutionary Guard didn't help. Its chief claimed the IRGC had invented a device that could detect coronavirus symptoms from 100 yards away. Amid nationwide hilarity, the Physics Society of Iran ridiculed the idea as a "science-fiction story." The clerics played their part. The learned Ayatollah Hashem Bathaei-Golpaygani announced he'd tested positive but had cured himself using an Islamic remedy. He died two days later. Another ayatollah told his followers to eat onions and brush their hair more to ward off the virus. There's a large market in Iran for the remedies of "Islamic medicine," but probably a bigger one which subscribes to the idea that laughter is a good tonic. The clerics were thoroughly ridiculed on social media with a variety of memes, jokes, and cartoons, which spread more quickly than the virus itself.

This is dangerous for the regime, because laughing at the revolutionaries is a revolutionary act in itself, and one it cannot prevent. However, this does not mean the fall of the regime is necessarily imminent, nor that, when it does fall, what follows will be an enlightened democracy. That said, as a highly educated and sophisticated country, with borders not drawn by Europeans, Iran has a better chance of becoming a genuine democracy than most other countries in its neighborhood, but probably not for some time.

We must look at the internal challenges facing the regime and the power it has to meet them. Economically it is in a hole that may yet get deeper, but the government appears to have officials with doctorates in getting around sanctions, and the economy staggers on year after year. Iran has forged good economic relations with China, which is more willing than many countries to ignore a number of the sanctions, as indeed is Russia. There will be more demonstrations, but the regime has shown a willingness to slaughter its people in their thousands to suppress dissent, and when you've gone that far, it's hard to turn back.

The Kurds have risen up in the past but are unlikely to make a move as long as the regime's grip remains tight. In the southwest the Arab minority of Khuzestan are angry that Iran's oil riches have not made their lives better. They are among the poorest of the minority groups, and resentment of this has resulted in occasional bomb attacks against government targets. In the southeast the huge province of Baluchistan is restive. Its 1.5 million people are mostly Sunni and poor, and many identify more with the Baluchis next door in Pakistan than with Iran. It is a busy drug- and people-smuggling route from Afghanistan and Pakistan to Europe. There have been bomb attacks against the Revolutionary Guard and government officials, but neither Khuzestan nor Baluchistan is an existential problem for the regime so long as it ensures that foreign powers are not organizing a revolt.

What of the middle class, the intelligentsia, and the arts? They continue a low-level campaign to retain an alternative civic culture in the country and are the inheritors of the centuries-long struggle to wrest control of power from royalty and religion. Music and films continue to be outlets for ideas and social commentary, and many younger people are no longer prepared to tolerate the hurtful interferences in their lives, such as how much of their hair they can show. During some of the recent antigovernment demonstrations an incendiary chant had been heard on the streets: "Oh, shah of Iran, return to Iran." It doesn't mean there is a genuine yearning for a return to rule by the old system—the liberal struggle has always been to escape the grip of royalty and religion—but it is one of many signs of discontent. Such protest worries the establishment; it chips away at their authority, but it has its limits. It is magnificent to see a young woman atop a monument, waving her head scarf in the air and challenging the police to stop her. It makes YouTube, it makes a difference—but it doesn't yet make a counterrevolution. Eventually, either there will be an uprising that replaces the current establishment or the establishment will slowly wither, but at the moment the authorities still have the upper hand.

I've seen firsthand the incredible bravery of young Iranians in challenging their tormentors, and the concept of martyrdom runs deep in their culture; but there are limits to how many people will sacrifice themselves. The dynamic would change if enough young soldiers and militia members were no longer willing to open fire on protesters. So far, the true believers, especially in the Revolutionary Guard and the Basij, appear to be holding firm. The regime keeps close watch on its armed forces, the secret police are inside law-enforcement agencies, and units of the Revolutionary Guard accompany the army when it is deployed.

Finally, there are the reformers working from the inside. For twenty years they have been trying to use elected institutions that were set up to give the appearance of democracy to counterbalance the real power—that of the clerics and Revolutionary Guard. They have tried to preserve the country's strong Islamic traditions and at the same time build a democracy. It remains a work, but not in progress.

In 2020, versions of a new phrase began to do the rounds. Instead of power flowing from the "crown to the turban" it was seeping from the "turban to the boots," meaning the military—specifically the Revolutionary Guard. The Majlis is full of ex-Guards, as are the boards of some of the big companies. Chief executives know that with a Guard on board, a contract might follow—after all, the elite force is not just full of influential generals, it is itself a major company. Its construction wing, Khatam al-Anbia, has built parts of the Tehran Metro, in addition to many other projects. This is akin to the Royal Marines making profits from extending the Northern Line of the London Tube, or perhaps the US 82nd Airborne Division moving into manufacturing cars. The IRGC talks the revolutionary talk and walks the money-making walk.

The Revolutionary Guard even has its own media arm, which runs dozens of newspapers, TV and radio stations, social-media outlets, and film production companies. Over the past few years, by no coincidence, all seem to follow three broad narratives: that the Revolutionary Guard and the Supreme Leader are really great guys and anyone who disagrees is a very bad person; that any economic or political failure or security excess is the fault of the reform administrations; and that outside forces are, at every waking moment, working to destroy the great nation of Iran.

Too often foreign news reports from Iran feature interviews with English-speaking university students and portray them as the voice of the youth. Things are far more complicated than that, as shown by the fact that many young people volunteer to join the Basij and the Revolutionary Guard. The reports should also point out that for every young dissident they find, there are other educated youngsters queuing up for jobs as graphic designers, scriptwriters, video editors, and production assistants at Revolutionary Guard–related companies. They pay well. If this side of Iran is not explained, the viewer might have trouble understanding why, when they've seen all these young people demanding change, change isn't happening. This is not to say that people employed by the Revolutionary Guard necessarily support the system, but it does show how the system is co-opting everyone it can in order to survive. Some of the tech-savvy younger generation are at the forefront of Iran's cyberwarfare project and are busy trying to spread Iran's point of view across the world or attempting to hack into hostile powers' military, commercial, and political computer systems. They're quite good at it.

This is how you do joined-up government: the Revolutionary Guard media arm employs thousands of people and keeps an eye on them via its intelligence wing. It sells its programs to the state broadcaster to amplify its message. It links its media operation with that of the Basij militia. One of its biggest media outlets, Martyr Avini, is headed by the Supreme Leader's representative in the Basij and is subordinate to the Revolutionary Guard. Nice work, and they get it.

This doesn't mean the Revolutionary Guard intends to take over—it's more fun pretending you are not in politics—but it's an example of how intertwined it is with the state, and how, should the clerics have to retreat, it is an alternative, with guns. The Revolutionary Guard could "course-correct" the revolution, but its name tells you what its job is, and its name and its job are why the regime has not bent, despite four decades of internal and external pressure.

One of the most important aspects of the Iranian regime is one that is often not taken as seriously as it should be. It was, is, and will remain a revolutionary theocracy. As such, it has fundamentalist principles and cannot change them without undermining itself. Imagine a French president declaring that he or she is no longer in favor of the equality part of the country's national motto *"Liberté, égalité, fraternité."* It's not going to happen. Now imagine that the ayatollahs, whose ideology is that Iran's Shia Islam is the manifestation of God's plan for humanity, announce a massive compromise with the "Great Satan" and a tolerance of sexual freedoms, conversion to other faiths, and a genuinely pluralistic political system. If you think you are enforcing God's will on Earth—that's not going to happen either.

Every American president since the 1979 revolution has tried the carrot-and-stick approach to achieve a "grand bargain" with the Islamic Republic. Such a deal would require each side to make what it would regard as huge compromises. Iran would have to allow robust UN verification that it is not building nuclear weapons, limit its ballistic-missile program, stop funding terrorist groups, end what the US regards as destabilizing behavior in Afghanistan, Yemen, Iraq, Lebanon, and Syria, and no longer oppose a negotiated settlement to the Arab-Israeli conflict. That's a big ask. Iran prides itself on being revolutionary and has always sought to export its revolutionary principles, to become the leader of like-minded movements. However, there is a scenario in which it might abandon that role in order to save the revolution at home. In return, the US would guarantee that it is not seeking regime change in Iran, end its unilateral sanctions, and, after diplomatic relations were restored, work with Iran economically to modernize its energy industry and diplomatically to ensure regional stability.

It sounds great, but tentative moves toward even agreeing to a framework of how to achieve these aims are consistently undermined by hard-liners on each side and mutual suspicion of each other. Barack Obama opened a few doors in his presidency but is accused of allowing the Iranians to continue working on a nuclear bomb due to the perceived weaknesses in the nuclear deal of 2015. President Rouhani walked through some of those doors, but was hammered by the hawks in Tehran.

Under President Biden, the Americans, and others, have given up on regime change and instead seek to simply change regime behavior. The ayatollahs can hold on to Fortress Iran as long as they let go of ideas of becoming a nuclear-armed state and pull back from the Arab world. The Arab governments may never warm to Tehran, but if it no longer interfered in Saudi Arabia, Yemen, Syria, Iraq, and Bahrain, they could come to terms with it. Conversely, if Iran looks to be close to having nuclear weapons, the Arab states will close ranks against it, seek ever closer ties to the US, and failing that, shelter under the umbrella of a future nuclear-armed Saudi Arabia.

The Islamic Republic, under its current system, is stuck in a Catch-22 situation. It cannot liberalize, because that would undermine the foundations of what legitimacy it has left among the millions of people who still support it. But if it does not, as each year passes, the increasingly young population will chafe against a system more in tune with the sixteenth century than the twenty-first.

The class of 1979 know that time and demographics are against them, but they have many cards to play. The nuclear issue remains alive and the Strait of Hormuz remains narrow. They have a range of proxy actors in the region they can call on in the worlds of politics and terrorism. To counter internal sub-version organized from within and without, they have much feared and brutal security services. And they are doing God's work. Therefore, to compromise is a sin, to resist is divine. The religious revolutionaries do not intend to give up their revolution.

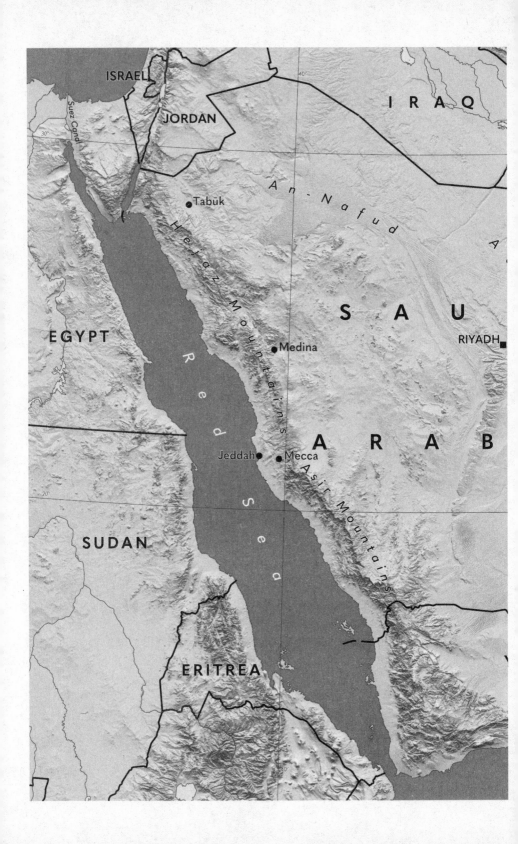

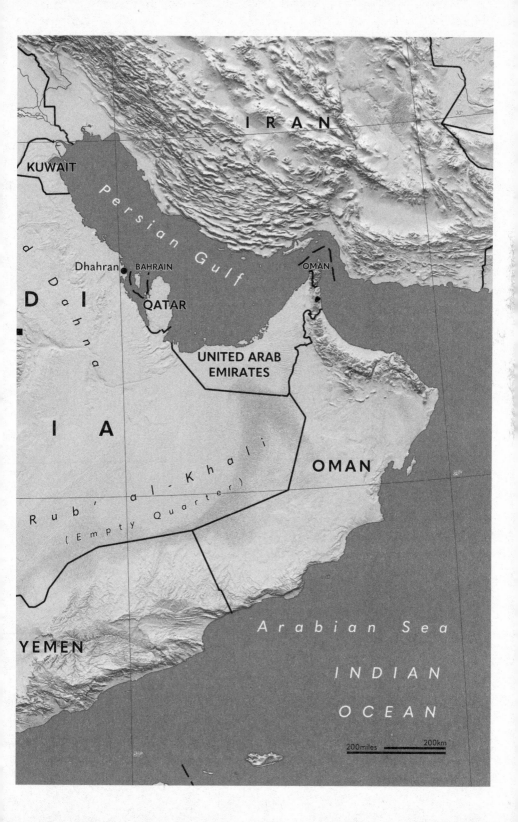

3

SAUDI ARABIA

If you keep walking, they have to follow you.

—Princess Reema bint Bandar Al Saud, first Saudi female ambassador

If you want to solve or manage a problem, you need to define it. In Saudi Arabia the problem is defined by two words: Saudi and Arabia.

In 1740, parts of the Najd region in central Arabia were controlled by a local emir named Muhammad ibn Saud. By 1930, one of his direct descendants had vastly extended that territory and renamed it Saudi Arabia. If a family names a country after itself, what about everyone who is not in the family? All citizens of Brazil are part of the Brazilian "family" and are equal in law, but not all Saudi citizens are from the House of Saud, nor are all equal. If I were to take over the United Kingdom and call it Marshland, some people might accept that it reflected the climate, but I wouldn't be confident of their loyalty to the country—by which I would mean me. (I hasten to assure Her Majesty Queen Elizabeth II, by the Grace of God, Head of the Commonwealth and Defender of the Faith, that I harbor no such treasonable ambitions.)

This identification of self with state creates difficulties, because historically the Sauds could make a reasonable argument to call parts of the Najd after themselves, but the rest of Arabia? Not so much. A large part of today's population has been under Saudi control for less than a century. If, 120 years ago, someone had told the Shammar tribe that the Emirate of Shammar would soon be turned into a mere province of the kingdom of the Sauds, they may have found themself at the wrong end of a scimitar. The Shia, most of whom live in provinces facing the Persian Gulf, would also have questioned the idea that they would be ruled by Saud Sunni Wahhabi fundamentalists, with whom they had clashed down the centuries.

This does not mean that the modern kingdom cannot survive, but it does explain the tensions that run beneath its surface. The center must hold the periphery if the ruling family is to retain its grip on power.

A century ago, the population of what is now a state with 34 million people was about 2 million, most of them nomads. Covering much of the Arabian peninsula, the country is mostly desert. There is still not much there except oil and sand. It was fossil energy sources that catapulted Saudi Arabia into the twentieth century and made it a major player. Oil is also the basis of the country's relationship with its major ally and protector: the US. Oil has given it vast wealth, and that wealth, in an oil-thirsty world, has allowed it to survive, even though elements within the power structure export a violent interpretation of its extreme brand of Islamic fundamentalism. The most famous Saudi of recent times is not a king or an oil multibillionaire, he is a terrorist—Osama bin Laden.

But there's a problem: the world is slowly weaning itself off oil. What is the ruling family to do, in a desert land with only sand and oil, a restive population, contested legitimacy, and beset by enemies within and without? It must modernize and use technology to harness renewable energy to adapt to the twenty-first century. It will not be an easy path, and its success or failure will affect the wider Middle East and beyond.

Saudi Arabia was created in the twentieth century using transport and communications technology, but the geography of the country meant the regions had distinct differences, many of which remain. Until recently, huge areas were uninhabitable. This is, after all, the world's largest country without a river and the interior is dominated by two vast deserts. In the north is the An-Nafud, which is connected to the Empty Quarter by a smaller, narrow corridor of sand. The Empty Quarter's official name is the Rub' al-Khali, although to the few nomadic Bedouin who live there it is simply called Al-Ramlah—the Sand. It is the largest continuous area of sand in the world, covering a region bigger than France, with dunes as high as 800 feet, and it stretches into the UAE, Oman, and Yemen. Summer temperatures in the deserts are frequently over 112°F in the shade, not that there's much of that. Conversely, if you've ever been in the desert at night in the winter, you'll have felt how bitterly cold it can be. Even now few people venture into it, and much of it remains unexplored. It's known that beneath the sands lie large quantities of oil and gas, but recent low oil prices mean it is too expensive to exploit them fully.

Saudi Arabia borders eight countries. To the north are Jordan, Iraq, and Kuwait. Saudi's eastern coastline then runs south toward Bahrain, Qatar, and the UAE, which also face the Gulf. To the south are Oman and Yemen; the latter is both the longest and most volatile of Saudi Arabia's borders. The Empty Quarter acts as a buffer protecting Saudi Arabia from land-based threats from the south, but also makes trading with its southern neighbors difficult. Crossing it was compared in difficulty with traversing the South Pole, and the first documented expedition came less than a century ago. In December 1931, the British explorer Bertram Thomas, accompanied by Bedouin tribesmen, set off from the coast of Oman and appeared 800 miles away in Qatar several weeks later. In 2018, a similar journey became somewhat easier when the first road across the desert was opened, connecting Oman to Riyadh, the Saudi capital. If you decide to drive it you may not need to be as intrepid as Thomas and his friends, but do bear in mind that there are no service stations along the way.

Climate and the ancient trade routes shaped by geography explain most of today's population centers. All of the high ground in Saudi is in the western half. The Red Sea coastal plains are relatively narrow, and a series of hills and mountains run inland parallel to the coast almost the entire length. Jeddah is on flat land but Mecca, which sits about 50 miles inland, is 900 feet above sea level, and some of the hills behind it are as high as 6,000 feet. There is a gap through the high ground leading to Medina and, with the ancient caravans unable to travel through the Empty Quarter, trade between Africa, the Red Sea, Persia, and India was funneled toward the three cities.

To the south, some of the highest mountains in the country lie just inland from the sea near the Yemeni border. The cooler climate there has long attracted settlement. This is why most Saudis live on the western side of the country, many in and around Mecca, Medina, and Jeddah, but the mountainous border with Yemen is the most densely populated part of the country.

Heading east, once you are over, or through, mountain ranges such as the Hejaz to the northwest, then it's flat all the way to the Persian Gulf in the east. Saudi Arabia is predominantly Sunni Muslim, but with a substantial Shia minority. Most of the Shias live in the Eastern Province and are from the Baharna tribe. This is the region most vulnerable to infiltration by hostile foreign powers, and, due to the hundreds of oil and gas pipelines crisscrossing the area, it is open to sabotage. The province is connected to Shia-majority Bahrain by a 15-mile-long causeway constructed by the Saudis in 1986. Officially it is for commuting, tourism, and trade; unofficially it is also for Saudi tanks to get there in a hurry if protests against the Sunni leadership get out of control. Large concentrations of Shia Muslims also live along the border with Yemen, and there are sizable populations in Mecca and Medina.

Toward the center of the country lie Riyadh and the Najd region. Although the capital is the biggest city and Saudi's political heart, it is isolated from the other population centers, a factor that partially explains why the inhabitants practice a form of Islam that most of the population find too extreme. While the arrival of camels, the "ships of the desert," had enabled traders to reach small oasis towns such as Mecca and Medina, Najd, where the Sauds lived, remained isolated by the three deserts surrounding it and the mountains separating it from Hejaz. Najd was a backwater without water. There was little reason to go there, except to get to Mecca from the east, but other routes were less arduous and so for centuries the world passed it by.

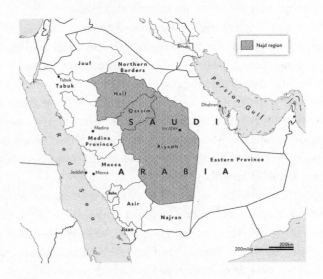

The modern-day regions of Saudi Arabia, and the historic region of Najd.

The fortunes of Najd began to change in the mid-1700s, when several hundred members of an ambitious minor clan called the Al Sauds took over some date groves around an oasis in Ad Diriyah. The local emir, Muhammad ibn Saud, turned it into a flourishing market town and the regional political center. If you are ever in Riyadh, it's worth making the 15-mile journey through the desert to get a feeling for the birthplace of the Saudi state. The mud-brick city walls of Ad Diriyah, a UNESCO World Heritage site, encompass half-ruined buildings, but also rebuilt clay houses and four-story palaces amid labyrinthine alleyways.

As the family grew in importance it forged a strategic relationship with the Wahhab clan, which exists to this day. In 1744 a religious scholar, Muhammad ibn Abd al-Wahhab, swore a *bayah*, or oath of allegiance, to Ibn Saud. He believed Muslims must give unquestioned allegiance to a leader, and in return the leader must rule according to strict Islamic principles. Islam has nothing comparable to Christianity's traditional demarcation of politics and religion. The bargain was that the Sauds would do the politics, but the religious aspects of politics and society were the Wahhabis' domain. It has mostly been that way, although occasionally each of these two pillars of Saudi Arabia has attempted to bend the other to its will. While most Saudis are Sunni, they do not all adhere to Wahhabism. For example, even in northern parts of Najd, in the lands formerly ruled by the Sauds' great rivals the Shammar, a less austere version of Sunni belief is practiced. This is also the case in the Red Sea coastal regions, which consider themselves, by Saudi standards, more cosmopolitan and outward-looking than the Wahhabi heartland. The creation of one of the most restricted societies in the modern world has not been entirely with the agreement of all the people.

To cement the Saud-Wahhab alliance, Ibn Saud's eldest son married the daughter of al-Wahhab. Al Saud publicly embraced Wahhabism, Wahhab embraced the Sauds, and together they set off to conquer Arabia. By 1765 they controlled Najd and were expanding in all directions, including Mecca and Medina, where they destroyed shrines, particularly targeting those used by the Shia minority. The Wahhabi referred to the Shia as Rafida, which means "rejecters," a slur still used by Wahhabis in the twenty-first century.

This expansion of power is known as the First Saudi State. At times it occupied most of the territory that makes up today's Saudi Arabia, as well as parts of northern Oman, Qatar, Bahrain, and the UAE. It fell in 1818 after the Ottomans sent an army from Egypt to recapture the Hejaz and then pushed on into the Najd, where it took Ad Diriyah, leveling much of the town. King Abd Allah al Saud was captured and sent to Istanbul to be publicly beheaded.

The kingdom was destroyed, but two years later the Ottomans withdrew most of their forces and a Saud survivor of the carnage, Turki ibn Abdullah, began to rebuild the empire and the family. By 1824 Riyadh was recovered, marking the beginning of the Second Saudi State, which lasted until 1891 but was constantly beleaguered by the Ottomans and the Sauds' near neighbors from the Shammar Mountains region of Najd, the Rashidi.

The Rashidi dynasty were the rulers of the Emirate of Shammar in northern Najd. The Sauds and Rashidi spent decades fighting each other for control of the interior of Arabia, culminating in a devastating defeat for the Sauds in 1890, when they lost Riyadh; they fled to Kuwait the following year.

And there they stayed, in exile, in poverty and a state of rage. And there they might have disappeared into history were it not for a man with a very long name whose surname would become a nation state—Abdul Aziz bin Abdul Rahman bin Faisal bin Turki bin Abdullah bin Mohammed Al-Saud.

Ibn Saud, as he is known, was fifteen when the extended family escaped to Kuwait; he spent his teenage years in poverty with barely a *riyal* to his illustrious name. In 1901, in his midtwenties, he succeeded his father as leader of the Saud dynasty, taking the title Sultan of Najd. There was a problem—Najd was ruled by the Rashidi and he was in Kuwait.

Ibn Saud was not the sort of man to let these details get in the way of a sultanate. In 1902 he led a party of just twenty warriors into the Najd and, on a moonless night in January, they went over Riyadh's city walls and killed the Rashidi governor. The young man was now sultan of the entire city, which measured about 250 acres.

It was a good base from which to begin the reconquest. By the outbreak of the First World War in 1914, Ibn Saud controlled enough of the rest of the region to really be the Sultan of Najd, and he had designs on regions in what are now Syria and Jordan, the kingdom of Hejaz (which included Mecca and Medina), and the parts of the Gulf coast not already under his control. However, all these could bring him into conflict with the British and Ottomans, so first he turned his attention to the Rashidi. They were allied with the Ottomans, so naturally he allied with the British, who gave him money and weapons with which to fight the rival tribe. "Thank you very much," said the sultan, who pocketed the money, stashed the arms away to create an arsenal, waited for the foreigners to stop fighting each other, and only then began a renewed campaign against the Rashidi. Ibn Saud mostly relied on the Ikhwan, an army of about 100,000 ultra-Wahhabi shock troops who actively sought any opportunity to fight non-Wahhabi Muslims. That gave them plenty of scope, so much so that eventually Ibn Saud had to suppress them by force.

In 1920 his well-armed forces marched on the Rashidi and within two years were victorious, doubling the size of Ibn Saud's kingdom. He then turned on another traditional enemy, the Hashemites, rulers of the kingdom of Hejaz. Mecca and Medina fell in 1925, causing the ruling family to flee to Iraq and Jordan. In 1927 Ibn Saud negotiated a treaty with the British; they recognized him as king of Najd and Hejaz, and in return he accepted that parts of northern Hejaz would be transferred to Jordan and he gave up claims to parts of eastern Jordan. Ibn Saud also took on the responsibilities of Khadim al-Haramayn al-Sharifayn

(Custodian of the Two Holy Mosques) in Medina and Mecca, Islam's holiest city and the birthplace of the Prophet Muhammad.

Ibn Saud was now the only truly independent Arab leader, and no one was in a position to challenge him for the title. His agreements with the British kept them off his back and allowed the House of Saud to consolidate control over most of the peninsula. In 1932 Saud again changed his title, and this time the name of the country; now he was king of Saudi Arabia.

Ibn Saud had united Saudi Arabia by force of arms; to hold it together he then married a daughter from each of the defeated tribes and senior religious families. He had about twenty wives but, in accordance with religious law, never more than four at a time. The result was more than one hundred children and the creation of a family network that dominates the state.

The official narrative is that Ibn Saud unified Arabia by reestablishing the Saudi states of previous decades for the good of all the tribes, with the justification that he was simply restoring authority over his land. This version of history cannot be challenged inside the kingdom. The extent to which other views exist in the country is hard to gauge, as it's hardly a subject local people will risk talking about to a foreigner—I know, I've tried. Saudi professor Madawi Al-Rasheed, writing from outside the country, gives an alternative view, arguing that the birth of Saudi Arabia marks "the emergence of a state imposed on people without a historical memory of unity or national heritage that would justify their inclusion in a single entity."

The debate matters because the grip of the House of Saud depends on levels of agreement about its legitimacy. In recent decades that legitimacy has been underpinned by efforts to improve the lives of ordinary Saudis, using the incredible wealth from the country's bountiful energy supplies.

In the decades before 1932, oil had been discovered in Iran, Bahrain, and Iraq. The oil companies suspected more was to be found in Saudi Arabia. They came knocking on Ibn Saud's door offering to explore the Eastern Province. The king was suspicious of the British companies, fearing that the UK government would be unable to resist its colonial tendencies and seek too much political influence. In 1933 the contract went to Standard Oil Company of California (SOCAL). The Saudis knew the Americans would meddle in their affairs, but not with the colonial mindset of London.

Drilling began in 1935, in 1938 oil was found, and in the same year Dammam No. 7—the "Prosperity Well"—began pumping out the black stuff and the change began. SOCAL built a new port, drilled for water supplies, constructed hospitals and office buildings, and brought in foreign workers, because few Saudis had even seen mechanical equipment, never mind knew how to use it. The capital of the new kingdom then had a population of about 40,000; within seventy years it had grown to 6 million.

The oil and money flowed, mostly to SOCAL at first, but as the years passed Riyadh managed to get more concessions and gradually buy a controlling interest in the company, which became Aramco.

During the Second World War Saudi Arabia remained neutral but leaned toward the Allies. The conflict demonstrated that the modern world now relied absolutely on oil, not just for industry and prosperity but also to fight wars. A single US mechanized division (about 250 tanks) was burning through 25,000 gallons of fuel just to travel 100 miles. Ibn Saud knew it, President Franklin Roosevelt knew it. It was time to meet.

Both men were pragmatists. In February 1945 they met on board a US warship in the Suez Canal. They were of similar age, both heads of state and each stricken with infirmity, and they appear to have bonded. The wounds Ibn Saud suffered in the battles he had fought were catching up with him and he had trouble walking, while FDR was in a wheelchair and had just weeks to live. They agreed that the Americans would be guaranteed access to Saudi oil, the Saudis would stay within their borders, and the safety of Saudi Arabia would be guaranteed by the Americans. Ibn Saud had many enemies—not least the Hashemites, who now ruled in Iraq and Jordan. It was only twenty years since he had pushed them out of Mecca and Medina; if they were strong enough and the right offer came along, they might try to retake the Hejaz, and that would be the end of Saudi Arabia and of Ibn Saud. Better to count the most powerful country in the world as your new best friend than have it making overtures to your enemies, especially as the British backed the Hashemites—now London would not dare support a Hashemite land grab.

Ibn Saud was good at timing. FDR headed home and a few days later Saudi Arabia declared war on Germany and Japan, thus earning a seat at the newly formed United Nations. The Saudis were now players on the world stage, oil made them important, and the Americans made them safe.

Ibn Saud died in 1953 aged seventy-three, having utterly transformed the fortunes of his family. He was succeeded by one of his many sons, Saud, whose extravagant spending habits, mostly on himself, depleted the government coffers and left little money for educational and health projects. Ibn Saud had built his first palace from the same sun-dried mud bricks ordinary people used; their new ruler was a very different sort of man. Public disquiet grew.

In the first few years of his rule, King Saud managed to fall out with almost everyone at home and abroad. By 1964 his many brothers had had enough. They went to the senior clerics, who, also taking a dim view of Saud's extravagance, issued a fatwa "suggesting" it was time to go and be replaced by his half brother Faisal. Saud left for Greece; Faisal headed for the royal palace.

During the new king's reign, oil revenues increased by more than 1,600 percent, enabling the building of a communications and transportation network and a generous welfare system. Slavery was finally abolished in law, although a modern version of it continues via the treatment of many foreign workers.

Faisal sent a token force to Jordan in the 1967 Arab-Israeli War, but when the next war broke out, in 1973, he sat out the fighting and limited the kingdom's direct military involvement. However, with the US supplying Israel, Faisal agreed to Arab League demands for an oil boycott to try to curtail American support. The Aramco oil wells closed, and world oil prices tripled. US president Richard Nixon then quietly suggested that American troops might have to show up in Saudi Arabia. That concentrated minds and Faisal began secretly to supply the US Navy with oil; the following year he dropped the oil embargo. The Saudis had crossed a red line and the reality of the "partnership" with the Americans was obvious.

At home, the introduction of television in 1965 sowed the seeds of Faisal's violent downfall and pushed the country further down the path toward religious extremism. Fearing this new contraption would lead the people astray, religious conservatives staged a large protest ahead of the first TV broadcast in 1965, despite its being a reading from the Koran. One of the king's nephews led an assault on the TV studios and was later killed in a shoot-out with security forces. No charges were brought against the police, which angered the religious establishment. To appease them, Faisal allowed religious extremists fleeing the secular regimes in Egypt and Syria to come to the kingdom and enter the education system. Saudi Arabia had its fair share of xenophobic religious characters already; Faisal inadvertently strengthened them. Many of the Saudi jihadists of the twenty-first century learned at the feet of this generation of extremist scholars.

In 1975, Faisal's past caught up with him. He was shot and killed by the brother of the nephew who died during the anti-TV protests a decade earlier. It is assumed this was revenge, although the authorities said the brother was mentally ill. Next up was Faisal's half brother Khalid. The fourth king of Saudi

Arabia had to contend with one of the most shocking events in the country's history.

On November 20, 1979, hundreds of armed dissidents stormed the Grand Mosque in Mecca. This is a place considered so holy in Islam that non-Muslims are not allowed into the city, never mind the mosque. There are signs outside the city limits telling non-Muslims not to come any nearer. It is forbidden to shed blood in the complex and the penalty for transgression is crucifixion. The insurgents had placed coffins in the center of the courtyard, a normal practice for those seeking blessings for the deceased, but inside were rifles that were quickly handed out. The insurrection was led by a man called Juhayman al-Otaybi, a descendant of the Ikhwan Wahhabi warriors who had fought for the Sauds in the 1920s. His grandfather had ridden alongside Ibn Saud, and his family was one of the most important in the Najd region.

The leadership was stunned. The insurgents had not only desecrated the holy place, they were using the mosque's loudspeakers to denounce the House of Saud for being corrupt and for allowing foreigners to come to Saudi Arabia and influence the population with their decadent ways. The royal family cleared the whole city of civilians, then went to the religious leaders to obtain a fatwa allowing them to use force to retake the mosque.

After nearly a week of fighting, with heavy losses on both sides, the authorities turned to the French, who had spent years building a solid intelligence-sharing relationship with the Saudis and selling them arms. Amid great secrecy, President Valéry Giscard d'Estaing dispatched three members of the GIGN, France's elite counterterror unit, to train the Saudi special forces. Two weeks after the takeover began it was over. Sixty-three survivors emerged, to be publicly beheaded in various city squares across the country.

The fallout was huge. The revolutionary leader of Iran, Ayatollah Khomeini, blamed "criminal American imperialism and international Zionism" for the takeover, leading to riots in several countries and the burning of American embassies in Libya and Pakistan. It was a routine reflex action by the Supreme Leader; he knew it would play well with millions of people gullible enough to believe that Muslims would never attack the mosque and that therefore the usual "hidden hands" must be responsible and the Saudi administration was probably complicit.

The long-term effect was that the panicked leadership reacted by snuffing out any ideas about modernizing the country in the social sphere. King Khalid was very aware that many of the insurgents were from tribes supplying most of the troops for the National Guard. His answer to the problem? More religion.

Photographs of women vanished from newspapers, female TV presenters were no longer seen on screen, the religious conservatives were given extra funds, cinemas were closed, and more hours of religious education were added to the national curriculum. The religious police had a field day for the following four decades. Schools and universities recruited greater numbers of clerics teaching young people that only Wahhabism was true Islam. No surprise, then, that for the next decade tens of thousands of young Saudi men traveled to Afghanistan to fight the invading godless Soviet Communists.

And it was no surprise that when they came home, they still wanted to use their military skills in the cause of international jihad. Among them was a man named Osama bin Laden.

It would be another decade before the bin Laden family became a household name. During that time Khalid died and his half brother Fahd took over. In 1990 Iraq invaded Kuwait and Saddam Hussein's next target looked to be the Saudi oil fields. Bin Laden, mostly unknown outside the kingdom, offered the services of his Afghan-trained mujahideen to defend the country. He wasn't taken seriously, and Fahd turned to the Americans.

This meant the Custodian of the Two Holy Mosques invited hundreds of thousands of "infidel" troops into the kingdom and some of them were even women! He needed a fatwa from the religious authorities to justify it. He got one, but Saudi Arabia got more than he bargained for.

The Americans came, saw, and conquered, insofar as their coalition, including Saudi forces, pushed Saddam's army out of Kuwait. But the Americans stayed in Saudi Arabia. It was too much for the bin Ladens of this world. Many people were asking why a government that had spent enormous sums on state-of-the-art defense systems required help from the infidel Americans. The US presence also emboldened reformers, meaning the ruling family faced opposition on two fronts. By far the more threatening was that from Islamists. The kings of Saudi Arabia partially base their right to rule on their religious credentials, but "king" and "kingdom" are not Islamic terms and the rulers are not theologians. Nevertheless, they claim to rule according to the principles of sharia law, and so the emergence of an Islamist opposition shocked the entire establishment.

In 1995 an explosion at the headquarters of a US training center for the Saudi National Guard killed five Americans and two Indians. Four young Saudis were arrested and executed after televised confessions that they were influenced by Osama bin Laden. In 1996 another explosion targeted an apartment block housing US personnel, killing nineteen. There were other attacks, but the intelligence services were able to break up several insurgent groups and sweep the problem under the carpet. In 2001 bin Laden lifted it, and beat it so hard that the Americans went to war and the House of Saud shook.

Out of the nineteen attackers on 9/11, fifteen were from Saudi Arabia, as was its mastermind, bin Laden. The Saudi authorities privately acknowledged that their shortcomings in tackling radicalism were partially to blame for the rise of Al-Qaeda, but could hardly admit to the public that they shared any responsibility for international terror. The outside world knows Riyadh has spent hundreds of millions of dollars opening Wahhabi-influenced mosques in places such as Bosnia and Pakistan, but Wahhabism per se is not terrorism and money talks, even if some of the mosques have dubious records on combating the sort of religious rhetoric that is a gateway to violence. The Saudi public was divided about America's subsequent war in Afghanistan, but the government quietly allowed the use of its air bases for US command-and-control operations. During America's longest war the Saudi media did not inform the public that, proportionally, Saudi fighters captured in Afghanistan were the biggest contingent of prisoners sent to Guantánamo Bay.

Some of the Saudi fighters in Al-Qaeda also wanted to bring the struggle home. The Sauds had rejected bin Laden's help and then assisted his enemies. Now he and others were not just going after American troops in the kingdom; they were going after the kingdom itself. The House of Saud had long ridden the tiger of Wahhabism—but it took 9/11 for it to realize that elements within it wanted to bite them as well.

In 2003 the Americans announced they were leaving Saudi Arabia. They'd pushed the Taliban out of Kabul and had swept into Baghdad. They knew their presence exacerbated tensions, and with "victory" in Afghanistan and Iraq they could afford to go. But bin Laden hadn't conceded.

That May three compounds housing foreign workers in Riyadh were stormed by gunmen who went from house to house looking for "cross and cow worshippers"—Christians and Hindus. Thirty-nine people were killed and more than 100 wounded. A spate of attacks followed: the American consulate in Jeddah was bombed, more compounds were hit, and an American, Paul Johnson, was kidnapped and beheaded and the footage uploaded to the internet. More than 100 foreigners were killed, among them BBC cameraman Simon Cumbers.

Simon was a great guy, always smiling, always willing to help, a generous, garrulous thirty-six-year-old Irishman. A few days before his death, we'd been chatting at a party in London; we were both heading to Saudi Arabia and were swapping tips on operating there. He was murdered in the same incident in which BBC correspondent Frank Gardner was shot and seriously injured as gunmen appeared on the street where they were filming. A few weeks later I was briefly on the same street, reporting on Al-Qaeda and Simon's death. We'd asked for a police car to follow us, but as we entered the neighborhood it disappeared. We spent about four minutes out of our vehicle, filmed a "piece to camera" in one take, and got going. Our driver was the same one Simon had used. He was on compassionate leave as he was so shaken by the event, but I'd found him after a few phone calls and he insisted on coming to help. He was in tears as he told us his story off camera, and despite his nerves was adamant he would help us. He wanted to show the real face of Arab hospitality to outsiders by which it is an honor to assist them. Less than 40 percent of Saudis are Wahhabis, and even most of them do not condone the savagery of the current generation of jihadists.

On the same trip Al-Qaeda's strategy became apparent: sow chaos and reap the rewards. From UK and US sources we found that about 20 percent of highly skilled foreign workers had fled the kingdom. A few months later, more had left and British Airways suspended flights to the country. If the trend continued, at some point the high-tech industries—most important, the energy sectors—would grind to a halt. If large sections of the population no longer received the generous subsidies provided by the government, opposition to the ruling family would grow. This would create a gap Al-Qaeda and others would try to force wider to collapse the state. The authorities went into overdrive, the crackdown surpassed that of the mid-1990s and again the intelligence services gripped the situation.

The kingdom survived, but the current leadership knows that the challenges have not gone away; indeed, new ones have risen, as has a new leader. In 2017 King Salman appointed his thirty-one-year-old son, Mohammed bin Salman, crown prince. He'd already made him defense minister, despite negligible military experience, and for many Saudis, especially within the royal family, the promotion to king in waiting was too much, too young. Tradition dictated that ascension to the throne should be based on seniority in both lineage and age. It is estimated there are about fifteen thousand members of the royal family, of whom two thousand or so are senior members who hold most of the wealth and power. Within the corridors of the royal palaces, there are ways and means of undermining the crown prince. He is vulnerable.

For better or worse, though, he is the designated future leader and already has many of the levers of power in his hands. As he looks around the kingdom, the man known as MBS sees problems in all directions and has acted.

To understand foreign policy under MBS, it's important to see the policies he has inherited, especially the regional cold war with Iran that has descended into proxy wars this century. The chaos unleashed in Iraq by the Americans produced a Shia-dominated government with ties to Iran, and Iran arms numerous Iraqi Shia militias. Riyadh refused to recognize the government and funded some Sunni militias to rival the Shia groups. The policy achieved little and in 2015 was reversed; diplomatic relations were restored and, in a bid to undermine Iranian influence, economic ties strengthened. What the Sauds want is domestic and regional dominance, preferably in as stable an atmosphere as possible.

The Arab uprisings of 2011 had upped the stakes in the confrontation with Iran. The Saudis sent troops to help put down protests in Bahrain, which they claimed were instigated by Tehran. Then, as the Syrian revolt descended into sectarian civil war in 2012, Riyadh joined the attempt to bring down President Assad, who was backed by Iran. It sent money and weapons to some of the more moderate units within the Free Syrian Army rebel alliance. The Saudis view Syria as an Iranian land bridge linking Tehran, via Baghdad and Damascus, to the Iranian-funded Shia Hezbollah militia in Beirut. It follows that if you break Assad, you break the bridge. However, with the Americans taking a back seat and Russia and Iran supporting the Assad regime, the bridge remains intact. The Saudi kingdom does not just fear Iran obtaining nuclear weapons, it fears its ability to project influence and violence across the region. If Iran does become a nuclear-armed state, Saudi Arabia will consider following suit.

As defense minister, MBS was on the front foot. In 2015 an economic blockade was imposed on Qatar amid accusations that it was not only siding with Iran but supporting Islamist groups such as the Muslim Brotherhood and Hamas. Qatar, with a population of 3 million, knows it can punch massively above its weight due to its wealth from gas supplies and, like other Gulf states, aspires to be a regional leader. The two have been at odds since the mid-1990s, especially since Qatar set up Al Jazeera TV, which the Saudis say is hostile to them. The frosty relationship is a major contributor to what has become another front in the Saudi/Iran cold war. The Qataris responded to the blockade by moving closer to Iran and another of Saudi Arabia's rivals, Turkey. The Saudis have long opposed the Muslim Brotherhood as it seeks to topple royal dynasties. In 2013 Riyadh supported the military coup in Egypt that deposed the elected Brotherhood leader Mohamed Morsi and replaced him with General Abdel al-Sisi.

They also supported the Libyan National Army against the Turkish-backed Government of National Accord (GNA) in the Libyan civil war. The Saudis and

UAE believe that the GNA is dominated by Muslim Brotherhood–influenced Islamists, and that Turkey's president, Recep Erdoğan, is connected to the Brotherhood, which seeks to overthrow their kingdoms. Hence, just as Riyadh supported the coup in Egypt that toppled the Brotherhood government, so it is attempting to block a Brotherhood government in Libya. Saudi money is used to fund the Libyan National Army, while Turkish money and forces have ensured that the Libyan National Army cannot take Tripoli.

MBS also sanctioned military intervention in Yemen via a coalition of mostly Gulf countries in Operation Decisive Storm. The coalition was fighting the rebel Houthi Shia forces, which are backed by Iran. Saudi Arabia does not want the Houthis in control of Yemen due to their ties with Tehran and because the Saudis fought a war with Yemen in 1934 during which they took several border regions. Some of the territory is populated by Shia, and some Yemenis would like it back.

By 2019 Decisive Storm had failed to achieve its aims. It did cause a storm of protest around the world as Yemeni civilian casualties mounted during a relentless bombing campaign, often in urban areas. The Houthis were also sending long-range missiles and drones into Saudi Arabia, targeting oil facilities, airports, and civilian areas. Late that year, two major oil-processing plants were hit, briefly shutting down half the country's oil production. The Houthis claimed responsibility, but the Americans said the missiles came from Iran, and the Saudis did not contradict them.

Escalation against Iran was an option, but the Trump administration made it clear the US was not willing to go to war over the issue and the Saudis knew they were in no position to go it alone, even if they wanted to. They let the crisis blow over and by 2020 were quietly trying to get out of the war MBS had got them into. They need to persuade the Houthis to end the relationship with Iran and in return receive Saudi money to reconstruct what is a failing state.

MBS's foreign policy has been seen as impetuous and aggressive. An example was the surreal incident in late 2017 when Lebanon's then prime minister, Saad al-Hariri, "chose" to announce his resignation during a visit to Riyadh. Hariri thought he was going on a camping trip with MBS, only to find himself separated from his bodyguards, relieved of his phone, shoved into a room by security officials, and handed his resignation speech. When he appeared on television to read it, he appeared to blame Hezbollah and Iran for his decision, at which point the clumsy machinations of the crown prince became apparent.

The suspicion is that MBS hoped Hariri's resignation would collapse the Lebanese coalition government and thereby weaken the power of Hezbollah, which is in the coalition. Riyadh does not wish to see a Shia movement, particularly one controlled by Iran, dominate Lebanon. There are even suggestions, less credible but not impossible, that Hariri was instructed to tell the militia in the Palestinian refugee camps in Lebanon that they should fight Hezbollah. Given that Hezbollah is stronger than even the Lebanese army, such a move would come at some cost.

Over the next few days, Lebanese officials made increasingly frantic phone calls to their counterparts in the US, Egypt, France, and elsewhere, suggesting their prime minister was being detained. According to the *New York Times*, several Western ambassadors demanded to see Hariri and were allowed access but only in the presence of two Saudi guards. After several days, and furious private interventions by foreign governments, Hariri was allowed to fly home, whereupon he promptly announced that, actually, he wasn't going to resign after all.

Riyadh has muscle when it comes to both Lebanon and its prime minister. Hariri's family business owes much to Saudi backing, and Saudi Arabia hosts 250,000 Lebanese workers; sending them home would severely damage Lebanon's struggling economy. Saudi officials deny that Hariri was coerced, but cannot offer an explanation as to why he resigned and then rescinded the decision.

The opprobrium heaped upon the crown prince in diplomatic circles for this escapade was nothing compared with the reaction to the 2018 murder of the Saudi journalist Jamal Khashoggi in the Saudi consulate in Istanbul. Khashoggi had fallen out with the regime over the behavior of the crown prince. On October 2 he was seen entering the consulate but not leaving, and was reported missing by his fiancée the same day.

The Saudis insisted he had left but provided no evidence, not even from the CCTV cameras that cover all exits. It quickly emerged that Khashoggi had been killed inside the building and his body dismembered. The Turkish government briefed the media that the killing must have been sanctioned at the "highest levels." It was established that fifteen Saudi men had flown into Istanbul that morning and left late at night.

It took the Saudi government until October 19 to admit Khashoggi had been killed inside the consulate, during which time state TV had broadcast an item claiming the fifteen Saudis seen arriving and leaving were tourists. Saudi officials then claimed Khashoggi had died after a fight, but no one had meant to kill him. Finally they shifted their story again, saying that he had died because of a "rogue operation" and they were shocked that such a thing could happen, and that Crown Prince Mohammed had absolutely no idea it was going on.

The idea that Saudi agents, from a rigidly hierarchical country, would assassinate a prominent figure abroad without its being sanctioned from the top stretches credibility. Whatever the truth, it was clear to Riyadh that someone had to pay for the crime—just not anyone senior. Arrests were made but Khashoggi's family, still in Saudi Arabia, "pardoned" five of the suspects, thus sparing them the death penalty. In late 2020 a Saudi court delivered a final ruling sentencing eight defendants to jail sentences of between seven and twenty years. Charges against the most high-profile figures were dismissed, but the government did say that it had been "a terrible act, a terrible crime."

The crown prince had initially been seen as a reformer, but this incident shattered that image. Many countries have held him at arm's length at a personal level, but if we're talking about the state, then it's almost business as usual. At a Group of 20 summit a few weeks after the murder, some world leaders appeared to shun MBS, but he was embraced by Russian president Vladimir Putin. The following February he was warmly welcomed in Pakistan and India, and in China he concluded an economic deal worth $28 billion. Even Turkey, a regional rival, and the very place where Saudi government officials had murdered the journalist, did not seek to punish the kingdom economically; trade dropped only marginally in the two years following the killing. Oil is money, money talks, and as long as the world wants what Saudi Arabia has, it will have diplomatic weight in the councils of the world. That, though, is finite.

The crown prince's actions on the domestic front have also made global headlines. In the same week that Lebanon's prime minister was "invited" on an extended visit to the kingdom, some of the most senior members of the royal household were being booked into the Ritz-Carlton in Riyadh. It's a fabulous hotel—opulent is an understatement; if you have a spare $10,000 or so for the night I can recommend the royal suite, which is to die for. Unfortunately, some of the guests that week may not have realized that could be part of the service. The bookings were made by the intelligence services, and many of the guests knew nothing about them until they were taken to their rooms. The purge had begun. Eleven princes and dozens of the political, military, and business elite were taken to the hotel, among them Prince Miteb bin Abdullah, a cousin of MBS and commander of the National Guard, which has the same troop levels as the regular army.

Sources suggest MBS feared that loyalty in a family of fifteen thousand might be stretched a little thin. There were many among the elite who did not want him as de facto ruler, and who thought there may be time to topple him before he became king. All those arrested were confronted with corruption charges, which are easy to find in Saudi Arabia if those in power want to find them, and almost impossible to find if they don't.

It took several weeks, but once confronted with evidence of corruption many of the detainees said something along the lines of "Good heavens, somehow millions of dollars are missing from my government accounts! Let me pay that amount to the state immediately." Prince Miteb was among the first to discover the shocking errors in accounting and paid about $1 billion to settle the matter. The government insists the arrests were entirely about its anticorruption drive.

On the domestic front, MBS doesn't just have family problems, he has country problems, among them the simmering resentment of its largest minority—the Shia. Most ordinary Shia do not seek the downfall of the Saudi state, but in recent years the failure of the "notables" to seriously improve their lives means many younger people are being radicalized by Shia Islamist preachers who argue that insurrection is the way to achieve change. In 2011, an uprising in the Eastern Province was put down with great brutality, including shelling the town of Al Awamiyah and later the demolition of dozens of people's houses. The tensions between state and Shia can be eased only by treating the Shia as equals in economic, social, and religious terms. The last of those is a particular problem for the Wahhabi population, which views Shia as apostates, some going so far as to say they are not Muslims. This prejudice goes back a long way. Even in this century, senior clerics have denounced Shia as unbelievers and sanctioned their killing.

However, despite all the criticisms of despotism, and worse, against Crown Prince Mohammed, he genuinely is a reformer. He has surrounded himself with young advisers, many of whom appear equally impetuous; but crucially, probably because of their age, they are more open to change. He has granted women the right to drive, reopened cinemas, modernized religious rulings, and is restructuring the economy. This may be because he is a feminist, a passionate supporter of the arts, a religious liberal, and a believer in the market economy, or it may be because he believes that without change the economy will sink, unrest will spiral out of control, the state will collapse, and he'll be out of a job and possibly out of a life.

Between 2014 and 2020 the price of oil halved, and Saudi Arabia's foreign reserves fell from $737 billion to $475 billion as the state tried to plug the gaps. The crash in oil prices and the limited future of fossil-fuel energy means there has to be change. In this context it makes sense to try to purge the state of corruption, even if it is window dressing for removing rivals and putting some serious money back into the government's coffers. It also requires a long-term plan—one called Vision 2030.

Vision 2030 accepts that the economy must be diversified, with the focus on technology and the service sector. Budget projections for the next few years envisage a steady draining of foreign reserves and the sovereign wealth fund. The state pays for an exceptionally generous welfare system. Rapidly declining income from oil and gas means that this is unsustainable; but without welfare, and with high unemployment, unrest is all but certain. To bolster the coffers during the change the government is prepared to sell off about 5 percent of the family jewels—Saudi Aramco. It values the company at around $2 trillion; the oil market suggests it's worth just over half that. Valuations shift due to market factors, but outside of Saudi Arabia few agree with the Saudis' original pricing.

Cost cutting with Vision 2030 has begun even as the grand enterprise slowly moves ahead, and some of the smaller projects within it are being curtailed. The "saudification" of the workforce is accelerating, a move connected to granting women driver's licenses. Many families do not allow women out without a guardian, and often they travel together in taxis or are chauffeured in cars driven by foreign workers, who send money out of the country. Allow women to drive and you save the money spent on drivers, increasing disposable income and bringing more women into the workforce to take the place of other foreign workers.

Exact numbers of the foreign population are unclear, but projections from embassies suggest that of the 34 million inhabitants there are over 12 million non-Saudis, including 2 million Bangladeshis, 1.5 million Filipinos, and 1 million Egyptians. This population growth, the presence of foreigners, and urbanization have happened relatively recently and at a pace not seen anywhere else in the world. On one trip to Jeddah, I went to the port and talked with the fishermen; they were mostly Bangladeshis, not a single one was Saudi, nor can I envisage a Saudi man wanting to relearn the old skills of his forefathers. Unemployment among those under twenty-four runs at about 28 percent, but that doesn't mean young men want to crouch on the Jeddah dockside mending nets.

Replacing these workers with Saudis, and oil with technology, is a gamble, a fast-forward into a future the conservatives in the country don't want; one that overrides religious and tribal identities. The plan also risks exacerbating regional tensions. Already investment seems to be drawn toward two of the kingdom's thirteen administrative regions—those housing Riyadh and Jeddah. If this continues, then regions such as the Shia-dominated Eastern Province and the borderland with Yemen will ask "What's in this vision for us?" and identify even less with central power.

The mega-projects are slipping behind schedule. With great fanfare, MBS announced the building of Neom—a $500 billion city by the Red Sea in which all vehicles would be driverless, robots would do most of the mundane work, sustainable energy would power everything, and men and women would mingle freely. Sounds great, but there's very little chance of its being ready on time, a fact that will become increasingly embarrassing as we approach 2030.

Covid-19 has set back the budget. In 2020 only a handful of Saudi citizens were allowed to perform the hajj pilgrimage to Mecca, and the ban on foreign pilgrims is estimated to have cost the economy about $12 billion in revenue.

It's not all doom and gloom on the economic front. Even a temporary increased demand for oil in a global industrial boom would mean a price rise, and in the medium term Saudi Arabia should be well positioned to maintain its supremacy in the energy market. This will offset some of the current losses as the country seeks to eventually wean itself off this energy source.

Even as the world slowly turns away from oil, Saudi domestic consumption has been on an upward trend. The country burns about a quarter of the oil it produces, and that burns through a huge part of the government's income. Petrol and electricity are supplied to the public at a fraction of even the lowest prices in most developed countries. For the less environmentally conscious this means there is no barrier to gunning your massive SUV down the highway to get back to your home where you've kept the air-conditioning on, even though you were away for the weekend. Saudi Arabia is the sixth-largest consumer of oil in the world and air conditioners use 70 percent of Saudi Arabia's electricity. Top tip: if you go to Saudi Arabia in the height of summer, take a jacket—the hotels are cold.

In the near term the Saudis have to burn their oil, not just to keep the lights (and air-conditioning) on but so they can drink water. The kingdom has the largest desalination operation in the world, which successfully produces the majority of its domestic needs. But there's a problem. The massive desalination plants require large amounts of electricity, which comes from oil. In a land without a river, desalination may be the only option, albeit an expensive and still polluting one.

Initially, to find a non-saline solution they went back to the experts—Saudi Aramco. The oil giant used its expertise to access some of the giant underground freshwater reservoirs found under the sands of the north and east of the country. In the previous century there was easily enough water to fill Lake Erie, but intensive farming practices have steadily reduced supplies, which, due to lack of rainfall, are not being replenished. The irrigated lands are used to grow crops and raise livestock for the domestic and foreign markets at prices achievable only because the government subsidizes the cost of the water. The farmers are not known for their careful use of this most precious of all liquids. To them it is a cheap resource, but for the state it is expensive. Experts fear that four-fifths of the water has been used, and it may run out in the 2030s. Oil paid for the subsidies, but if there's little water left to subsidize, then there are no cheap crops and no foreign markets. Instead there would be a lot of Saudis grumbling about rising food prices. The government intends to severely reduce the amount of wheat grown, since it is a water-intensive crop, and instead some of the sovereign wealth fund is going toward buying land in other countries and growing produce there.

Because of these subsidies to the public, the more power they consume, the more it costs the government. To escape this spiral, it is plowing money into renewable energy. Diversification has begun. For example, Saudi Arabia owns 5 percent of Tesla and has invested heavily in General Motors' push toward electric cars, as well as dozens of other projects around the world. At home, Riyadh hopes it can create 750,000 jobs in the industry and that at least 7 percent of electricity will come from renewables, mostly solar, by 2030. The Saudis have the factories to build solar panels, the space in which to put them, and the sunshine to fuel them. They've even got the right type of sunlight, as levels of solar radiation in the kingdom are among the highest in the world. The government has also floated the idea that by 2032 the figure could rise to 20 percent. That is, in business jargon, an aggressive target.

When announcing its solar plans, the government enjoys talking about "historic moments" and sets what turn out to be overly ambitious targets. Bureaucratic wrangles and technical difficulties have caused some projects to collapse and others to stall, but the authorities are well aware they need to act. Time is running out.

Economically there's another balancing act: diversifying from oil, but balancing the books without causing economic hardship in the population by too sudden a withdrawal of the subsidies the oil pays for. Renewable energy, investment abroad, tourism, and the successful development of infrastructure such as the Red Sea ports will all help, but turning the oil tanker around is a massive challenge.

Strategically, Saudi Arabia surely has to stick with the Americans for many years to come, assuming, that is, that the Americans stick with them. Without a security guarantee from the US, the country's maritime borders are insecure because the Persian Gulf and the Red Sea are narrow, and each has choke points. In the absence of a strong Saudi Arabian navy, a hostile power could block Saudi exports from reaching the Indian Ocean or the Suez Canal.

However, despite the security relationship with the US, economic ties with

China will strengthen. China has sold the kingdom intermediate-range ballistic missiles, its oil imports have grown rapidly in the past few years, and Saudi Arabia has signed one of the twelve 5G contracts Huawei has won in the region. Unlike the US, China does not take an interest in promoting human rights in countries it does business with. As Mina Al-Oraibi, one of the Middle East's foremost political analysts, told me, "The Chinese model of 'state capitalism' is appealing to most Arab politicians. 'Economic liberalism' decoupled from political liberalism is a model most governments in the region pursue, and in the past two decades the Chinese model is lauded as a success."

In recent years, again reading the future, verbal attacks on Israel have been muted and business contacts quietly forged ready for a potential normalization of relations between the two states. Such a move is no longer dependent on the formation of a Palestinian state; Crown Prince bin Salman was one of the first Arab leaders to lose patience with what he sees as a refusal by the Palestinians to compromise with Israel. He was, though, content to let others take the lead. MBS has a very close relationship with the de facto ruler of the UAE, Crown Prince Mohammed bin Zayed, who in 2020 normalized ties with Israel, as did Bahrain. King Salman was against the move, but MBS is said to believe that most young Saudis do not care about the issue as much as the older generation does. Israel has defense capabilities and technology that the Gulf states can use, and it is prepared to deal. Its Iron Dome missile defense system is coveted, especially because of the perceived threat from Iran, and its technology in "making the desert bloom" can benefit the agricultural industries. This rapprochement by several Arab countries is a sea change in policy and proves wrong most of the Middle East experts, who said the Arab countries would never agree to peace with Israel without the creation of a Palestinian state. While they were watching a tiny piece of land, the rest of the world was moving on. The Biden administration will not change this; the American president may take a hard line on settlements in the Palestinian West Bank, but there's no reason to think he wants to unravel the new reality.

The UAE-Israel agreement was put together with the full knowledge of MBS (although his father was kept in the dark). He approved it because he has one eye on the day-to-day political machinations required to keep him in power and the other on the future.

Saudi Arabia takes a similar hardheaded, pragmatic approach to pan-Arab nationalism. The idea of a single Arab state stretching across the region has never attracted the Saudis. During the 1960s and 1970s, as Arab intellectuals and politicians in Egypt, Syria, and elsewhere advanced the idea, the Saudi ruling class instead encouraged loyalty to the monarchy. It also has little time for democracy—after all, the people might choose the wrong leaders. It is more interested in creating loose economic and political forums across the region, which is why in 1981 it was the key founding member of the six-member Gulf Cooperation Council, an organization designed to simplify trade.

This all forms a very mixed picture as we head toward the crown prince's vision of the country in 2030. Domestically he walks a tightrope between reform and conservatism, relative liberalism and repression. The ruling class cannot allow regionalism to grow stronger, and yet it knows that there is such a thing as regional identity and that those identities want a say in how things are run. They cannot allow Shia separatism to gain a foothold on the peripheries of the Eastern Province and the Yemen border, as instability there not only would cause economic damage but could spread. Discontent simmers, and there's the permanent danger that incidents could spark renewed violence.

MBS is offering the people a new social contract. They will get a less bureaucratic country with reduced corruption, an economy that will be able to survive the slow end of the oil era, and one in which they will be free to enjoy some of the leisure pursuits most of the modern world takes for granted. In return, they have to get to work and realize that some of the subsidies they receive will end. The religious conservatives must accept that they will be free to practice religion as they see fit, but that their hold on society must be weakened if the country is to modernize in order to survive. The export of Wahhabism may also have to be scaled back. If the Saudis are less crucial to the global economy, the rest of the world will be less tolerant of an ideology that partially spawned the likes of bin Laden and eventually ISIS.

This is breaking the founding principle of the Saud-Wahhab alliance forged almost three hundred years ago. The contract later offered by MBS's grandfather, Ibn Saud, was that the people would obey, and the oil money would give them a good life. MBS offers a twenty-first-century model of this, but one in which oil money plays a diminishing role.

If the reforms are not implemented, and the world moves on from oil, what does Saudi Arabia offer to that new world—sand?

The Saudi leadership has to build a new society, a new economy, and a functioning military. We are still in a time in which the Americans will fight for Saudi Arabia to keep the black stuff flowing to grease the wheels of the world economy, but we are approaching a time in which there is no way the Americans will fight to defend Saudi Arabia's solar panels.

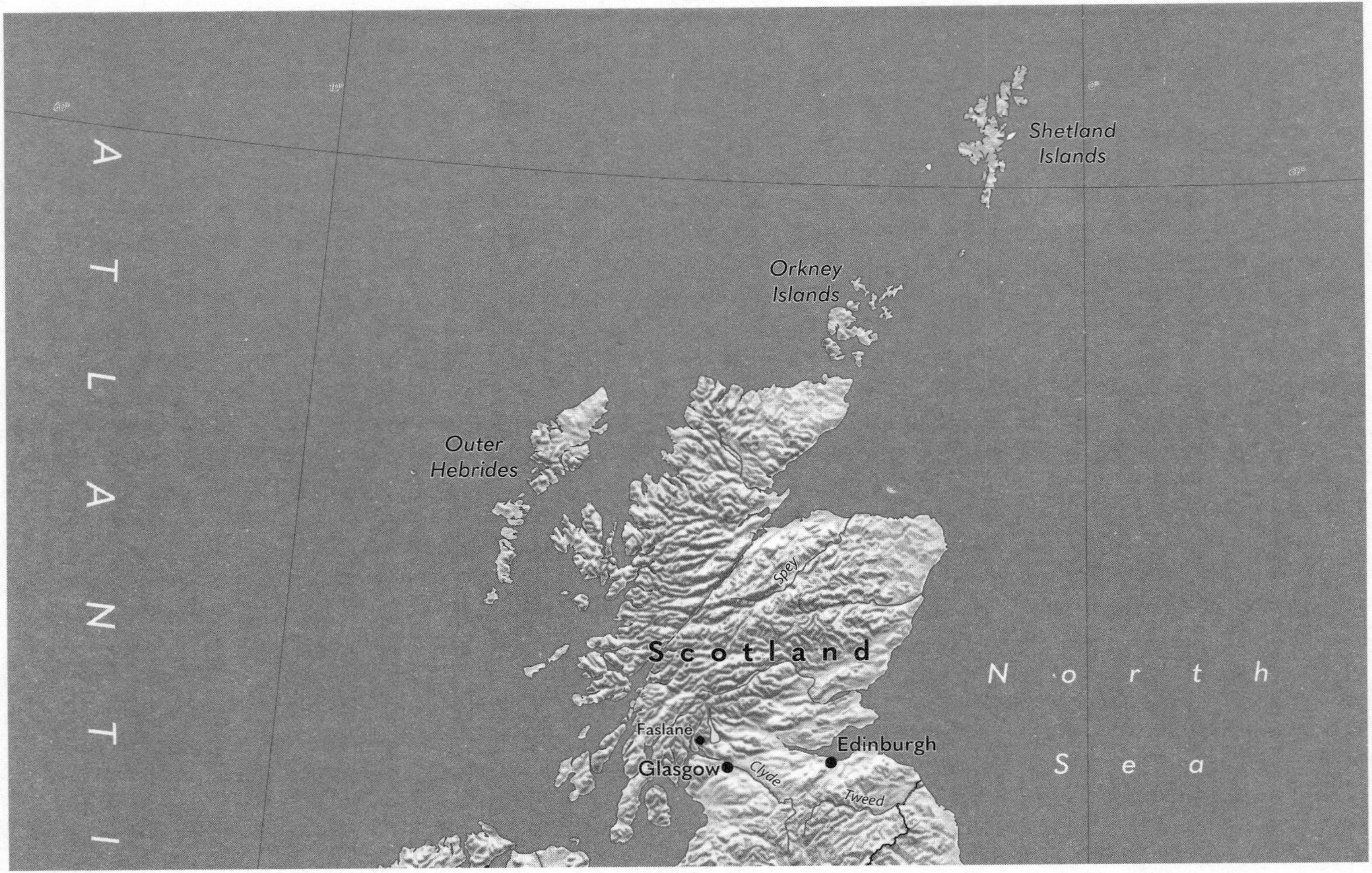

Shetland Islands
Orkney Islands
Outer Hebrides
Scotland
Spey
Faslane
Glasgow
Clyde
Edinburgh
Tweed
North Sea
ATLANTI

OCEAN
IRELAND
Northern Ireland
Belfast
DUBLIN
Irish Sea
UNITED KINGDOM
England
Wales
Newcastle
Tyne
Tees
York
Leeds
Sheffield
Manchester
Liverpool
Mersey
Trent
Nottingham
Birmingham
Severn
Wye
Great Ouse
Thames
LONDON
Cardiff
Bristol
Exe
Isle of Wight
English Channel
Isles of Scilly
Channel Islands
FRANCE

4

THE UNITED KINGDOM

The British are coming! The British are coming!

—Paul Revere (attrib.)

"The British are coming" is a phrase that might have been uttered in much of the world over several centuries, during which they built an empire that controlled a quarter of the globe. Now it might be heard again, but with a very different meaning. Following the 2016 Brexit vote to leave the EU, the British are looking for alliances—but they've been searching for a global role since the mid-twentieth century. The UK lost a lot as the maps changed during the drive to decolonization; now it must navigate a new world in which empire is becoming a distant memory.

So the British may not be sure of what they're coming to, or indeed where they're going—but these new times will still be influenced by being an island at the western end of the north European plain. Britain is a place that, for most of its history, was cold, windswept, and backward, and yet it became the center of one of the world's greatest empires. How it did so is partially due to its geography—notably, its access to the oceans.

The waters around the UK continue to play a central role in its culture and national psyche. In recent centuries they have protected it from the excesses of politics and warfare on the European mainland. This partially explains why the sense of belonging to a common European home is not as strong on the island as it is in many EU countries. The carnage of the two huge world wars did not shake the UK in the way it did the mainland. The psychology of separateness had an influence, albeit unquantifiable, on the Brexit vote.

In recent years, the UK has been a bridge across the Atlantic between Europe and the US. It will remain so, but one used less as time passes and national interests change. Nevertheless, despite its current uncertainty, the UK still has a huge potential consumer market in Europe, direct access to the sea lanes of the oceans, and a long history of innovation, quality education, and commercial prowess that means that it remains one of the top ten economies in the world. To stay there will require making the right calls for the future in a world in which change has gathered pace. It may also require unity.

Britain's economic and military power accelerated after the 1707 Acts of Union joined Scotland and England as a single entity. For the first time in its history, one authority alone controlled the island. Not only did the English no longer have to worry about Scottish armies heading south, but the back door to potential invasion from a European power was locked. Three centuries later, the Brexit vote has endangered the Union, and although London no longer fears an invasion from France, it is deeply worried about the economic and military effects of an independent Scotland.

The political union of 1707 had been preceded by a natural one over 400 million years earlier. England was attached to a small continent called Avalonia, drifting northward across the ocean. At the same time, several thousand miles away, Scotland was heading south as part of the Laurentia continent. It was a slow-motion crash of continents that took place pretty much along the line where, somewhat later, in 122 CE the Roman emperor Hadrian would build a wall. This north-south collision failed to create mountains but did result in the Cheviot Hills, which run along the English-Scottish border. Fast-forward past rain forests, dinosaurs, and mammoths and eventually, about 800,000 years ago, humans show up. Then it gets cold again, so they leave, and come back, and leave, and repeat the process until it gets warm enough to stay.

In about 10,000 BCE, Ireland was separated from Britain by rising sea levels, which also flooded the land between what are now Britain and Continental Europe, making Britain an island. To be more accurate, Britain is made up of islands—thousands of them if you count by size and what is above water at high tide; but of these only around two hundred are inhabited. The United Kingdom of Great Britain and Northern Ireland includes the Shetland Islands to the far north, the Isles of Scilly about 700 miles to their south, and the island of Anglesey, off the Welsh coast, to the west. It has direct access into the English Channel, the North Sea, the Irish Sea, and the Atlantic. At its widest it is only 300 miles across, and because of its jagged coastline no part is more than 75 miles from the sea.

The first record of its existence came around 330 BCE, when a Greek explorer named Pytheas made an astonishing voyage north, possibly as far as Iceland, and along the way circumnavigated what we now know as Britain. He wasn't believed by everyone, but that's because he also returned with stories of white bears sitting on ice caps and the sun shining at midnight.

The rough, cold waters of the North Sea are not for me, and so when, a few years ago, I decided to explore Europe's largest island I did so on two wheels, cycling its length on the route known as LEJOG—Land's End to John O'Groats. It's 1,000 miles long, and usually done from south to north as you have a better chance of having the wind at your back. It took twelve days, each one a painful joy. What struck me more than anything was how much, at the end of each day, the accents, dialects, and type of place-names had changed. Even over as little as 30 miles there are marked differences. This is due to both geography and history. The regions developed in relative isolation, and were influenced by the arrival of Romans, Anglo-Saxons, Vikings, and Normans. For example, the Scandinavians settled in what is now called East Anglia; the suffix "-by" is thought to originate from the Danish word for "town," and this explains why names such as Whitby and Grimsby are found on the east coast of England. To this day, in Yorkshire words someone from the south might not even understand are spoken daily—"bairn" for child and "beck" for stream, for example. Most countries have regional differences, but few are as pronounced over such small areas as those of the UK.

The main geographical divide in the country is not north-south, as is often thought, but east-west, and it is defined by highlands and lowlands. If you draw a line from the River Tees in the northeast down to the River Exe in Devon, you see the divide between the high and low ground of England and Wales. To its west are the hard rock and high areas of the Lake District, the Cambrian Mountains, and moorlands such as Dartmoor; to its east the terrain is flatter, and the rock is softer, with more chalk—hence the White Cliffs of Dover. This divide is why the western side of the UK is warmer than the east and has more rain. Gulf Stream waters, originating in the Caribbean, cross the Atlantic and arrive at the UK's western coastlines. The winds above the Gulf Stream pick up moisture, hit the high ground, and drop the water. Overall this means that the UK is hardly a tropical paradise, but it has more temperate weather than many other places at a similar latitude (e.g., Russia and Canada), which has benefited agriculture.

There is also a north-south divide. The mountains are indeed mostly on the western half of the main island, but the farther north you travel in England, the higher they become. In Scotland too, the majority of the Highlands are in the northwest. Because it is easier to build on flat ground, this divide has contributed to a difference in infrastructure development. The northwest,

Yorkshire, and the northeast of England include places made famous by the Industrial Revolution, such as Leeds, Sheffield, Manchester, Liverpool, and Newcastle. The decline of cotton manufacturing, coal mining, and heavy industry hit these regions hard. The south's milder climate, flatter rivers, land conducive to farming, and influence from the capital are some of the reasons it is more developed than the north, and why England, which makes up just over half of the landmass, contains 84 percent of its population. The majority of Scotland's inhabitants and its industry are to the south, closer to the English border, but overall its populace is much smaller—5.5 million compared with 56 million in England, 3 million in Wales, and just under 2 million in Northern Ireland. The south of England is the hub for international and domestic rail and air travel via the major London train stations and Heathrow and Gatwick Airports. It also has some of the busiest ports and the Channel Tunnel. London is at the center of the southeast and the hub of the region's motorway system, which radiates out in all directions. The capital hosts Parliament and the headquarters of many of the UK's biggest companies, especially in the financial sector. This is the modern state. It took a long time and much bloodshed to get there.

Where to begin? The year 43 CE and Roman occupation is as good a time as any. It marks a break from what came before, it clearly shaped the following centuries, and its imprint is still on the land in many ways.

Before our wine-drinking, bathroom-building, and lawmaking friends from across the Channel showed up, Britain was simply a huge, cold, wet island on the periphery of where history happened. And it was full of wild tribes who couldn't read or write and, instead of learning, spent their time fighting one another.

The Romans had a vague idea about what they considered to be blue-painted barbarians from reports brought back by Julius Caesar a century earlier. They knew what they were getting into, so Emperor Claudius sent forty thousand crack troops for the invasion. He needed them. The fictional Asterix the Gaul gets all the headlines, defending a tiny piece of territory in what is now France, but he had nothing on the Celtic Britons.

It took decades to subdue the plethora of tribes in the southern half of England: even after twenty years Rome's legions faced a massive rebellion led by Queen Boudicca of the Iceni. Historians use the shorthand "Roman Britain," but the legions never conquered what are now Wales and Scotland and this helped retain the separate identities we see even today. The areas they did dominate roughly follow England's east-west split. Also visible are the layout of some of their roads; many of Britain's motorways follow the ancient routes they carved into the landscape.

The structure of the occupation had lasting effects—perhaps nowhere more so than at the head of the estuary of the River Thames. The Romans knew they needed a crossing point to connect territories they would take south and north of it. It had to be close to the estuary to handle their vessels, but at a narrow section. They came across a spot between two small hills on the north bank where the river narrowed and there was solid land on each bank. Rome may have been built on seven hills, but when they first came to Britain the Romans built on just two, Ludgate Hill and Cornhill, and in so doing founded Londinium—London. They built the first London bridge—a bridgehead into what they called Britannia. The fledgling town prospered; all major Roman roads connected to it, and from it goods were shipped to the empire. By the end of the first century, London's population was in the tens of thousands.

Three hundred years later, the legions left in a hurry to attend to a more pressing concern than a rain-swept island—trying to save the Roman Empire. By so doing they collapsed the economic system they'd imposed, urban areas were quickly abandoned, and literacy disappeared. Despite its weather, covetous eyes were on post-Roman Britain as it quickly splintered back into warring factions. Without the Pax Romana it made easy pickings for waves of invaders. First came the Angles, Saxons, and Jutes from Denmark and northern Germany. The regions they conquered roughly correspond with those of the Romans: the east-west divide is seen again, as is the fierce resistance of the tribes in Scotland, Wales, and Cornwall. The faint outline of the boundaries of modern England were emerging at the same time as a new name for the southern half of the island—Angleland. Celtic tongues were disappearing, replaced by Germanic Old English, from which much of modern English is derived.

By 600 the Anglo-Saxons had established several kingdoms, even as the Scotti tribes of Ireland were invading and settling in western Scotland, which explains how the northern third of Britain got its name.

After that—well, in the south it was just one king after another at first. Most of them seem to have been called Edward, or Egbert, or some other name beginning with an "e" sound such as Æthelred, and all had issues with invading Vikings. There was an Alfred, though. He managed to unite the kingdoms of Wessex and Mercia, and retook London from the Vikings in 886. His son, Edward, and daughter, Æthelflæd, then expanded their territory to encompass the Viking capital, York, up to Northumbria and across toward Wales. Edward was described as "king of the English"; some went so far as to say "king of Britain," which was a bit of a stretch. In fact, it was a stretch of a couple of hundred miles and years before any such thing was a reality.

An Edmund, Eadred, and even an Eadwig followed, before we arrive at King Edgar the Peaceful who reigned from 959 to 975. Apart from his demeanor, his contribution to history was to establish the system of dividing the kingdom into counties, or shires, the names of which are still used today. There was now a recognizable England, with a distinct culture and growing sense of itself, while north of the border, the kingdom of Scotland was also starting to emerge from various warring tribal groups.

Enter the Normans, and a date which is probably the best known in the UK: 1066.

From across the Channel, the Norman ruler William the Conqueror landed on the south coast, won the Battle of Hastings, marched on London, and crowned himself king. The city would not become the capital for almost a century, but under William it grew rapidly. He built the Tower of London and established London as the conduit between Norman and English territories.

The invasion was the most influential moment in British history since the departure of the Romans. It broke England's links with Scandinavia and oriented it toward Western Europe. French words began to make their way into the language, great cathedrals were built, and castles appeared across the country as the new landowners sought to defend themselves from what was often a hostile population.

Tensions lasted for decades, with rebellions led by the likes of Edgar the Ætheling (son of Edward the Exile), but the Normans were able to maintain their grip on their new land. William was soon followed by the Plantagenets, a royal French house whose kings held power in England from 1154 until 1485. Among them was King John, who, in a bid to avert a civil war, agreed to reduce the power of English monarchs by signing the Magna Carta in 1215. The charter is part of the foundation of the modern legal system. At the time it did little to further the rights of ordinary people, but it has become an iconic document and a symbol of liberty still invoked in political debate in the UK. It also had a strong influence on the American Constitution. One of Britain's most respected judges of the twentieth century, Lord Denning, described it as "the greatest constitutional document of all time."

Over the next centuries the English warred with Scotland, with France, and with one another. The Plantagenets were replaced by the Tudors in 1485.

The best-known Tudor king, Henry VIII (r. 1509–1547), signed into law what was de facto reality. The English already controlled Wales, but Henry's Acts of Union stated that the law of England was now that of Wales too, and English the language of the courts. As most people in Wales spoke only Welsh, this had several effects: interpreters got a lot of work, the Welsh language almost disappeared over the following centuries, and a legacy of resentment toward London was cemented. It was, though, another step toward the creation of the United Kingdom.

Henry's main claim to fame is having had six wives. In 1533 his marriage to Catherine of Aragon was annulled, allowing him to marry Anne Boleyn, with whom he went on to have a daughter named Elizabeth. His subsequent excommunication from the Catholic Church led to the English Reformation, during which Henry created the Church of England, closed eight hundred monasteries, and decided their lands and treasure were now his.

His daughter Elizabeth I (r. 1558–1603) propelled England more firmly into Protestantism amid much intrigue and opposition from Catholic powers in mainland Europe and Scotland. She even executed the Scottish queen, her cousin Mary, in 1587 for conspiring against her. Elizabeth took England forward to greatness. This was the era of voyages of discovery (and piracy) by Francis Drake and Walter Raleigh, the defeat of the Spanish Armada, and the writings of Shakespeare. Next up: King James I of England. The thing about James I was that he was also James VI—of Scotland. These united crowns were the next step toward the United Kingdom, but first the English had to endure the beheading of a king (Charles I), civil war (1642–1651), a military dictatorship (Oliver Cromwell), and the restoration of royalty before finally, in 1707, the unification of England and Wales with Scotland was achieved. This was the key; it unlocked the door to what followed because it changed the geography of the threat to England and Scotland.

For centuries the English understood that the Continent had a population far bigger than their own and thus could muster armies capable of overwhelming them. This had happened with the Romans, Vikings, and Normans. The threat was more acute if one dominant force could coerce others to join it, and worse still if it allied with Scotland. That brought the possibility of an unopposed landing by enemy forces in the far north, or even simultaneous invasions from the north and south.

Various strategies flowed from this. The English always sought to ensure a balance of power in Europe to prevent a dominant power emerging, or, if one looked like doing so, siding with its opponents. Concurrent with "offshore balancing" was the desire to control the whole island.

Scotland's perspective was very different. With its small population and limited resources, Scotland could never hope to defeat, or even dominate, England. Instead, to try to ensure its security, it sought alliances with England's enemies, notably France.

The first Scottish-French treaty came as early as 1295, in which it was agreed that if England invaded France, Scotland would invade England, causing a two-front war. When the English got wind of this, they promptly invaded Scotland—which didn't go down too well. Every Scottish and French leader, apart from Louis XI, renewed the agreement all the way up to 1560, by which time it was known as the Auld Alliance. Thousands of Scottish soldiers were sent to fight alongside their French counterparts, while the French funded Scottish armies and encouraged incursions into England.

However, by 1707 a number of factors had aligned to bring about the Acts of Union. Because the crowns had been unified a hundred years earlier, tensions were reduced and trade between the two countries increased. The previous century had seen the English establish colonies and settlements in North America, the West Indies, India, and Africa, and they were growing wealthier even as the first sparks of what would develop into the Industrial Revolution were appearing. But Scotland had no colonies, and during the 1690s suffered successive crop failures, which led to thousands of people dying from starvation. It was not equipped to face the new century.

There was an ill-fated attempt at Scottish imperialism. In 1698 a fleet of five ships sailed from Scotland to establish a colony in Panama. It was funded by public subscription amid a wave of national fervor. However, few of the hundreds of settlers survived, many dying of disease before the colony was abandoned following a siege by the Spanish navy. It was supposed to bring riches, allowing Scotland to compete with Spain, Portugal, and England. Instead it brought death and contributed to the end of Scottish independence. You can find a reference to the sorry episode on current Panamanian maps: look for Punta Escocés—Scottish Point.

Historians differ over the financial costs, but Scotland is said to have lost at least one-fifth of its wealth in the misadventure (some say much more). So by 1707 an impoverished Scotland needed access to England's overseas markets on favorable terms. England, meanwhile, aware that the population of France was double its own, needed the strategic guarantee that Scotland would not look to

France for a renewal of the Auld Alliance. In the subsequent treaty, England gave Scotland the monies required to pay off its debts, each parliament passed the Acts of Union, and for the first time in its history the island had a single government.

It's no coincidence that the next two centuries saw Britain grow to the height of its power. Whereas beforehand the Scottish and English governments each had to fund a standing army to keep watch on their land borders, now the money could be used to secure Britain against invasion from the Continent, and to expand the empire. There was a larger population from which to form the military, and the resources, energy, and time spent looking inward could be focused outward—and by outward, the British meant the world.

The British Empire grew rapidly, and the more it grew, the harder it was to challenge. Sea power was the key, and only a wealthy power could build a navy capable of either controlling the sea lanes or challenging the navies that did. Britain made use of its oak forests to build ocean-worthy ships. The trees supplied extremely strong wood of the type required when your enemy might be firing cannonballs at you, or when you risked running aground exploring strange new worlds where no big ship had gone before. Oak is also resistant to insects and rot, and so allowed the navy's ships to spend more time at sea and less in dry dock. Lord Horatio Nelson's HMS *Victory* and Captain Cook's HMS *Endeavour* were both built from oak, and the Royal Navy's official march is titled "Heart of Oak." Britain's shoreline is heavily indented, which allows for deepwater ports and thus oceangoing trade. To compete with Britain, any potential rival needed stability, a huge navy, excellent ports, wood, and cutting-edge technology.

The two main candidates, France and Spain, diluted their wealth and focus by continually waging land wars in Europe. They also industrialized more slowly than Britain. As early as 1780, there were 20,000 cotton-spinning machines in Britain and only 900 in France. The size of France and Spain, each more than twice as large as the UK, increased their transport costs. The British made use of the narrowness of their island and its many rivers and canals to move raw materials more easily into the towns, and the finished products out to domestic and foreign markets. Britain's abundance of coal was mostly close to the industrial cities, and once the rail network began to develop in the 1830s the pace of movement accelerated.

In 1801, Ireland formally came into Britain's domain through another set of Acts of Union. In reality, though, England had controlled Ireland for over 250 years, but the move officially created the United Kingdom of Great Britain and Ireland. The UK tried to sit out most of the seemingly never-ending wars in Europe, content to see its rivals busy weakening each other, but when feeling threatened it stepped in. The greatest challenge was from Napoleon, who was eventually beaten by the familiar policy of allying with the enemies of whichever Continental power was the strongest. In Napoleon's case this was pretty much everyone. In 1803 he'd decided it would be a good idea to use the money the Americans had given him for the Louisiana Purchase to fund an invasion of Britain. This saw a mobilization of British troops and civilians on an unprecedented scale.

Napoleon was the British nightmare made flesh. He was dominating the Continent and planning to impose a French-led political, economic, and military system whose combined power would almost certainly have been able to defeat Britain, or at least impose its will on it. Even before the direct threat of invasion, London's perspective was that war was not a choice but a necessity.

The geography of both the invasion and the defense plans bears a remarkable similarity to those at the beginning of the Second World War. Barges to carry French troops across the Channel assembled along the coast on either side of Boulogne. Napoleon's intention was to land at Sheerness and Chatham and head straight for London, arriving within four days. The bulk of British troops and militia were positioned along the Kent and Sussex coastlines behind a line of newly built fortifications (some of these gun emplacements and forts can still be seen today). In the non-event, the invasion was called off, Napoleon went on to meet his Waterloo, Europe's armies were exhausted, and the British were free to concentrate on their empire again.

The continuing supremacy of British sea power allowed the dominance of British willpower around the world. A hundred years earlier the British had captured Gibraltar, commanding the gap between the Mediterranean Sea and the Atlantic Ocean. In the nineteenth century, it was used as a staging port on the way to the harbors on the west coast of Africa, before docking at the Cape of Good Hope. From there it was up along Africa's east coast and on to the jewel in the crown—India. After that, Malaysia gave the British access to the Strait of Malacca, the maritime gateway to China. This unrivaled geographical power was increased by the opening of the Suez Canal in 1869: British ships could then cut through the canal to reach India, and the empire was at its height.

It was, at least for Britain, a virtuous circle: increased wealth led to increased military and political power. The UK dodged most of Europe's wars and revolutions, but its army was busy elsewhere: south Africa, Burma, Crimea, and

India are some of the many faraway places about which the public knew little, but from which the country benefited a lot. Raw materials flowed into Britain's factories, creating wealth for the owners and jobs for the workers.

Sea power underpinned an empire based on the usual power building common to all countries, but also the racist assumptions of colonialism. There was, however, one bright point of moral light in the navy's role. In 1807, having played a prominent role in the slave trade, Britain outlawed it. For the next few decades the Royal Navy actively pursued slave traders, liberating about 150,000 people, while the government paid subsidies to African chiefs to persuade them to end the practice. Slavery itself, though, continued to be "legal" (although it never had been within Britain itself), but in 1833 was made illegal throughout all parts of the world controlled by the UK.

It was said that the sun never set on the British Empire. That actually remains true, given that the remnants of it are the fourteen British Overseas Territories. There is always at least one of them in daylight. It might be dark in the Cayman Islands at midnight, but it's still daytime in the Pitcairn Islands of the South Pacific. Nevertheless, all good things, and bad things, come to an end. The beginning of the end for the British Empire came as two powers rose to meet it: Germany and the US.

In 1871 the Germanic states finally became tired of fighting one another and unified to become Western Europe's biggest and most populous country. It was soon also the most economically dynamic, with an arms industry to match that included shipbuilding. For the first time since Napoleon, the British could see a power that might dominate the Continent. Simultaneously, the American Industrial Revolution gathered pace. This fueled both the production of goods to compete with the markets of the major powers in the world and the emergence of a blue-water navy capable of global reach.

An Anglo-German arms race ensued, adding to the myriad factors that, with hindsight, made the First World War inevitable. It was a catastrophe for all concerned. The history books say that Britain was on the winning side, but in reality everyone lost—and lost in a manner that led to the Second World War. Britain was weakened by war, as was a vengeful France; and Germany was still the largest country, and one in which many people felt betrayed by both its wartime leaders and the terms of surrender in 1918.

Twenty-one years later, Europe again teetered on the brink of the abyss, and fell in. This war surpassed even the barbarity of the previous one; it also broke the back of the British Empire.

By 1940 the UK was in a similar position to that of 1803. An all-conquering power had forced British troops into a humiliating retreat at Dunkirk. It then positioned its troops within sight of England, intent on invasion. Even though this never actually happened, both the attack and defense plans give a fascinating insight into how the geography and economy of the UK were intertwined in the military strategy. In the unlikely event of such a threat today, the thinking would be along similar lines.

The initial plans for Germany's Operation Sea Lion were to set out from Rotterdam and Calais and make an amphibious assault on the Kent and Sussex coasts. Parachutists would simultaneously take Brighton and the high ground above the port of Dover. A second assault would be made from Cherbourg, landing on the Dorset/Devon coast. With bridgeheads established, the two forces would approach London. A feint would be made as if Scotland was also to be invaded, thus drawing troops from the south.

The British didn't know this plan but made some educated geographical guesses. The front lines were the beaches in the south. Many of the potential landing points were mined, pillboxes were built above them, and between them ran lengths of barbed wire. Piers were dismantled and parts of Romney Marsh were flooded. This was the "coastal crust," but behind it lay the "stop lines" to protect the capital, the industrial heartlands of the Midlands, and the north if the Germans managed to break out from their bridgeheads. These lines were designed to slow the enemy and deflect it from industrial centers. The key was to stop the German tanks, which had caused such havoc in the blitzkrieg through Belgium and France.

The core of the strategy was the general headquarters line. It ran east from Bristol to just south of London, then wrapped around the capital, running north past Cambridge, the Midlands, and the industrial cities in Yorkshire, such as Leeds, before heading toward Scotland. The line linked obstacles to tanks such as woods, rivers, canals, and railway embankments. Bridges were wired, readied to be blown up, and airfields and gas stations were prepared for destruction. Hundreds of thousands of civilians were evacuated from the potential invasion zones, and from those who stayed the Home Guard was formed.

The British government then had a change of mind. Instead, the focus would be on preventing the landings or any subsequent German breakout. That summer the Royal Air Force won the Battle of Britain, retaining control of the skies over the planned invasion zone and the Royal Navy maintained control of the sea. Hitler postponed the attack and, following the invasion of Russia, the German military was busy elsewhere. When an amphibious assault came, it was four years later and in the other direction. The Allies fought their way to Germany, the Russians advanced from the east, and once again a power that had risen to dominate Europe was defeated.

Part of the price Britain paid for this was its empire. It was not only on its knees financially, it had handed over most of its bases to the Americans in return for ships with which to fight. That was fine with Washington; it had plenty of ships, and now it had plenty of bases. The balance of power had shifted across the Atlantic and the ability to maintain an empire was crumbling. Now what?

Now to find a new role. Plan A was never going to work. The British may have thought they could hang on to the empire by being America's best friend—but the Americans didn't think so. They'd never been keen on the British Empire, and with a Cold War to fight it really wasn't useful for the Soviets to be able to remind revolutionary movements the world over about British colonialism. So the UK may have signed up to American-designed postwar organizations such as NATO, but when it landed troops to occupy the Suez Canal in 1956, it was bluntly reminded that the days of empire were over. Amid a catalogue of misjudgments, the British had omitted to tell the Americans that they intended to invade, seize the canal, and reverse Egypt's action of nationalizing it. Dwight Eisenhower, the furious American president, quickly ensured that the British withdrew instead.

Time for Plan B: still be America's best friend in order to have influence, but this time without the empire bit. That didn't go too well either, at least not at first. In 1962, Dean Acheson, the former secretary of state who was a special adviser to President John Kennedy, made a famous remark that "Britain has lost an empire but has not yet found a role." Ouch.

Plan C ensued from the truisms of the next lines of Acheson's speech: "The attempt to play a separate power role—that is a role apart from Europe, a role based on a 'special relationship' with the United States, a role based on being Head of a 'Commonwealth' which has no political structure, or unity or strength . . . this role is about played out." Acheson believed that it was time for the British to engage with the Continent.

The new role was something of a hybrid—one foot in the American camp, one in the forerunner of the EU—and it lasted for over four decades. Even as it shifted toward involvement with what would become the EU, Britain made sure its armed forces outstripped those of everyone else in NATO, apart from the US. Of equal importance, it demonstrated a willingness to use them if the Americans came calling. (Vietnam was an exception, due to British public opinion and opposition within the governing Labour Party.) It also contributed formidable intelligence assets and frequent diplomatic support to the US. Critics have long sneered at the term "special relationship"—but it did exist, and to a lesser extent still does. This does not mean that the realists on either side were dewy-eyed about it. Anyone sensible knew (a) who, by far, was the senior partner, and (b) that the Americans did not buy all the guff about Britain being Greece to their Rome. But it was a relationship based on a shared language, history, and political culture, and, compared with what America had with any other European nation, it was special. As indeed was the UK's relationship with Europe, albeit in a different way.

The British were as uncertain about joining the European Economic Community (EEC) as the French were suspicious. In the 1960s France twice vetoed Britain's entry, on both occasions led by President Charles de Gaulle. He wanted an EEC dominated by France, and UK membership would make that more difficult. He also felt that the ways of the Anglo-Saxons were incompatible with "the project." Vetoing Britain's first application to join in 1963, he said: "England in effect is insular, she is maritime, she is linked through her interactions, her markets and her supply lines in the most diverse and often the most distant countries; she pursues essentially industrial and commercial activities, and only slight agricultural ones. She has, in all her doings, very marked and very original habits and traditions."

De Gaulle believed that even inside the EEC the UK would continue its centuries-old policy of forming alliances to balance against a dominant power, in this case France. He didn't want an influential country inside the bloc that had very different ideas about economic affairs. The British economy was dominated by private finance, with the state taking a back seat; France was the opposite. De Gaulle also feared that the UK might be a Trojan horse for the Americans to have eyes and ears inside the EEC. He was right on all counts.

By 1973 de Gaulle was gone, and the British were in. A bit. The UK never embraced the project in the way many member states did. This was partially due to ancient history, but also the recent past. For all its suffering and loss, the UK did not experience the horror of the Second World War in the way that

Continental countries had, nor did it have borders with those countries. The founding members of the EEC believed that this was the way to permanently end centuries of warfare, but Britain joined due to an early bout of economic FOMO—fear of missing out—specifically from the growing markets available on the Continent. It spent the next forty-three years resisting full integration, opting out of various laws, and allying itself with smaller states to balance what became the Franco-German engine of the EU. Whenever the EU tried to deepen political ties, Britain backed the widening of economic ones, and was always keen to see more countries join the union in order to dilute the power of the larger nations. They weren't the only ones; several EU countries were suspicious of ever closer union and were happier with the concept of the single market bringing prosperity while retaining whatever fiscal and political sovereignty remained to them.

For Britain the arrangement worked for several decades, helping it to regain economic stability while still cozying up to Washington. The Americans were happy enough with this, and the UK served as the geopolitical knot tying together the American-led NATO and the EU. However, in the present century several factors changed, and public opinion in the UK changed with them.

The launch of the euro signaled another step toward a single European political entity. Along with Sweden and Denmark, Britain opted not to adopt the currency. The rumblings about creating a European army continually caused unease in London, even if the debate rarely broke through into public discourse. What was probably of more influence in the 2016 Brexit vote than the currency or the army was the economy.

The financial crash of 2008 triggered questions about the benefits of globalization and transnational organizations. For most countries, the deal for EU membership, second only to keeping the peace, was swapping sovereignty for prosperity. But, for many British people, if you weren't experiencing prosperity, the second part of the bargain had less value. This caused much anguish and division in the UK, and the result of the Brexit vote has continued to split public opinion in vitriolic fashion.

The reasons for Brexit are more complicated than outlined above, but the turmoil after 2008 played a role, along with questions about the viability of the EU and Britain's long history of engaging with, but keeping its distance from, the European mainland.

Post-Brexit, new strategies are emerging, but they are in flux because so many other countries are feeling their way as the post–Second World War order fades.

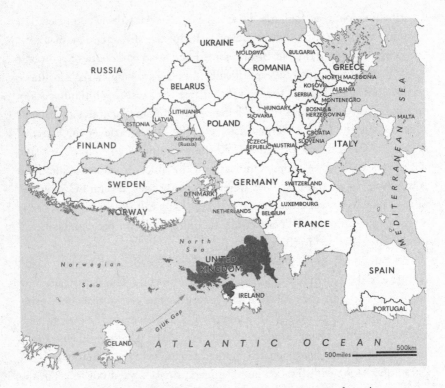

The traditional map view of the UK emphasizes its separation from the rest
of Europe, but considering it from an alternative angle offers a strategic
perspective of the UK from the surrounding European countries.

Britain's instinct post-2016 has been to look to the United States. Given America's continuing political and economic power, this makes sense; but there are now differences to the twentieth-century rationales for doing so. In the Cold War, it wasn't just politically unacceptable to do major trade deals with Russia, it was of limited economic value. But this is not the case with twenty-first-century China, which, along with the EU and the US, is one of the three modern entities with massive purchasing power. So another hybrid strategy will be required, one that sticks with Washington, but somehow leaves the door open for good political and economic relations with Beijing. It will be, as the diplomats in the Foreign Office like to say, by way of understatement, "challenging." However, a clear indication of what the British believe to be their best option was seen in the summer of 2021 when its new aircraft carrier, the HMS *Queen Elizabeth*, was dispatched to the South China Sea with ten US Marine Corps F-35 jets on board.

The US still has significant interests in a stable Europe, Middle East, and Africa, but its pivot to the Pacific is real, and to attract Washington's attention and ensure access to its consumer market on favorable terms will require supporting it in all four regions mentioned. The US wants all the European states to take more responsibility for the defense of Europe and the stability of nearby regions, so that it can concentrate on the Pacific. The costs of maintaining a military capable of fighting abroad are huge but will be part of the price of an alliance with what remains the global superpower.

The UK will likely continue to attempt to slow, or somehow even reverse, the long goodbye between Washington and London. The demographic trends in the US mean that as each year passes, there are fewer Americans whose heritage looks back to the Old World, including Britain. The emotional ties that bind the two nations are loosening at the same time as the geopolitical priorities of the US change and it focuses on the Pacific region. There were glimpses of this in the Obama presidency. If it wishes to remain relevant to the US, the UK will at times need to play a supporting role to the superpower's grand strategies, sometimes economically, sometimes diplomatically, sometimes militarily. As we saw in Iraq, this does not always turn out for the best. In chess terms, the king will still be the US, and the queen will be American foreign policy as it moves around the board. Britain can be a knight, capable of making its own moves, but major British decisions will have to be referred to the king and queen to see how they fit with America's game strategy. The lessons of the Suez debacle in 1956 showed that Washington is prepared to sacrifice its own ally. However, that is an extremely rare event and Britain does have a built-in advantage in remaining a key player—the geography and politics of the last three centuries are still relevant. As mentioned in chapter 1, the UK is a member of the Five Eyes intelligence-sharing community, along with the US, Canada, Australia, and New Zealand. There's nothing quite like this elsewhere in terms of its scope and abilities, and it gives each member unparalleled access to information to guide decision making.

As part of a wider economic policy, the UK would like to broaden Five Eyes into a loose trading partnership with deals conducted on favorable terms. Some British enthusiasts see this as an alternative to the EU. The flaw in that argument is distance. Five Eyes may collectively have a bigger population and more dynamic economy than the EU, but it is not located 20 miles from the southern coast of Britain. Nevertheless, there are elements to the idea that would attract all parties, such as guaranteed markets, commitment to trading standards, and dealing with states at the cleaner end of the corruption scale.

The UK is now free to seek individual trade deals with whatever countries it chooses, and places such as Japan have shown that it is possible to go it alone. The UK reached an agreement with the EU at the end of 2020 and negotiates with it as a single bloc, and dozens of other deals have been concluded as well—for example, with Mexico and Canada. But when it comes to China, the US, and the EU, the UK is at a disadvantage. It may be the second-biggest economy in Europe, but it will remain far smaller than the three twenty-first-century economic giants, and it will struggle to win future economic concessions in trade deals with them without substantial political concessions in return. The following are only theoretical models, but, for example, the EU might link future agreements with a commitment to the UK signing up to "associate" status in an EU army, whereas the US might insist that it stays out of it. China, totally opposed as it is to Tibetan independence, would probably scupper a deal with the UK if a British prime minister invited the Dalai Lama for tea and biscuits in Downing Street. David Cameron did just that in 2012 and the following year, in April, while setting up a visit to Beijing, found that no senior leaders could find time to meet him. The visit was canceled, Downing Street let it be known that it had "turned a page" in its relationship with the Dalai Lama, and lo—Cameron went to Beijing in November in order to allow China to invest in Britain's nuclear power plants.

Politically, London now has much less influence within the EU; but that is not to say it won't have friends in individual countries. One of them is likely to be Poland. It looks destined to be the "leader" of Eastern Europe, and it shares some of the British views on the value of the EU and NATO, such as that the former should be structured to restrain Germany within a successful trading bloc but not become a single entity, and that the latter ensures that the Russians do not head west. When the UK was an EU member, the two countries frequently voted for or against the same policies; their shared worldview has not changed just because one is no longer in the union.

Poland is not the only ally that can make a good fit for post-Brexit Britain. The EU is not Europe and Europe is not the EU. On the military and political front, there's a strong case to be made for close relations not just with Poland but also with France.

The UK and France are easily the two strongest military forces in Europe. Both are concerned about Russian activity on many fronts, and both share concerns about instability in the Sahel and Sahara regions in North Africa and the associated effects of the mass movement of people northward. They already share a Common Security and Defence Policy, which, as long as it does not weaken NATO, the UK is happy to build on. There are several examples of France and the UK operating militarily together outside the EU and NATO frameworks. They were involved in Libya, remain active in Syria, and recently the UK moved to support the six thousand French troops in the Sahel.

There is also the well-established E3 format in which Germany, France, and the UK work together diplomatically to achieve common aims, the most notable example being the Iranian nuclear agreement. Looking north, it is in the interests of the UK and Norway, Denmark, Finland, Iceland, and Sweden to cooperate on a range of issues. Of those six countries, only three are EU members—a reminder that the UK may be able to construct power blocs outside the EU. If EU countries that are also in NATO do not take a robust line with perceived Russian aggression, the Baltic states, Poland, Romania, and, to a lesser extent, the Nordics will all welcome the support of the UK. The past decade has seen the emergence of "post-Atlanticist" thinking in Berlin and Paris, which makes many of their neighbors nervous. French president Emmanuel Macron's declaration that NATO was "brain-dead" didn't help confidence in the alliance, and has sparked a debate about whether Europe has to decouple from the US in its defense thinking and instead forge a robust European military. Given most European countries' reluctance to spend on defense and inability to make quick decisions, such talk worries EU and NATO states east of Berlin.

Britain sits off the coast of Europe, watching carefully and assessing options. It is not in its interest to see the union disintegrate. A strong EU helps to maintain a prosperous market for UK goods and stability on the Continent. Dismantling the liberal and legal principles of countries that were, in living memory, dictatorships would encourage a return to the bad old days. In recent memory, Greece, Portugal, Spain, Poland, Hungary, Croatia, parts of Germany, and several other countries were ruled by dictators. If the EU does fail, Britain can attempt to forge the new balance of power that will emerge. If the EU succeeds, Britain will work with it, albeit somewhat at arm's length. In 2018 Brussels denied the UK access to the secure parts of its Galileo satellite navigation system, built to rival America's GPS. This forced London to look at alternatives to achieve "strategic autonomy" in the satellite field, something it has yet to accomplish.

The opportunities and challenges for Britain will present themselves and change as countries adjust to the post–Cold War multipolar world, and we'll find out if Britain has finally got past the days of empire and positioned itself to take advantage of these shifts.

The UK remains a leading second-tier power in economic, political, and military terms. It retains its place among the Permanent Five members of the UN and is a senior partner in NATO, the Group of 7, and a founding partner of the Commonwealth. London is a global financial powerhouse; were it a nation-state, it would have the twentieth-largest economy in the world, bigger than that of Argentina. It is the capital of a country that continues to be a leader in soft power, with a quite astonishing output of culture attracting attention around the globe.

This is partially driven by the English language, which is spoken as a first tongue by upward of 400 million people and by more than 1 billion people as a second. It remains the main language of commerce and international legal contracts. The UK's higher-education system continues to attract some of the brightest and best (and richest) students. Britain is home to three of the world's top-ten-ranked universities—Oxford, Cambridge, and Imperial College London. This contributes to the wealth of the nation and to its future soft power, as many foreign graduates go on to high political office when they return home.

The BBC's influence has declined, and Britannia no longer rules the airwaves, but its output is still listened to and watched around the world. Many of the UK's former print-based media outlets such as the *Economist*, the *Guardian*, and the *Daily Mail* now have global audiences, with the latter two gaining a huge following in the US.

Sport continues to be a revenue earner, especially the English Premier League, as is the music industry and, despite Covid-19, tourism. People still come in droves, some fascinated by the institution of royalty, others by a different throne: a 2019 report from Northern Ireland's tourist board said that 350,000 people had visited that year to see the Mourne Mountains, Cairncastle, and other locations where much of *Game of Thrones* was filmed.

That level of soft power is partially dependent on a strong economy, and maintaining it will allow the UK to remain a second-tier political and military power. To what degree depends on the choices it makes.

The UK faces many challenges. It has political divisions of a sort the public are not used to, and it is searching for a clearly defined diplomatic and military role. Of possible roles the defense of the realm is the easiest to assess, although, as we will see, that could change with Scottish independence. In the 1720s, the advantages of the Acts of Union uniting Scotland and England were kicking in. The 2020s may be a new era for Britain, but its geography hasn't changed.

The UK has no current direct existential military threats. Russia may not be friendly, but its troops are not about to pour across the north European plain and arrive on the western coast of Europe. Germany and France are allies, and likely to stay that way for the foreseeable future. Indeed, as we have seen, there's a scenario in which France becomes Britain's strongest military ally in Europe.

Even if a threat appeared on the horizon, the UK's current geography remains, for now, in its favor, as it has for three hundred years, ever since the union between England and Scotland. The list of potentially hostile countries capable of mounting an invasion is short: China and, at a push, Russia. As for the rest, if an enemy did not have a fleet of aircraft carriers, it would have to base itself close to the UK in order to gain air superiority; it would need to invade nearby countries, or dominate them over a long period. During that time, UK defenses would be upgraded, as they would also be if a neighboring country gradually became an enemy. In any event, in order to land forces you'd have to overcome two hundred UK combat aircraft and the Royal Navy.

The navy may have shrunk considerably but it is still a formidable armada, with two brand-new aircraft carriers and six destroyers that are among the most advanced in the world. To get to the UK would require getting past them. Among its fleet of submarines are four Vanguard-class vessels armed with nuclear missiles. At least one of them is always at sea, and well hidden. In the event of an amphibious assault the defender usually has the advantage, and even if you get ashore you still have to gain control of the entire island—something the Romans, Vikings, and Normans never quite managed.

It's a situation that requires constant monitoring, but not one that keeps defense chiefs awake at night. What does disturb their sleep is the threat of mass-casualty terrorism, nuclear and cyber threats—and a restless Scotland.

What if Scotland became independent? What if it took with it, as it would, its share of the UK's fighter aircraft, helicopters, tanks, and ships? It gets more complicated. What if it insisted, as it would, that the Royal Navy remove its nuclear-armed submarines from its base at Faslane, on the west coast of Scotland, and close the nearby storage and repair base at Coulport? Faslane is a perfect sub base: it has deep water and quick access to the North Atlantic, where you can head up to the GIUK gap (Greenland, Iceland, UK), the old Cold War "kill zone," in the event of a Soviet naval attack, or round to the North Sea and then down toward the English Channel. It's not just Faslane, though; the questions keep coming: NATO membership? The air bases in the far north? Five Eyes? And so on.

The division of tanks, ships, etc., is relatively straightforward. It would be worked out on the basis of population, economics, and need. Faslane is a whole different world of pain. The Royal Navy can't just power up and sail out. Where would the subs go? At a stroke the UK would lose its "continually at sea" nuclear deterrent. It would take many years and billions of pounds to replicate the base. The Ministry of Defence has done scenario planning for the event, but not at a serious level. In evidence to Parliament in 2013, Rear Admiral Martin Alabaster said, "It would be very difficult—in fact, I would almost use the word 'inconceivable'—to re-create the facilities necessary to mount the strategic deterrent, without the use of Faslane and Coulport, somewhere else in the UK." The loss of the air bases at Lossiemouth and Leuchars would give the RAF a headache. Most of the frequent interceptions of Russian aircraft heading toward the UK to test its defenses are in the airspace north of Scotland. Negotiations for temporary basing rights would require huge concessions from the rump UK and entail anger on both sides of the border.

A Scottish application to join NATO would take years and be complicated by the Edinburgh government's position on nuclear weapons. NATO would want assurances that nuclear-powered, possibly nuclear-armed, vessels could access Scotland's ports. As for Five Eyes, it's very much a give-and-give relationship, and a fledgling Scottish intelligence-gathering operation would not be in a position to give very much in return for what it was given, and is thus unlikely to be invited to join. Scotland would have its own armed forces, of course, and it's likely that there would be a degree of cooperation with the UK; but whichever way you cut it, the island would no longer enjoy the strategic and geopolitical benefits of being a single entity.

In short, the rump UK (name and flag to be determined) would lose 8 percent of its population, 32 percent of its landmass, and 12,000 miles of coastline (according to Scottish government figures). It would face threats to its security: its military capacity would be reduced and there would be a shorter time frame for its early-warning systems as it would have to withdraw some of them from Scotland, which is closer to the potential threat of Russian jets coming in over the Norwegian Sea. The UK's nuclear deterrent, in the shape of the submarines, could be parked in the US while another naval base was built, but this is not the sort of logistical headache the service chiefs want. As for why Britain needs such a deterrent, supporters point to the potential threat of Russia, North Korea, and Iran. The prospect of Iranian nuclear-tipped missiles heading toward London seems highly unlikely, but that's not how state strategy works. Times change: in 1932 Germany's Weimar Republic was on its knees and its military restricted in strength by the Treaty of Versailles. Nine years later, Nazi Germany was at the gates of Moscow.

Scottish independence might not be the end of the breakup. It would accelerate the slowly growing trend in Northern Ireland that unification with the Republic of Ireland might be a good idea. The republic was formed in 1922 after a campaign of violence achieved independence—an early example of the long-drawn-out roar of the dying British Empire.

These modern independence scenarios are directly connected to Brexit. The Scottish independence referendum of 2014 saw a 55 percent vote to remain in the UK, but that was when the UK was in the EU. In the Brexit referendum, support for the EU was considerably higher in Scotland and Northern Ireland than in England. One way to stay in that union is to leave another.

This is not an argument for or against Scottish independence, nor do the economic arguments for and against it concern us here; but a case can be made that if Scotland does leave, the damage to the UK's international standing would be worse than that caused by it leaving the EU. Russia would be the country most pleased with the breakup as it would militarily diminish one of the two main powers in Europe. Few other countries would actively welcome it, but Paris and Berlin would note the reduced economic power of the nation that traditionally disrupted plans to create a unified force on the Continent.

It is, for now, speculative, but these are some of the choices facing the UK. It won't be easy, and it will not go unchallenged as Britain heads out once again into the great sea lanes of the world.

In 1902 the UK's most famous geopolitical analyst, Sir Halford Mackinder, wrote, "Great consequences lie in the simple statements that Britain is an island group, set in an ocean, but off the shores of the great continent; that the opposing shores are indented."

Some people dislike Mackinder's writings because he was an imperialist and focused on the importance of geography on strategy. But he was also a supporter of democracy and of the League of Nations to help reduce great-power tensions, and he was horrified at the rise of Nazism, despite having inadvertently influenced some of its leaders' thinking. The misuse of his ideas does not mean that the above quote is wrong. The reality of being an island off the coast of a continent has not changed; the shorelines of both are indented, providing deepwater ports which allow oceangoing trade. The way to look at Mackinder's work is to accept geographical realities without seeking in them anything to justify aggression.

Two and a half centuries after the American War of Independence, the British are coming again—to as many places as they can. Post-empire and post-Brexit, they will try to come as friends and equals. It won't always be friendly, or equal.

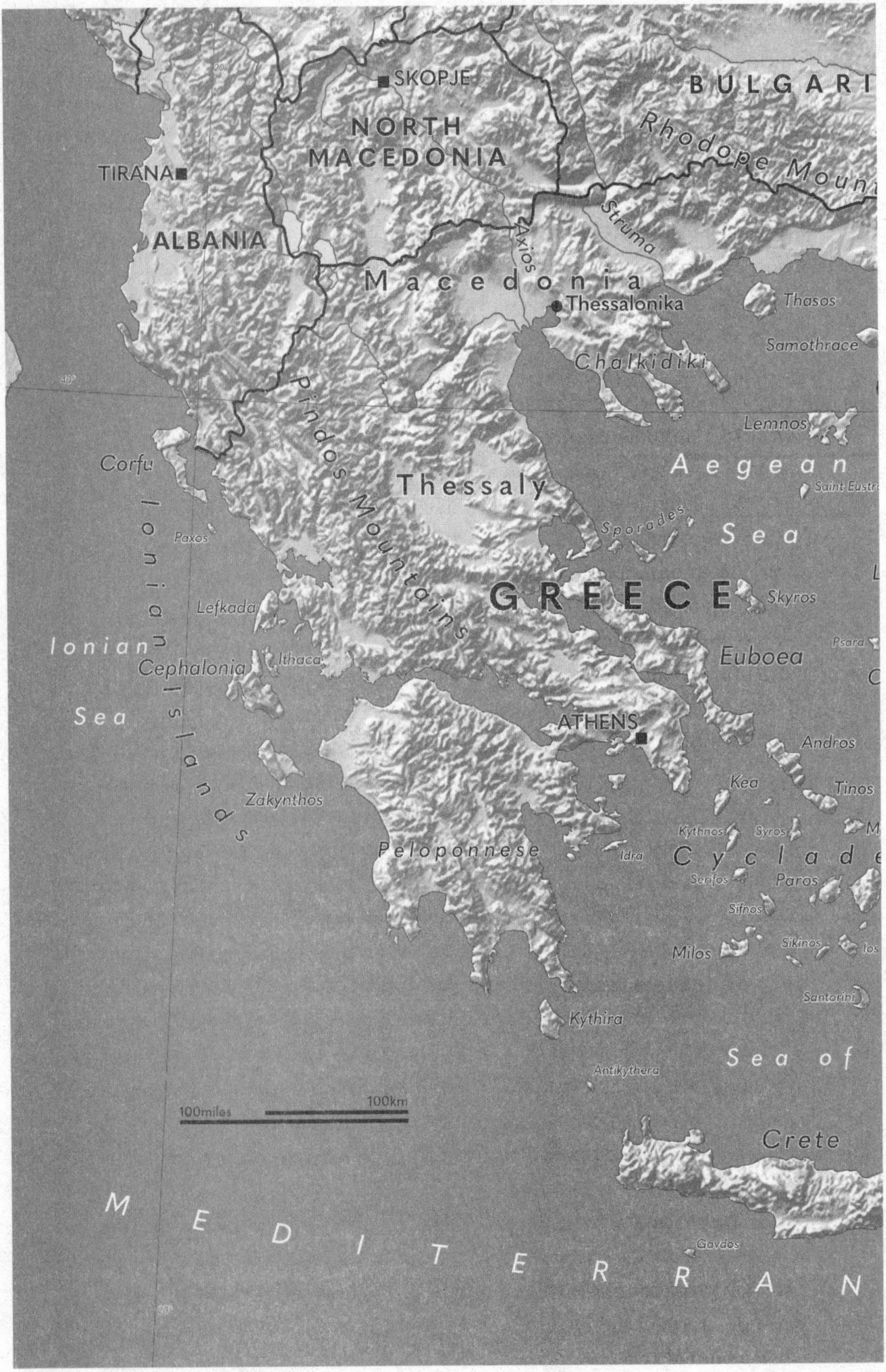
SKOPJE
BULGARI
NORTH MACEDONIA
Rhodope Moun
TIRANA
Struma
ALBANIA
Axios
Macedonia
Thessalonika
Thasos
Samothrace
Chalkidiki
Pindos Mountains
Lemnos
Corfu
Aegean
Saint Eustr
Thessaly
Sporades
Sea
Paxos
GREECE
Skyros
Lefkada
Ionian Islands
Ionian Sea
Psara
Ithaca
Cephalonia
Euboea
ATHENS
Andros
Kea
Tinos
Zakynthos
Kythnos
Syros
Peloponnese
Idra
Cyclade
Serifos
Paros
Sifnos
Milos
Sikinos
Ios
Santorini
Kythira
Sea of
Antikythera
100miles
100km
Crete
MEDITERRAN
Gavdos

Black Sea
Bosporus Strait
Istanbul
Sea of Marmara
TURKEY
Anatolia
Izmir
Lesbos
Chios
Samos
Ikaria
Patmos
Leros
Kalymnos
Naxos
Amorgos
Kos
Astypalaia
Nisyros
Symi
Tilos
Anafi
Dodecanese
Rhodes
Kastellorizo
Crete
Karpathos
Kasos

5

GREECE

Let there be light! Said Liberty,
And like the sunrise from the sea, Athens arose!

—Percy Bysshe Shelley, "Hellas"

Summer in the eastern Med, or perhaps the Aegean? Sounds lovely, but in recent years it has become a little too hot for comfort.

After decades of relative calm, the region is once again a volatile geopolitical front. The discovery of undersea gas fields has merged old and new conflicts with Greece and Turkey at their heart, and numerous countries are being dragged in. These waters were a source of potential dispute between the two before the gas discovery, but this has added a new toxicity.

Greece has a special place in the hearts of many students of geopolitics. It is the place that gave birth to the study of the subject. The father of the discipline in the Western canon is Thucydides (c. 460–400 BCE), and his *History of the Peloponnesian War* has inspired scholars of international relations over many centuries. His work is still used when discussing current events (the term "Thucydides trap," originally about the growth of Athenian power and the fear that this caused in Sparta, now refers to the rise of China and the emotions this evokes in the US).

Thucydides knew then what remains true now: the mountains to the north of the Greek mainland make trade in that direction arduous, but they are also a barrier to land-based threats. However, to feel secure and to prosper, Greece must be a maritime power in the Aegean Sea. These two factors—mountains and water—are the key to understanding the past, present, and future of Greece.

Modern Athens is the capital of a country that includes more than six thousand islands. Nowhere in Greece is more than 60 miles from water. Greece is at the southeastern tip of the Balkans; to its north are borders with Albania, North Macedonia, and Bulgaria and to its northeast is the border with Turkey.

This totals almost 750 miles of land frontier, but the majority of Greece's border length is maritime.

Surrounding the mainland are the Aegean, Mediterranean, and Ionian Seas. The Aegean sits between mainland Greece and Turkey, leading via the Sea of Marmara into the Bosporus Strait and on into the Black Sea, where Russia is the dominant power. The Aegean is therefore crucial not only to Greek security but also to Turkey, NATO, the Americans, and the Russians. The Aegean's largest island is Crete, which is Greek. It is also where we find the Dodecanese islands, including Rhodes, just off the coast of Turkey. Their location is why the Aegean is sometimes called a "Greek lake." Under international maritime law, a country has 200 nautical miles of exclusive economic zone (EEZ) from its coastline (shared if another nation is within 200 nautical miles). Therefore, the waters around islands such as Crete, Rhodes, and Lesbos belong to Greece, meaning that most of the Aegean is Greek territory—a fact that Turkey does not accept.

The other major islands are to the northwest in the Ionian Sea, which borders Italy and Albania. They include Corfu and Paxos. Southeast of Crete is the eastern Mediterranean, bordering Turkey, Syria, Lebanon, Israel, Egypt, and Libya. It also contains the island of Cyprus, with which Greece has a special relationship and which is partly occupied by Turkey.

In antiquity these seas linked the known world, connecting civilizations and allowing trade to bring new ideas, wealth, and conflict. Today they mean that Greece must have as much of an eye on the Middle East and North Africa as on Europe. Since the days of ancient Greece, geography has both restrained Greece and made it the subject of great-power play. At the southeastern corner of Europe, and facing off across the Aegean against its larger neighbor and nemesis, Greece now finds itself at the crossroads of the EU, Russia, NATO, the turmoil of the Middle East, and the ongoing migrant crisis.

As legend tells it, the country was formed when God was distributing soil around the world in a sieve, presumably a large one. Job done, he found himself with a lot of leftover rocks and stones and used them to build Greece. This sharp handiwork is apparent as you approach mainland Greece from almost any direction: apart from a few coastal plains, often the mountains rise straight up out of the water. Four-fifths of the Hellenic Republic is mountainous, characterized by jagged peaks and spectacular deep gorges. The mainland's core is the Pindus mountain range, which sweeps down from the Albanian and North Macedonian borders. At its widest, from east to west, it is 50 miles across, parts of it impassable. It features rocky peaks with extreme slopes where you could make a living herding goats perhaps, but not in large-scale farming. On the eastern side of the range, by the coastline, in the Greek Macedonian and Thessaly regions we find the narrow, fertile plains that can sustain intensive farming. It's no coincidence that the place capable of providing enough food to grow a large population is also the region that produced the empire of Alexander the Great. However, most Greek land either is mountainous, is covered in forest, or has poor soil.

As the ancient Greek city-states formed, they were hemmed in by the hills to their backs, giving little room to expand and even less for the sort of scaled-up agriculture required to sustain large numbers of people. The developing centers of antiquity were not well connected to one another, thus hampering internal trade, communications, and population growth and making central control difficult. This is partially why to this day, although politically unified under the nation-state of Greece, the regions have distinctive characteristics.

This limited scope for large-scale farming is why today only about 4 percent of GDP comes from agriculture, and it would be difficult to expand it in the narrow plains, which means Greece imports significantly more food than it exports. Even now, building roads and railways between land regions is tricky. There is also a lack of good river routes up into the Balkans and on to other EU countries. For example, the Axiós River comes down from North Macedonia into Greece before emptying into the Aegean, but at its maximum it is only 13 feet deep. This is not conducive to shipping. It's a similar story with the Strymon River, which flows south from Bulgaria.

On the other hand, as numerous invaders both ancient and modern have discovered, this same terrain makes Greece difficult to invade. This is a twist on the traditional concept of strategic depth. In classic terms it refers to the distance between an invading army and the main centers of gravity in a country, such as its industrial heartlands. The greater the distance, the better chance of defense the country has. One of the best examples is Russia: not only does an invading force have to travel a long way to get to the center of gravity, but Russia has so much depth that, in extremis, defending forces can retreat huge distances behind the center of gravity.

Greece does not have this luxury, but its twist is that defending forces can fall back to the high ground and fight on. That is, of course, if the invading forces get to the Greek centers of gravity in the first place. To prevent that possibility, Greece looks not only to its natural defenses in the north but also to the sea.

The inhospitable terrain of the peninsula was what ensured that Greeks became skilled seafarers. Land trade within the mainland was (and is) challenging, so traders took to the water to ply their wares along the coastline. This geography meant that as Greece emerged, relying on its maritime trade, the trade routes had to be defended, and that required a navy; it still does.

This was the landscape in which the city-state of Athens arose. Of all the Greek city-states, Athens is the one that, for many, is synonymous with ancient Greece as it grew to become the Western world's most advanced civilization. The city developed around the high ground where the Acropolis now stands. The location was chosen because it was a defensible position with commanding views of the surrounding plains leading to the Aegean, about four miles away; indeed, the word "Acropolis" means "high city." It was first settled in about 4000 BCE, major building on and around the Acropolis, including a palace, came around 1500 BCE, and there is evidence of a defensive wall from about 1200 BCE.

High ground, access to the sea, and the determination to be a naval power gave Athens the edge over similar city-states such as Sparta. By the sixth century BCE, Athens was a regional power, but it was not powerful enough to withstand an onslaught from a far superior enemy—Persia.

In 480 BCE, the Persians landed a huge army 85 miles from Athens. Tens of thousands of men advanced a few hundred yards to a narrow coastal path, believing it to be the only way to the interior and conquering Greece. What followed, the Battle of Thermopylae, has become one of antiquity's best-known confrontations and has fought its way out of the history books to become a Hollywood blockbuster—300 (2006).

Greek soldiers from a Spartan-led alliance, commanded by King Leonidas, arrived at the pass to block the Persian advance. The vastly outnumbered Greeks inflicted massive casualties before their enemy found a shepherds' pass, which they used to begin infiltrating behind Greek lines. Leonidas ordered a retreat before staging the famous last stand by 300 of his men. In reality there were probably up to 2,000 defenders, including 300 Spartans, but "up to 2,000" does not make for a good film title.

The upshot was occupation, but the following year the Persians were defeated. Athenians then realized they could make their city impregnable if they extended its walls in a 200-yard-wide corridor down to the port of Piraeus, four miles away. Accompanied by a strong naval presence, this meant that Athens could be supplied even if it was under siege. The key, though, was sea power, a lesson the Greeks never forgot.

Between the end of the Persian Wars (449 BCE) and the opening of the Peloponnesian War (431 BCE), Athens was the leading Greek power, especially in intellectual capital, producing ideas and people whose influence has been maintained over twenty-five hundred years. It was an exhilarating moment in human civilization, one in which education, building, science, debate, arts, and experiments in democracy were practiced during a time of peace and prosperity. The author Eric Weiner notes in *The Geography of Genius* that "other Greek city-states were larger (Syracuse) or wealthier (Corinth) or mightier (Sparta). Yet Athens produced more brilliant minds—from Socrates to Aristotle—than any other place the world has seen before or since."

Athenians loved to venture abroad and learn from other cultures. As the philosopher Plato put it in an indelicate phrase, "What the Greeks borrow from foreigners, they perfect." What they perfected has given us so much— for example, Hippodamus, the father of urban planning; the great philosophers such as Aristotle; in medicine, Hippocrates; in mathematics, Pythagoras; and the world's first known female mathematician, Hypatia. An estimated 150,000 English words derive from Greek—"democracy," "acrobat," and "sarcasm" among them. We can also thank Greek antiquity for the term "hippopotomonstrosesquipedalian"—relating to long words.

The three-decade-long Peloponnesian War between Athens and Sparta brought misery but ended with Athens controlling large areas, including some of the western coast of Anatolia, across the Aegean in what is now Turkey. This was to prove a source of friction and conflict through the centuries and remains the basis of dispute today. A century later, Athens was again at war with a neighbor, this time Philip II of Macedon, who went on to unite Greece under Macedonian leadership. The city-states looked upon Macedonia as a backward region, but it had one thing they did not: enough river-fed agricultural land to sustain a growing local population without having to rely on sea trade. Philip, and then his son Alexander the Great, parlayed this into an empire.

However, the Greek mainland still did not have land capable of producing enough food to feed a major regional population, whereas across the Ionian Sea a power was rising that was fed and watered by the expansive fertile valleys through which the Rivers Arno, Tiber, and Po flow. Rome moved into the

Greek neighborhood first by capturing Corfu, which sits across from the heel of Italy's boot. The island guards the western approaches to mainland Greece and in the hands of a powerful enemy is a useful base for invasion. Rome took it in 299 BCE and used it for just that purpose.

And that was the end of ancient Greece. Under Roman rule the city-states were given substantial autonomy, Athenian institutions significantly influenced Roman thought, and being part of the Roman Empire helped the Greek language to spread throughout the Mediterranean, ensuring that Greek culture was handed down through the generations. But as for power—those days were over, and it became a backwater as greater states fought their way into the pages of history. The American humorist David Sedaris has quipped that Greeks "invented democracy, built the Acropolis and called it a day." It's a little harsh given that over the next two thousand years the Romans, Byzantines, Ottomans, British, and Russians worked tirelessly to prevent Greece from taking charge of its own destiny and getting back in the geopolitical game. They all wanted to control the Aegean and eastern Mediterranean, and a weakened Greece suited these aims.

In the fourth century CE, the Roman Empire split, with the eastern half centered on the Greek-speaking city of Byzantium (renamed Constantinople, now Istanbul). The culture of the city and region was Hellenic and remained so for centuries. It was the capital of the Byzantine Empire for a millennium during which Greece was "ruled" from the city, although actual control was of the coastal plains, major cities, and most islands, while in the mountains tribes often held sway. Subsequent years saw a series of unfortunate events as parts of Greece were held by, among others, Franks, Serbs, and Venetians, but the constant, until 1453, was Byzantium.

The year 1453 is when Constantinople fell to the Ottomans. During the rise of this new dominant force, Greece was on the margins and remained there. It was now cut off from Christian Europe, although most of the population retained their Christian faith. For more than two hundred years the Ottomans would dominate the islands, the seas around the mainland, and some of the land above, ensuring that Greece remained peripheral. The mountainous interior of the mainland meant that some regions were never under Ottoman control, but the most important thing to them was control of the Aegean islands. The Ottomans conquered the Balkans and got as far north as Vienna. But in 1683 they suffered a major military defeat there, beginning the long decline of the empire and helping to clear the way for Greek independence.

Over the following century, the expanding Austro-Hungarian and Russian Empires exposed the weakening Ottoman grip on the Balkans and in the 1800s rebellions broke out in Greece. This was the beginning of a long drive to create a modern idea of a Greek identity in the territories ruled by the ancient city-states. Recognition of sovereignty by the great powers came in 1832, although as sovereignty goes it left a lot to be desired. Greeks were not involved in the agreement and less than a third of Greek speakers were within the new state borders. The country would spend the next 115 years trying to change this through the Megali Idea—the Great Idea—the concept of uniting all Greeks within the borders of an expanded state exemplified in the slogan "Once more, as years and time go by, once more they shall be ours." Its more radical proponents took the idea as reviving the Byzantine Empire and including the Black Sea, Constantinople, and central Anatolia, territories central to the Ottoman Empire (and, later, Turkey).

"Dream on," said the European powers, who decreed that Greece would be a monarchy of limited size, that its king would be a seventeen-year-old Bavarian, Otto of Wittelsbach, and its army would be made up of Bavarians. This didn't go down well. Still, he survived in office until 1862 before being deposed. The answer to this turmoil was another seventeen-year-old foreigner in the shape of Prince William of Denmark (King George I of the Hellenes). The Greeks had wanted a Brit, hoping that Europe's dominant power might help expand their territory; but disappointment at Queen Victoria keeping her son Alfred at home was assuaged after she gave George a present, the Ionian Islands, which were then a British protectorate. They included Corfu, the same island the Romans had used as the launchpad to destroy ancient Greece twenty-two hundred years before.

George used his relationship with the royal families of Russia and the UK to gain more territory for Greece, a policy that had some success, including the incorporation of most of the Thessaly region. The Olympic Games returned to Athens in 1896, after a sixteen-hundred-year interruption, and were regarded as symbolic of the revival of sovereignty. It helped that the marathon event was won by a local shepherd, Spyridon Louis, as King George stood and applauded him down the home stretch.

Even following its independence from the Ottomans, the other great powers had Greece in their sights. In 1841, the British ambassador to Greece, Sir Edmund Lyons, had said, "A truly independent Greece is an absurdity. Greece can either be English or Russian, and since she cannot be Russian, it is necessary that she be English." During the great-power play of the nineteenth century, one of the main aims was to block the expansion of the Russians in the Mediterranean basin. During the 1870s, relations between the empires worsened as they squabbled over Afghanistan, with the British worried that Moscow would use it as a back door to the jewel in its imperial crown—India. The British also did not want Russia in a position to block the Mediterranean entrance to the Suez Canal and thus endanger access to India. Throughout this period and into the twentieth century, the British regarded themselves as the "protectors" of the Greek nation. The underlying reason was the protection not of Greece, but of their own empire.

By the end of the nineteenth century the Ottoman Empire, known as the "sick man of Europe," was pretty much on its deathbed. Numerous nationalist conflicts were breaking out in Ottoman territories and the resultant land grab had repercussions that are still being felt in the Balkans in the form of border disputes. For most people in Western Europe, the years 1914 to 1918 bracket the war years; for Greeks the period is more like 1912 to 1922.

In 1912 the First Balkan War broke out, with Montenegro opening hostilities against the Ottomans and encouraging the Greeks, Serbs, and Bulgarians to join in. The Greeks had spent the first decade of the twentieth century putting together a well-trained military, and within a few weeks they marched into the port of Thessalonika (Salonika), beating the Bulgarians to the city by a matter of hours. A few days later King George led a parade through what would become, once the great powers recognized it as part of Greece in 1913, the nation's second-largest city. By then George was dead, shot in the back at close range. The headline in the *Times* of London was "King of the Hellenes Murdered. Shot by a Madman in Salonika." The killer, Alexandros Schinas, was arrested and died six weeks later, when he appears to have been mad enough to fall out of a window at a police station.

The Second Balkan War started in 1913. The first was everyone against Turkey; the second was everyone against Bulgaria, which was still smarting over being beaten to Thessalonika. Bulgarian forces attacked Greek and Serbian positions but were soon pushed back. The Romanians joined in, followed by the Turks, and with the Romanian army approaching Sofia the Bulgarians, realizing they'd got it horribly wrong, sued for peace, subsequently losing territory to all four opponents.

The two wars cost Greece 9,500 men but extended its land by 70 percent and its population grew by 2 million people, to 4.8 million. The Megali Idea was becoming real; however, the First World War would present Greece with a dilemma: hold its cards and consolidate, or play a hand and maybe win part of the jackpot.

From 1914 Greece spent three years sitting out the war, which caused severe political tensions as the country split on the issue of participation. Eventually it entered on the side of the Allies and sent its entire army to the Macedonian front to fight alongside British, French, and Serbian forces, helping to break the Bulgarian defenses. This earned it a place at the table at the Paris Peace Conference, which it used as the diplomatic springboard for further territorial gains, including the port city of Smyrna, now Izmir, in Turkey. In 1919 Greek forces landed in Smyrna, which had been ceded to Athens as a reward for joining the Allies. At the time there were substantial Greek-speaking populations there, along the coast and in the interior. With Allied troops occupying Constantinople, Greek nationalists saw Smyrna as a stepping-stone to capturing the Ottoman capital and reviving the Byzantine Empire, dominated by Hellenic culture.

Conversely, Turkish nationalists saw the arrival of Greek troops as the opening shot in their war of independence, and by the summer of 1922 the Greeks, who had pushed well into the interior, were in headlong retreat with the Turkish army, led by Mustafa Kemal (Atatürk), pursuing them to the coast. The war was over when Kemal's forces entered Smyrna, which erupted in flames, killing tens of thousands of people and reducing the city to ash, along with Greek dreams of a reconstituted Byzantine Empire.

The Greeks of Turkey didn't wait for politicians to decide their future. The massacre of civilians and razing of villages led at least 1 million of them to flee months before the Treaty of Lausanne (1923) dictated a compulsory population exchange after both Greece and Turkey stated they were not confident that minorities could be protected. In total about 1.5 million Greek Orthodox left Turkey, with approximately 400,000 Muslims going the other way. The tragic events of the first two decades of the twentieth century, built on the foundations of history, continue to frame the current antagonism between Greece and Turkey.

For Greece, this influx of people had profound political effects. Thessalonika was the largest Jewish city in the Balkans; but increased competition for jobs, which arrived with the refugees, spurred antisemitism, leading to interest in the Zionist movement and migration to the Palestinian Mandate. Many of the newcomers were settled in poor living conditions in what was known as New Greece—the areas incorporated over the previous decade. In later years many began to support the Communist party, ultimately contributing to the rise of military coups and authoritarian regimes.

The 1920s and 1930s were a story of continuing division, instability, and military rule that flirted with fascism. Greece went into the Second World War under the leadership of a dictator, General Ioannis Metaxas. He'd hoped to keep Greece neutral, but following two failed Italian invasions, Greece surrendered to the Germans and endured a brutal occupation by German, Italian, and Bulgarian troops. Thanks to Greece's geography, the occupying forces never fully controlled the interior, and the formidable Greek Resistance was able to take advantage of the mountainous terrain to carry out a sustained guerrilla war. But tens of thousands of people starved due to food being requisitioned, seventy thousand people were executed, and hundreds of villages were destroyed to punish the resistance attacks. About sixty thousand Greek Jews were killed, many at Auschwitz; only 9 percent of Thessalonika's Jews survived the war.

In October 1944, the Germans withdrew and the British arrived in Athens amid wild celebrations. But joy and relief lasted only a few weeks. In December gunfire again rang out in the streets of the capital; the sound presaged the Greek civil war. Its roots went back at least to the beginning of the century and a royalist/antimonarchist split within the population. Despite occasionally cooperating, neither of the two main resistance groups—the Communist EAM-ELAS and the right-of-center EDES—was prepared to see the other control Greece after the German withdrawal.

Following an election in 1946 in which the royalists won a majority, the Communists, who abstained, refused to accept the result. A full-scale civil war broke out, which the Communists may well have won had it not been for a confluence of regional and global events, notably the alarm in Western capitals about the reach of Soviet power into the Balkans to the north.

In 1947 the British accepted they could no longer commit to the defense of Greece and their role was taken up by the Americans. The US began to supply the Greek army, which, thus strengthened, cleared the mountains of Communist strongholds. As in previous centuries, an outside power directed events, and, as in the previous century, the prime rationale was to block the Russians—now the Soviets—in the Mediterranean basin.

Yugoslavia's break with the Soviet Union dealt another blow to the rebels as Belgrade ended support and in 1949 closed Yugoslavia's borders to the Communist forces. In October most retreated into Albania, bringing the war to a close. It's estimated that more than fifty thousand combatants died and half a million people were displaced—this in a country of less than 8 million.

So a devastated Greece emerged into the 1950s and 1960s with a divided population and a military class that saw itself not just as defender of the nation but as the guardian of political culture. The fallout from the civil war and subsequent lack of economic development meant Greece was falling behind the rest of Europe, but the military focused on subverting democratic institutions even as the population became more exposed to Western European culture. Elections scheduled for May 1967 were expected to be won by a centrist-left party intent on curbing military influence, and as polling day approached sections of the army were concerned. Early in the morning of April 21, the residents of Athens were awakened by the sound of tanks rumbling through the streets and the occasional gunshot. Most would have known what was happening. With the radio playing military music, it was no surprise when eventually came the announcement "The Hellenic Armed Forces undertake the governance of the country." The only surprise was that it was lower-ranking officers who were behind the coup.

"The colonels," as they were known, arrested key politicians and the commander in chief of the army. They went on to round up those on a list of ten thousand names drawn up in advance of the coup, and many of these detainees were tortured. Despite becoming a dictatorship, Greece remained a member of NATO, which it had joined in 1952—testament to its location still being strategically important for outside powers.

Democracy was reintroduced in 1974, and in 1981 Greece joined the EEC (later the EU). Membership helped the economy and, although the lack of good road trade routes remained a problem, things were looking up for Greece—until the twenty-first century, when geography and politics have placed Greece at the forefront of the two major crises to strain the EU.

In the first decade of this century, steady economic growth and a successful hosting of the Olympics papered over some structural cracks in the economy, but the financial crash of 2008–2009 laid bare how much money successive governments had borrowed, using smoke and mirrors to pretend it was sustainable in an economy in which the public sector was 40 percent of GDP. To join the euro, Athens cooked the books, and the other eurozone members turned a blind eye.

The economy went into meltdown amid riots, strikes, and societal hardship not seen for decades. The International Monetary Fund stepped in with loans, but insisted on strict austerity measures. The old Greek fear of being dominated by the outside world quickly resurfaced and the political center ground shrank as far-right and far-left parties gained significant support.

The relationship with the EU has been strained by this, and also by Greece's position at the southeast corner of the union. Greece has been angered by what it sees as the lack of help from the EU and other member states over the waves of migrants and refugees arriving in the hope of getting to richer countries via the Balkan route. Greece, like Italy, believes it is being asked to be Europe's border police, but without EU funding. Both fear they will be hosting refugees in squalid camps for years to come, without their EU partners alleviating the burden.

Many make the dangerous journey across the short stretch of Aegean Sea between Turkey and the Greek islands, some of which are visible from the Turkish shoreline. Samos is just 1 mile from the Anatolian coast and in 2015 it became the focal point for those desperate to get to an EU country. More than 100,000 migrants and refugees arrived on the island, which is just 8 miles wide and 27 miles long. They contributed to the more than 850,000 who made it to Greece that year. But among the hundreds who perished in the Aegean was a three-year-old Syrian refugee named Alan Kurdi, whose body was pictured washed up on a beach—a shocking image that came to represent the human cost of the crisis.

Greece is the main entry point to Europe for many migrants,
mostly coming from Turkey.

Greece struggled to deal with the situation, which developed during its economic collapse. The islands simply couldn't cope with the number of people arriving, the state did not have the capacity to deal with another crisis, and the outside world did not come to its assistance. The situation eased slightly in 2016, when the EU basically bribed Turkey to work harder to prevent migrants from setting out across the sea, and to accept the return of those who had made it to Greece. The price was several billion euros to fund refugee aid, and visa-free EU travel for Turkish citizens. The numbers crossing fell dramatically, but tens of thousands of people remain trapped in squalid camps on the islands, and a steady trickle of newcomers arrives almost every day. It's hard to see the way out of this. Hardening attitudes farther north make it unlikely that most EU states will take larger numbers willingly, and the push factors of conflict, poverty, and climate change will take years to deal with, if indeed they can be. In the meantime, parts of some of the Greek islands look destined to be, in effect, prison camps.

The issue has been a source of great tension between Greece and Turkey. Greece believes the Turks open their frontier to allow migrants and refugees through, at a time and place of Ankara's choosing, in order to destabilize Greece. Ankara denies this, but there has been evidence of local authorities effectively escorting migrants out of urban areas and to the border, which has led to violent scenes as people try to cross. Proof that this is government policy has not been found, but without doubt Turkey's power over the movement of people gives it distinct leverage over the EU countries in general. Athens has responded by deploying extra forces to its land and sea borders.

The many disputes between Greece and Turkey exacerbate a mutual antagonism rooted in antiquity. In the popular imagination of some Turks, the first major confrontation between them came more than three thousand years ago with the siege of Troy, in which the Greeks gambled on a horse and won. Whether there was such a battle and whether or not the Trojans were the forebears of modern Turks is subject to historic debate, but in this context it is less important than the idea of an almost primordial enmity. We are on firmer historical ground in eastern Turkey at the Battle of Manzikert in 1071, even if what is often thought of as Byzantine Greeks fighting Seljuk Turks actually involved a more complicated array of combatants. The "Greeks" lost, setting the Byzantine Empire on the road to losing Constantinople. In the Greek telling, Greece then endured four hundred years under the yoke of Turkish occupation. In the modern era, the Greek War of Independence and the Greco-Turkish War of 1919–1922 remain fresh in the memory of each side.

Riding into this was Turkey's nationalist president, Recep Erdoğan, whose rhetoric fuels Turkish xenophobia and Greek anxieties. Turkish state TV likes to show maps depicting "Turkey's National Pact," a 1920 document identifying which parts of the defeated Ottoman Empire the new Turkish republic would fight for. They include many of the Greek Aegean islands and part of the mainland. Erdoğan has appeared in an official photograph of a 2019 visit to Istanbul's National Defense University standing in front of a map showing half of the Aegean as belonging to Turkey.

From the Greek perspective, national defense is centered on the mainland and control of the Aegean. Without control of the sea, the mainland's supply route can be cut and it would be open to invasion. The Greek geopolitical writer Ioannis Michaletos described the Aegean islands to me as "unsinkable aircraft carriers giving Greece power-projection capabilities into the Anatolian hinterland and up to the shores of East Med countries by placing aeroplanes, rockets and mobile troops on the islands. Without them Greece becomes just a rugged Balkan peninsula not easily defended from the east and susceptible to landing operations and naval blockade. In short—militarily doomed."

It is probable that much of Erdoğan's rhetoric is for Turkish domestic consumption as it plays to his base of support, but talk of "a just need to correct the wrong flow of history" keeps the military planners in Athens awake at night, as well as providing them with the ammunition they need when they lobby for the defense budget each year.

Greece's defense costs have contributed to the economic and social nightmare it has suffered since the debt crisis began in 2010, which in turn has led to defense cuts. In 1981 the military budget as a percentage of GDP was 5.7 percent—easily the highest among NATO European allies. In 2000 that figure was 3.6 percent, but by 2018 had fallen to 2.4 percent.

The majority of Greece's 10.5 million people live on the mainland and peninsulas; indeed, about a third of the entire population are in the greater metropolitan Athens region. But there are hundreds of thousands of citizens on the islands—for example, Crete has over 600,000 people, Rhodes has about 100,000, as does Corfu. Many more live in smaller communities dotted around the Aegean. These include twenty-one islands with between 5,000 and 50,000 residents, and thirty-two with between 750 and 5,000 people. There are even thirty-five islands with fewer than 100 people. Each is sovereign territory, and each must be defended.

Simply patrolling six thousand islands is expensive enough and requires a large navy, but when you factor in the history between Greece and Turkey the costs soar, because successive Greek governments over the generations have viewed Turkey as a threat. The result is a modern navy and a large army, above which flies an advanced air force whose fighter pilots are considered among the best in Europe. They need to be, as they are frequently involved in mock dog-fights with Turkish pilots in the skies above the Aegean.

On land the priority is to defend the major population centers and to hold as much as possible of the Axiós River valley, leading up into North Macedonia, in order to protect agricultural land and the routes into Europe. The twenty-first century has seen Greece involved in a number of disputes in addition to the issues with Turkey. Fearing territorial claims on its own province called Macedo-nia, it refused to accept the existence of the neighboring country the Republic of Macedonia, which emerged from the breakup of Yugoslavia in the 1990s, and so imposed an economic embargo. The issue was settled only in 2018, when both sides accepted the term "North Macedonia," and even this sparked nation-alist rioting in Greece at the perceived appropriation of the name. The move did, however, pave the way for North Macedonia to join NATO.

The other main defense objective is to maintain control of Corfu in the Ionian Sea, but there are no threats to this for the foreseeable future, and, in contrast to antiquity, Greece has no desire to project military power any farther west. Therefore the concentration is on the Aegean, specifically Rhodes and Crete—and farther east, in the Mediterranean, Cyprus.

Cyprus, of which Greece still sees itself as a protector, sits in the middle of a geostrategic highway—the main sea lanes of the eastern Mediterranean, and a series of newly discovered gas fields.

Following three centuries of Ottoman rule, the British assumed adminis-trative responsibility for the island in 1878 and then annexed it in 1914. Like every great power before it, Britain knew Cyprus's strategic value in monitoring military and commercial movements in the Aegean and Levant. During the Cold War it was a vital radar listening post, not just to keep watch over the Mediterranean but to monitor Soviet nuclear tests as far away as Central Asia. The UK still has an air base there, garrisoned by several thousand troops.

Independence in 1960 led to sectarian violence between the Greek Cypriot majority and Turkish Cypriot minority, resulting in a UN peacekeeping force arriving to police a border, known as the Green Line, between the two commu-nities. What happened next has to be seen in the context of the Cold War. The Soviets were still seeking influence and a port in the Mediterranean, and in the early 1970s the Cypriot president, Archbishop Makarios, was playing the risky game of cozying up to Moscow. In 1974, with the tacit support of the US, the Greek military junta replaced the archbishop in a coup designed to lead to the union of Greece and Cyprus.

Instead it brought a Turkish invasion. After several weeks of fierce fighting, the Turks established a bridgehead around the northern port town of Kyrenia and then linked it to the main Turkish Cypriot region to control 37 percent of the island. Unlike Turkey, Cyprus was not a member of NATO (it still isn't), and there was little room for the Western powers to intervene militarily. The debacle led to the fall of the Greek military government and ushered in the current Greek democratic era. In 1983 the northern region declared itself to be the Turkish Republic of Northern Cyprus. It is recognized as such by two countries: itself and Turkey. The United Nations considers it a territory of the Republic of Cyprus currently under Turkish occupation.

The discovery of potentially huge reserves of natural gas in the eastern Mediterranean has complicated what was already a potential source of conflict between Greece and Turkey. Gas fields have been found off Egypt, Israel, Cyprus, and Greece. Turkey, anxious that its own waters have not yielded energy, is scouting around in Cypriot and Greek territory and has signed an agreement with Libya to drill there. Lebanon has a maritime dispute with Israel over part of one gas field; the energy companies BP, Total, Eni, and Exxon Mobil have all become involved; and Russia is watching the whole scene nervously as its dominant position supplying natural gas to Europe comes under threat.

As a sovereign state, Cyprus has drilling rights around its coastlines, so Turkish plans to develop a major naval base in the north set the alarm bells ringing in Nicosia and Athens even before a new crisis centered on energy supplies erupted.

In the summer of 2019, Turkish drilling ships showed up off the northern coast, escorted by a warship. Ankara said they were in the sovereign waters of the Republic of Northern Cyprus and "within Turkey's continental shelf." Cyprus appealed to the EU, which said Turkey's actions were illegal and could damage future relations between it and Ankara. Cyprus, Greece, and Egypt, which are cooperating on energy exploration in the Mediterranean, issued a joint statement saying that Turkey had violated international law.

In June 2020 Turkey announced it intended to begin drilling off islands, including Rhodes and Crete. Its ambassador to Athens was summoned to the Foreign Ministry and informed that Greece was "ready to respond" to what it regarded as a provocation if drilling took place. Turkey's position is based on an astonishing agreement it came to with Libya in late 2019. It "created" an exclusive economic zone (EEZ) stretching in a corridor across the Mediterranean from Turkey's southwest coast down to the northern tip of Libya, despite its cutting through part of the Greek zone. At a stroke it theoretically blocked a proposed pipeline running from Israeli and Cypriot waters to Crete, on to the Greek mainland, and then into Europe's gas network. The agreement was made with the government of Libya, which is why Turkey intervened militarily in Libya's civil war: if the Tripoli government fell, so did the agreement. Turkey doesn't recognize the UN's EEZ delineations and falls back on claims of sovereignty based on its continental shelf, which extends out into the Mediterranean. Russia, meanwhile, would prefer both projects to fail and for everyone to remain reliant on its supplies.

Turkey's moves in the Mediterranean are designed both to try to secure resources for itself and as a way to destabilize Greece. Wars have begun over less than this high-stake game, and the next decade looks set to provide numerous flashpoints that could get out of hand even if neither side wants a full-blown conflict.

Militarily the two NATO powers are fairly evenly matched, although Turkey upgraded its navy during the years of the Greek bailout in the knowledge that Athens did not have the funds to respond. The Greek navy has a clear advantage in submarines, but the Turks have been investing in antisubmarine warfare. Turkey also has greater available manpower, which is partially why Greece still has conscription.

What Greece also has, and Turkey does not, is friends in the neighborhood. In 2019 it helped set up the Cairo-based East Mediterranean Gas Forum along with Egypt, the Palestinian Territories, Israel, Cyprus, Jordan, and Italy. The forum focuses on energy but, interestingly, has a security component, which has resulted in naval cooperation and joint training exercises. This does not mean that if Greece and Turkey should come into conflict, the other members of the forum would join in, but it is clear whom they would assist in other ways. The Egyptians and Turks are already at loggerheads over other regional issues, such as Libya.

The potential for escalation has been shown several times, sometimes from surprising quarters. In February 2020, when Turkish frigates were sailing close to the Cypriot gas fields, France dispatched its aircraft carrier, the *Charles de Gaulle*, to shadow the naval forces of its NATO ally. French-Turkish relations have been, at best, cool since President Giscard d'Estaing condemned the 1974 Turkish invasion of Cyprus, and became frosty after France held its first National Day of Commemoration of the Armenian Genocide thus signaling that it accepted that the Ottoman Empire set out to intentionally destroy the Turkish Armenian minority population during the First World War; Turkey does not accept the charge of genocide.

In June 2020, the French alleged that during a confrontation with the Turkish navy off Libya the Turks locked their weapons systems onto a French frigate. The Turks were attempting to slip through another illegal arms shipment to their ally in Tripoli, with which it had signed the EEZ agreement the year before. Mistakes can happen in such highly charged moments; even if shooting had broken out, it doesn't mean that war would have followed, but it does show just how tense the situation is between several NATO countries and outside actors. NATO has a clause in its charter that states "An attack on one is an attack on all"; it was never envisaged that an attack on one might be by a fellow NATO ally.

President Macron used the incident as another example of his belief that NATO is "brain-dead." That is more an attempt to switch off the life-support machine and build a better European fighting force than a statement of reality. Macron is leading the charge for an EU army, but given German hesitancy, the British withdrawal from the EU, and with an Atlanticist in the White House in the shape of Joe Biden, he's finding it tough going. However, it is the case that Turkey is now at best a semidetached NATO member. Successive governments in Athens have spent the last decade watching with interest as its principal rival has become increasingly alienated from NATO, to the point where its very membership is in question. Greece knows the Americans are looking for a more reliable partner, and it hopes to replace Turkey as the key NATO member in the Aegean.

Public-opinion polls in Greece have for decades suggested that there is a coolness toward the US, but recently this has begun to shift and at government levels there is a growing consensus that Greece needs to attach itself at the hip to America diplomatically and militarily. It already hosts a US naval base, strategically located in Souda Bay in Crete, and in 2020 updated a defense agreement allowing American forces access to Greek military bases for training, refueling, and, crucially, emergency response. Included in the deal was "unimpeded access and use" of the northern port of Alexandroúpolis, which is close to the entrance of the Sea of Marmara, which leads to the Black Sea.

This port's location plays into the centuries-old strategy of the British, and for the past seventy years the Americans: keep the Russians away from Greece. The Russian military base of Sevastopol in Crimea sits on the Black Sea coast, which links to the Bosporus, leading into the Marmara, on to the Aegean, and out into the Mediterranean. Neither the Brits nor the Americans want the Russians to have a power base from which to project influence into the Balkans from the south, something it has been attempting for centuries. This is also why Cyprus has been such a strategically important island and part of the reason the UK hangs on to its military base there. Moscow consistently lobbies for Cyprus to be free of foreign forces, knowing that this would weaken NATO's ability to link its power bases in the eastern Mediterranean down to the Middle East's western and northern coastlines.

Greece is positioning itself to become the indispensable US ally in the region. The Americans are hedging: they are ensuring reliable access for their military while also being able to use this fact to pressure Turkey to reestablish itself as a reliable NATO partner and guarantee that the Americans can continue to lease its air base in Incirlik, near the Syrian border.

Despite the pain caused by the financial crash, because of its geography and history Greece will continue to spend more on defense than countries with similar-sized economies. This plays well in Washington, where many voices can be heard demanding that NATO powers pay more to alleviate the military and financial burden the alliance places on American blood and treasure. In the event that the Turkish-Western relationship becomes so bad that Ankara leaves NATO, then Greece becomes the most southeastern flank of the alliance. The Russians are trying to play both sides, sometimes allying with Turkey, but also courting Greek leaders. President Putin knows it's a long shot—but a nice Russian naval base in the Mediterranean to complement the small one Russia now has in Syria would be most welcome to Moscow's strategic ambitions.

Greece no longer has to be English, Russian, or indeed American—it is Greek. However, it is again an important piece of real estate for foreign powers. In a crisis it can be a secondary defensive position if a hostile Russian navy tries to break out of the Black Sea; it is on the front line of Europe's migrant crisis and looks destined to become a crucial transit route for the gas pipelines coming out of the eastern Mediterranean.

All three issues are likely to occupy strategic thinking for the foreseeable future. There are no signs that Russia seeks rapprochement with the NATO powers, Greece will be corralling large numbers of migrants and refugees for years to come, and the long hostile relationship with Turkey is unlikely to improve, meaning the potential for military action will remain present.

On the domestic front, the ancient geographical divisions are still there, different regions are still suspicious of Athens, and parts of the interior remain isolated from the day-to-day business of the modern state. All Greeks are still within 60 miles of the sea, and as a people they remain close to the water in spirit, in enterprise, and in commerce. At a strategic level what concerns them is much the same as when they looked up to Zeus, Apollo, and Aphrodite on the heights of Mount Olympus. The gods have gone, empires come and go, alliances shift, but the constants for Greeks remain what made them—the mountains and the seas.

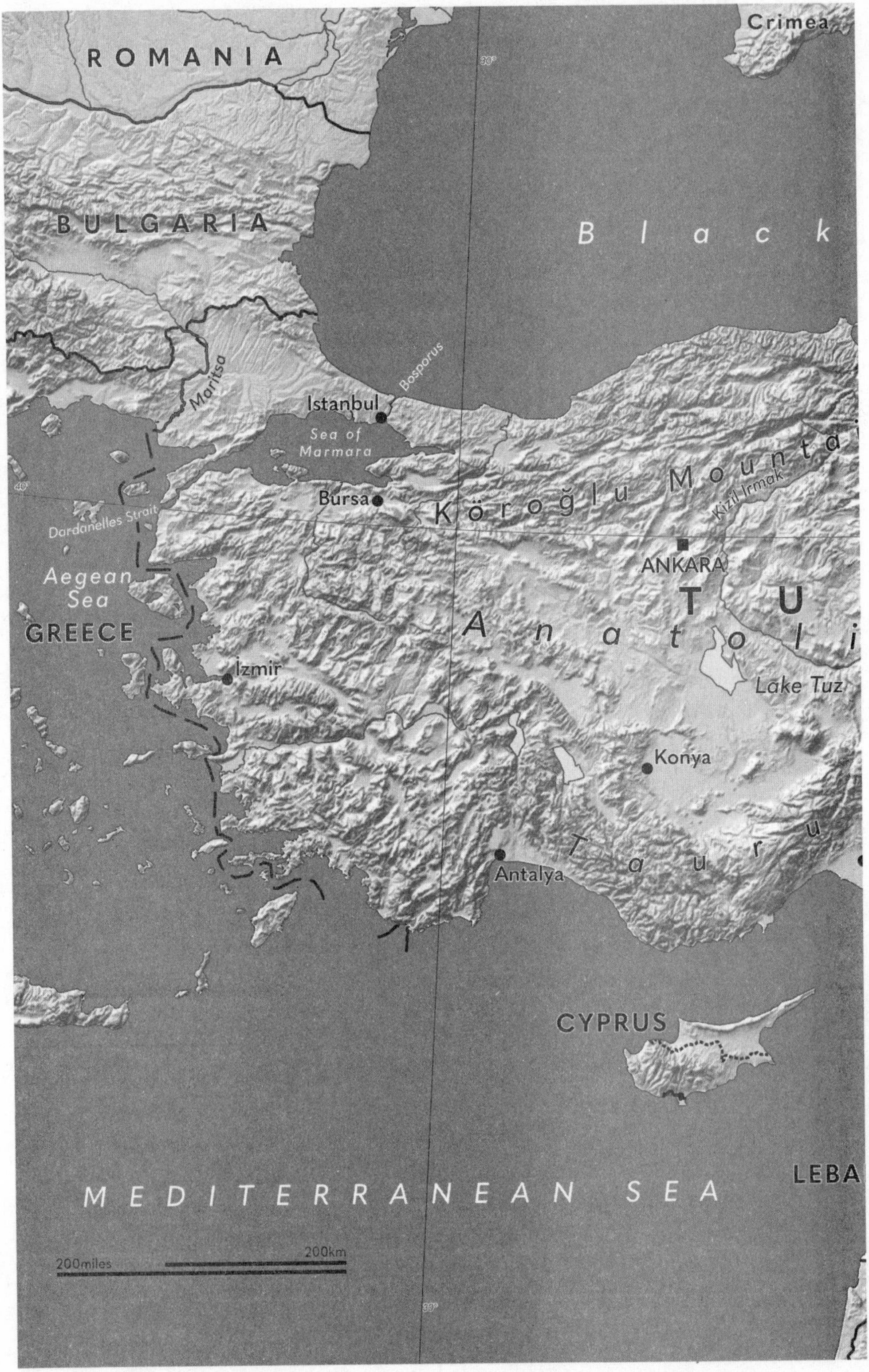

Crimea
ROMANIA
BULGARIA
Black
Bosporus
Maritsa
Istanbul
Sea of Marmara
Bursa
Köroğlu Mountai
Kizil Irmak
Dardanelles Strait
ANKARA
Aegean Sea
GREECE
TU
Anatoli
İzmir
Lake Tuz
Konya
Taurus
Antalya
CYPRUS
LEBA
MEDITERRANEAN SEA
200miles
200km

6

TURKEY

We resemble ourselves.

—Mustafa Kemal (Atatürk)

The Turks—you'd think they originated in Turkey, wouldn't you? After all, Türkiye means "Land of the Turks." But no, the original Turks came from far away, east of the Altai Mountains in Mongolia. Getting to what is now the homeland, and then ensuring it was called Turkey, was quite a journey.

First they had to cross the large plateau of Anatolia to what, despite being on the westernmost point of Turkey, is actually its core—the Sea of Marmara and the low-lying regions on that body of water's eastern and western shores. The area may not have vast plains, or long, flat rivers along which to transport goods, but it is fertile land with sufficient freshwater to supply a major population, and the sea is more a lake across which you can trade. It helps that the major urban area, Istanbul, is defensible if attacked from the water. At the western end of the Sea of Marmara is the Dardanelles, the strait giving access to the Aegean Sea, and at the eastern end is the Bosporus, which at its narrowest is less than half a mile wide. Control of these two choke points is a huge defensive advantage.

This amounts to what could sustain a small nation-state—let's call it Marmaria. The problem is, Marmaria probably wouldn't last very long. Prime real estate such as this always draws covetous glances from outside powers, especially if trade heading east, west, north, and south has to pass through it, quite possibly attracting taxes. That's certainly how the Greeks saw things when they controlled the area, as did the Romans, then the Byzantines, and indeed the Turks in the shape of the Ottomans.

The Ottomans used this real estate to project power outward, controlling areas across the Middle East, Africa, and much of southeastern Europe before contracting and bequeathing a shrunken state to their successors. But modern Turkey is again at the crossroads of east and west, as it determines its role on the world stage. It holds the keys to one of the gates through which migrants flow to Europe, and being a gatekeeper gives it power. Turkey has increasingly become involved in conflicts throughout the Arab world, including in Syria and Libya, where it bumps up against the interests of other regional powers. There are clear signs of neo-Ottomanism in its ambitions to expand its control and influence as power is once more being projected in all directions with significant repercussions in Europe, the Middle East, and Central Asia.

From west to east, Turkey is about 1,000 miles across, and from north to south between 300 and 500 miles. Around 97 percent of this land is in Asia, and most of it consists of Anatolia. Its modern land borders are with eight countries: Greece, Bulgaria, Georgia, Armenia, Azerbaijan, Iran, Iraq, and Syria. This was the neighborhood the early Ottomans saw as they set out to build an empire.

From about the ninth century, nomadic Turkish tribes had roamed out of the eastern steppes (Mongolia), over the Altai Mountains, and across the western steppes (Kazakhstan), taken a hard left through Central Asia, and arrived at the Caspian Sea in time to meet the Byzantine Empire. By then they had encountered Islam in the region around Persia and converted from pagan beliefs. They appeared on the eastern fringes of the empire in the eleventh century and began raiding Anatolia. In 1037 the Turkish Seljuk Empire was formed in what is now Armenia, bordering Byzantine territory. Its sultan then took a shine to Georgia, which was a steppe too far for the Byzantine emperor Romanus IV Diogenes. Something had to be done.

In 1071 the Byzantine army met the Seljuks at Manzikert, near Lake Van, about 75 miles from what is now the Turkish-Iranian border. It was badly beaten, leaving the gate open for various Turkish tribes to pour into Anatolia and establish a patchwork quilt of emirates. Within a decade they were nearing Constantinople and named their new territory the Sultanate of Rum, which, given that this was their name for Rome, may be an early form of trolling.

At the time the inhabitants of Anatolia mostly spoke Indo-European languages and, following the conquest of Alexander the Great, had adopted Greek customs, including, during the Byzantine period, Christianity. They were a mixture of ethnicities, including Armenian, Kurdish, and Greek. Over several centuries many assimilated into Turkish culture, some converting to Sunni Islam and speaking the Turkish language even as the Turks assimilated genetically with the Anatolians. Most modern Turks are more closely related to Armenians and Greeks than they are to Turkic peoples such as the Kazakhs, but studies show that 9 to 15 percent of their genetic mix is of Central Asian origin.

One of the many emirates established in northwestern Anatolia in the late 1200s was that of a man called Osman Ghazi (Osman the Warrior). He expanded his writ by overrunning Byzantine territory along the Black Sea coast and pushing into central Anatolia. In honor of this founder, people began to call themselves Osmanli, meaning "followers of Osman," which in Western Europe became Ottomans. They were by no means the biggest of the Turkish powers, but they used their gains as the jumping-off point from which to take more territory from the Byzantines and the other Turkish emirates.

By 1326 the emirate had taken control of Bursa, about 100 miles south of Constantinople, which was now also in its sights. The Ottomans had hacked away bits of the surrounding area and by 1453 the icon of the remnant of the Byzantine Empire was isolated. The city's immense walls had stood for a thousand years, but for fifty-three days the Ottoman army battered the defenses, eventually opening gaps through which its soldiers poured.

Now they had to get rich, or die trying. They needed to ensure that no powerful regional force capable of raiding the rich lands around the Sea of Marmara could arise on the high Anatolian plateau, while also being confident that they could block any major force arriving from the Middle East.

The weakest spot in this prime territory is where the flat land funnels down to the isthmus housing Istanbul. If you can mass enough land forces and march on the city, the entire core is in trouble. So the key to defense is first to have a decent navy capable of blocking the marine choke points, and then to keep hostile land forces as far away as possible from the core. To do that, you expand the core.

"Marmaria" had to be consolidated and then expanded, so the Turks first had to secure the route they themselves had taken to get to the prize. They'd conquered large areas of Anatolia, but, other than strategic depth, it didn't offer them much. It is mostly dry, rugged, and mountainous, with limited scope for agriculture. A lot of the southern Anatolian coastline is smooth and has a few good ports for trading but, with narrow coastal plains, little room for crops. Populating and developing the interior was therefore of little interest to the Ottomans. That still left the often restless power bases in the interior to deal with, but they just needed to keep these subdued. Throughout most of its history, the Ottoman Empire struggled to contain rebellions in Anatolia, a problem modern Turkey has inherited in the shape of the Kurdish uprisings.

However, using Anatolia for defense was a priority. With the region under control, the back door to a major invasion was mostly closed, and anyway there were now few challengers keen to venture across the high plateau to get to them. To their immediate northwest, the Ottomans had reached the Balkans, giving them a barrier against threats from that direction. Now they could consolidate Constantinople as the empire's capital—the city walls were rebuilt, and the urban areas repopulated with thousands of Muslims, Christians, and Jews—and then look to the horizon.

The Ottomans already had territory in Europe; as early as the 1300s they'd been raiding the Balkans. Then in the 1480s they captured ports on the Black Sea in what is now Ukraine, and with increased naval skills could keep the slowly increasing power of the Russians at bay. They could now concentrate on the west, where the Ottomans faced the same geographical opportunities and problems as do modern states in the region. If you head due west from Istanbul you enter the Maritsa River valley. Then, skirting around to the east of the Balkan Mountains, you arrive at the Danube, the second-longest river in Europe. Specifically, you reach a section of the river lying between the Bessarabian Gap and the Iron Gate.

The Bessarabian Gap is the lowland between where the Carpathian Mountains finish and the Black Sea begins. The Carpathians run in a 950-mile-long arc all the way north to the lower reaches of Poland, and the two longtime routes around them are the north European plain as it runs along the Baltic Sea and the Bessarabian Gap by the Black Sea. Thus, if you hold the gap, you control the southern east-west route.

The Iron Gate is where the Carpathians have swung round through Romania and meet the Balkans in Bulgaria. The Danube flows in a narrow valley through this bottleneck, where, prior to a dam built in the 1960s, there was a feared stretch of rapids tumbling down through four thin gorges spread along several miles. The waters are calmer now, but the Iron Gate remains a choke point that, if you control it, can be either a fixed point of defense or the next stage in an advance. The Ottomans chose the latter.

Vienna sits north of the Iron Gate in the Pannonian plain between the Carpathians and the Alps. The Danube passes through this plain on its way toward the Iron Gate, and then on to the Black Sea. The Ottomans were confident that their empire south of the Iron Gate was secure, but if they wanted to be sure of taking and holding the huge, fertile Pannonian plain, they'd also have to take Vienna.

They tried three times, and by the third attempt were not just north of the Iron Gate—they were north, south, east, and west of "Marmaria." In the 1500s the Ottomans were in control of most of the Balkans, had made forays as far northwest as Vienna, and controlled present-day Hungary. In the north they commanded the Black Sea, and in the south and east were in what is now Syria, Iraq, Saudi Arabia, Egypt, and Algeria. It was a multiethnic, multicultural empire prone to absolute savagery, yet it did not always insist its subjects convert to Sunni Islam, although Christians and Jews were considered inferior. The Christians and Jews were granted *dhimmi* status, usually translated as "protected," but this meant they had to pay the special *jizya* tax, which perhaps should be translated as "protection racket." Arab Muslims in the Ottoman colonies had an easier time, but all the conquered peoples were left in no doubt of who was boss. This is why there is such resentment in Arab countries now that Turkey is again pushing its way into their world. In Saudi Arabia, for example, one of the main thoroughfares in Riyadh, Sultan Suleiman the Magnificent Street, was renamed in 2020 following Turkey's involvement in Syria and Libya.

For the Ottoman rulers it was a glorious period that has been compared with the Roman Empire. But they had reached their high-water mark, and defeat by the Habsburg Empire at the gates of Vienna in 1683 marked the beginning of a long but steady decline, leading to the collapse of their empire in 1923.

Without being able to plug the gap at Vienna, the Ottomans were eventually forced to retreat to the Iron Gate and then fall back south of that. These were the most profitable parts of their empire and were closer to its capital than the far-flung outposts in North Africa. Imperial overstretch was catching up with them. The rise of increasingly industrialized Western European nation-states left the Ottomans unable to compete technologically or militarily, and those powers, notably Britain and France, began to push them out of the Middle East.

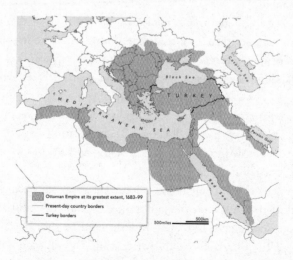

At the height of its power, the Ottoman Empire extended through large parts of Europe, Asia, and North Africa.

The Balkan Wars of 1912–1913 showed just how ill the "sick man of Europe" was, especially when the Bulgarians almost captured Constantinople. And when the Ottoman Empire then chose the wrong side in the First World War, it signed its own death warrant. The defeat of the British at the Battle of Gallipoli is part of the Turkish founding story, but it was not enough to prevent losing a war and an empire. Under the terms of the 1918 armistice, the capital was occupied by British, Italian, and French troops, the empire was broken up, and the sultanate was abolished. Some Turkish-speaking people were left outside the new borders, notably in Greece and on the island of Cyprus, and more than a million Greeks found themselves inside Turkey.

The Greco-Turkish War (1919–1922) resulted in a decisive win for the Turkish forces led by General Mustafa Kemal. A population swap followed, but there were still Greek and Turkish minorities living in the two countries, a fact that has resulted in tensions over the past century. The Turks signed the 1923 Treaty of Lausanne, which left Greece in control of most of the islands off the Turkish coast, and codified the loss of Kurdish and Arab territory in Syria, but it has never been accepted as fair and still rankles.

Kemal was the first president of the newly proclaimed Republic of Turkey, established in 1923. Ankara was chosen as the capital and Constantinople's name was officially changed to Istanbul (it's thought that the name comes from Greek speakers referring to visits as *eis ten polin*—"into the city"—which transmuted into Istanbul).

Kemal, who was granted the surname Atatürk ("Father of the Turks") by the Turkish parliament, ruled for fifteen years during which he transformed his country, introducing a series of radical reforms to modernize Turkey after concluding that modernization meant Westernization. Some decrees appear superficial but were serious statements of intent, signaling a break with the past that would include separating the state from religion. For men, the wearing of fezzes was outlawed, while women were discouraged from wearing veils; the Western (Gregorian) calendar was introduced; and reading and writing were switched from Arabic to the Latin alphabet.

Atatürk understood that language is culture. He was in the business of forming a new culture based not on the multiethnic and multilinguistic Ottoman Empire, but on Turkishness. Ottoman Turkish, used by the educated classes, was a mixture of Turkish, Arabic, and Persian, while Turkish was for the poorer, mostly illiterate, classes, which caused a language gap emphasizing social division. The president led the way in bridging the divide, touring the country and showing up in village squares and schools armed with a portable blackboard on which he chalked the new alphabet. It was a smart move, helping to create a cult of personality and also freeing ordinary people from relying on religious scholars to tell them what was what.

Part of this "Turkification" of Turkey was the denial of the annihilation of the Christian Armenian communities between 1915 and 1923. Many Turks resented the fact that Armenians had hung on to their language and culture, and viewed them as the enemy within. Occurring mostly in eastern Anatolia, pogroms involved the massacre of hundreds of thousands of men of fighting age, and then the forced-march deportation of similar numbers of women, children, and the elderly toward the Syrian Desert, where they were left without food or water. The greatest atrocity of the First World War was wiped from history as told by the new state, helping to build the founding myths of the new country. Most historians argue that the events were carefully planned and amount to genocide. Even today, Ankara acknowledges that atrocities were committed but still vehemently denies genocide, claiming there was never a plan to wipe out the Armenian population. The suppression of facts and the Westernization of culture all served a purpose as Turkey began to evolve into a modern state and emerged into the modern world.

There was, however, a problem. The world had changed. The Turks' empire had shrunk—now it comprised only "Marmaria" and Anatolia—and although Turkey was still the land bridge between Europe and the Middle East, it was a bridge that had become less useful during the dying days of the empire. The Suez Canal had opened a new sea route for trade, and the rise of the US as a mass consumer society made America a more attractive market for many European merchants.

In the 1920s Turkey was still a relatively agrarian society, although under Atatürk it began to industrialize, and between 1929 and 1938 industrial production increased by 80 percent. But the US stock market crash of 1929 triggered an economic crisis for Turkey after the prices it could charge for its agricultural products plummeted. With its status as a major transit zone diminished, falling income, and a need to fund campaigns to suppress rebellions by the Kurds in the east, Turkey struggled to establish itself as a major power.

As the Second World War approached, its military was in poor shape, armed mostly with weapons left over from the First World War. Once the conflict broke out, both sides attempted to draw Turkey in. There were temptations, especially once the Nazis had overrun Greece. An alliance with Germany might have resulted in regaining lost territory, but Ankara held its neutral stance up until February 1945, when, with the Soviets approaching Berlin and a German defeat inevitable, Turkey declared war on Germany and Japan. It was a smart if cynical move, one that earned the Turks a place at the subsequent conferences convened to shape the postwar world order. They may not have been a major player, but at least they were at the top table.

In 1946 the Turks looked around their neighborhood and saw very little they liked. Turkey still wasn't back as a major trade route and its neighbors were not exactly wealthy. Meanwhile the Russians, whom they'd been fighting for centuries, now had troops in the Balkans as part of the Soviet expansion, they were giving aid to Kurdish rebels as both worked to weaken Turkey, and they were gaining influence in Syria and Iraq. "Splendid isolation" wasn't really an option—within six years, Turkey was a member of NATO.

It was a marriage of convenience. The Cold War was heating up and, for NATO, getting Turkey on board guaranteed it wouldn't hedge its bets and lean toward Moscow for the foreseeable future, while simultaneously guarding the alliance's southern flank. Greece joined NATO at the same time, in 1952, for the same reasons, and together they substantially increased NATO's options and firepower, although the two remained at odds with each other. Turkey's navy was given the job of "bottling up" the Soviets in the Black Sea, while the army tied down its ground forces on the edge of the Soviet bloc—the Bulgarian border. Such was its strategic importance that the alliance managed to over-look military coups in Turkey in 1960, 1971, and 1980. Amid some embarrassed throat clearing and muttering about "internal matters," Turkey's geographical position trumped its dictatorship status in the minds of the Western powers. It would take until the 1990s before civilian rule began to be considered the norm in Turkey.

The end of the Cold War brought in a new age, but one with some old problems. In the 1990s Turkey reestablished itself as a major trade route after building gas and oil pipes, running from Iraq and the Caspian Sea through Anatolia, to supply Europe. It had also put together one of the largest and most efficient militaries in NATO, giving it confidence as it assessed the new world around it. The Cold War had either put a lid on or frozen many issues around the globe including several in Turkey's neighborhood. As the bipolar world order of the USSR and the US shattered into a multipolar one, the lid came off and the ice melted. Small- and medium-sized countries quickly sought to establish new realities in the new age.

By the time the Balkan wars began again in 1991, Turkey had already watched in alarm as Operation Desert Storm in Iraq resulted in hundreds of thousands of Iraqi Kurds fleeing to its border regions to escape Saddam Hussein's army. It wasn't that Turkey opposed the intervention against Saddam; it was more that it helped create a semiautonomous Kurdish region in northern Iraq (which, as we will see, was problematic since Turkey was trying to suppress its own Kurdish nationalism). Then another part of the old Ottoman Empire descended into conflict as Yugoslavia broke apart and Bosnia, Croatia, Serbia, Kosovo, and Macedonia all suffered the consequences of ethnic tensions fueled by cynical nationalist leaders. Ankara wanted to export goods to these places, not import the ripples of insecurity and violence. The savagery of the breakup overshadowed another conflict in former Ottoman territories as Armenia and Azerbaijan went to war over the disputed territory of Nagorno-Karabakh. Ankara also became increasingly anxious over Russian and Iranian influence in the Caucasus and Central Asia, which sought to block its own.

At that point Turkey was still Western-oriented and hanging on to dreams of joining the European Union, but, as the century turned, it became unlikely that Ankara would ever be invited to join the club. Economically, Turkey did not meet enough criteria for entry, its record on human rights fell well short of requirements, and there was an unquantifiable, but identifiable, degree of prejudice that it was not "European" enough. The country slowly set out in a new direction under a new leader.

The direction was a turn to the past in order to shape the future, and the leader was a man who has become the embodiment of religious nationalism and neo-Ottomanism: Recep Tayyip Erdoğan. First as prime minister and then as president, Erdoğan has sought to turn Turkey into a stand-alone power playing all the sides. For the first decade of the twenty-first century, it seemed as if Ankara might continue on the path of being a good NATO ally and aspiring EU member. However, there were geographical, historical, and ideological roots at odds with this strategy, and subsequent events saw them emerge to influence a very different way of thinking.

There's an argument about the extent to which Erdoğan is an Islamist who believes that a radical interpretation of Islam should both guide and be involved in politics. He certainly was one when he emerged from a tough upbringing in a run-down district of Istanbul and won a place at university. By 1994 he was mayor of the city, representing the Islamist Welfare Party, but in 1999 he served four months in jail for reciting an Islamist poem in an officially secular country that included the lines "The mosques are our barracks, the domes our helmets, the minarets our bayonets, and the faithful our soldiers."

On his release, Erdoğan formed the Justice and Development Party, whose acronym in Turkish, AKP, is often shortened to *ak*, meaning "white" or "clean," a useful term to suggest a difference from other political groups. The AKP won power in 2002 and Erdoğan became prime minister the following year. His past does not prove he is an Islamist—he's canny enough to appeal to whichever demographic he requires for support—but there's little doubt he is an overt nationalist whose lack of respect for democracy was shown when he said: "Democracy is like a bus ride. Once I get to my stop, I'm getting off." The AKP's rise to power was a major shift in modern Turkish history. The country had been built on Atatürk's secularism; now it was led by a party rooted in Islam, whose ideologues were lukewarm about NATO and frustrated about their lack of influence in the former Ottoman Empire. Erdoğan was street-smart enough to know that the liberals in Istanbul did not reflect the country—indeed, they didn't even reflect a lot of Istanbul, especially as the preceding decades had witnessed an influx of conservative and religious rural people seeking work in the big cities.

A good guide to Erdoğan's foreign-policy thinking is the career and words of Professor Ahmet Davutoğlu, the former leader of the AKP, who served as foreign minister and prime minister. Davutoğlu's 2001 book, *Strategic Depth*, is seen as the architectural structure upon which the foreign-policy aspect of Erdoğan's "New Turkey" is built. His basic argument about how to expand Turkey's strategic depth is based on a "dynamic interpretation of geography" and boils down to "end the status quo and get on the front foot."

Erdoğan, like Davutoğlu, is a neo-Ottoman, believing that Turkey's destiny is to emerge as a global superpower as the West declines. The 1990s had been a period in which Turkish power had grown. With the Soviets out of the way, there was no one in the neighborhood capable of defeating the formidable and increasingly well-equipped Turkish military. For the first time in seventy years, the option of using military force was a choice, not an existential necessity.

However, in the post-9/11 world, Turkey had to tread carefully, with the US on the warpath. The foreign-policy narrative of the early 2000s was "zero problems with neighbors," and for the first decade of the twenty-first century Ankara maintained cordial relations with the Western powers, while simultaneously increasing its influence in the Balkans and the Middle East by using trade, soft power, and diplomacy. It made attempts to help reconcile Bosnia and Serbia, it brokered

Israeli-Syrian talks, it tried to bring the Palestinian factions of Fatah and Hamas together, and it even reached out to traditionally hostile Armenia. However, in almost all cases its efforts made headlines but not progress. And ultimately this approach was not going to end the status quo. Having zero problems requires not interfering in other countries' affairs; but if you see other powers shaping events in the territory of your neighbors, you are hardly likely to stand idle.

As the second decade of this century began, the softly-softly approach was wearing thin. It would be threadbare after the Arab uprisings broke out in 2011. "Zero problems with neighbors" became more like "zero friends."

By then Turkey's relations with Israel had soured after twenty years of cooperation. The Islamists and nationalists (Davutoğlu among them) had been arguing for years that being friends with Israel was alienating Turkey from its people and its past. The two countries had enjoyed a close relationship based on a shared concern about the Arab states and Iran, both of which were on occasion hostile to them—but that relationship was under previous administrations. The AKP's political support did not include many who also supported Israel, and so the 2008 Israel-Gaza conflict was the excuse to begin cooling relations. Within a few years, joint military exercises were canceled, Hamas leaders were being courted in Ankara, and Turkish television was showing anti-Israeli films while Erdoğan spouted antisemitic rhetoric.

Turkey viewed the Arab uprisings as an opportunity to extend its influence back into the region ruled by its predecessor, but it consistently backed the wrong horse. Ankara felt there was space to project power into the Middle East but less so in the Balkans, where countries were tempted more by the attractions of the EU than by what Turkey had to offer. Saudi Arabia, the UAE, and Egypt felt differently about how much "space" there was. As the Custodian of the Two Holy Mosques (Mecca and Medina), Saudi Arabia sees itself as the spiritual leader of Islam. Along with the UAE it also has the wealth to project power across the region, so the moment Ankara decided it wanted to become a player in the Middle East, it set itself on a collision course with the Saudis. Egypt, which has traditionally seen itself as the leading Arab power, was also not about to see the neo-Ottomans gain influence.

Erdoğan has always had close ties with the Muslim Brotherhood, a transnational Sunni Islamist movement that operates via a cell structure as it seeks to create a sharia-led global caliphate. As such, it is loathed by most of the Arab governments because they know they are in its sights for being either monarchies or too religiously moderate. The Brotherhood was founded in Egypt in the 1920s and when, after years of brutal oppression, it won the 2012 election following the overthrow of Hosni Mubarak in the Arab uprisings, Erdoğan was delighted. He hoped to build a strategic relationship with new Islamist governments in Egypt, Libya, and Tunisia, with Turkey as the senior partner. But the following year, after months of mass protests against it, the Brotherhood government fell to a military coup. This was roundly condemned by Erdoğan, putting him at odds with the new Egyptian president, General Abdel al-Sisi. Along with other regional leaders, Sisi viewed Turkey as a threat that supports Islamist terrorism, not only through the Brotherhood but also through its questionable links with other Islamist groups. Within weeks Turkey's ambassador to Cairo had been expelled and relations have not really recovered, although it's worth noting that both countries are usually pragmatic enough to maintain economic ties.

Both Erdoğan and Sisi are nationalists whose romantic views of their countries' history and regional roles are in opposition to each other. Their ideological and strategic differences have led to confrontation between them in Libya and competition in the eastern Mediterranean. For Sisi, Libya is his backyard and a place where he will not allow a Muslim Brotherhood–linked government to triumph. For Erdoğan, it's a place to support a Muslim Brotherhood–linked government and a chance to play in the former Ottoman territory.

They were also at odds during the Syrian civil war, which broke out in 2011. After various Islamist organizations hijacked much of the mostly Sunni uprising against Bashar al-Assad, Syria's (non-Sunni) president, Ankara was quick to offer them support. This was a chance to pose as the savior of the Sunni Muslims and install a pro-Turkish government in Damascus. Cairo, on the other hand, began to normalize relations with Assad almost as soon as Sisi took power, because although the two countries do not share the same branch of Islam, they are both more concerned about opposing Islamists. Besides, for Sisi, rather Assad than a Turkish-dominated government in Damascus. When Turkish forces invaded northern Syria in 2016, and then again in 2018 and 2019, the moves played into the Egyptian narrative that the Arabs faced a threat from the neo-Ottomans.

From the Turkish perspective, its incursions into Syria were necessary mostly to prevent an autonomous Kurdish region forming that might try to join itself to Kurdish-majority provinces in Turkey. But Turkey also moved to block Russian influence following Moscow's military assistance to Assad in 2016, and it hoped to prevent further waves of refugees, having taken in more than 3.5 million desperate people. The Turks resent the fact that they have not been given enough credit for hosting so many refugees, especially in comparison with Europe. However, in recent years antirefugee sentiment has grown, and Erdoğan has embarked on a plan to get as many of them as possible out of the country. He was also openly bitter after NATO sent extra troops to Lithuania to deter potential Russian aggression there, but then refused to help Turkey in what it felt was its hour of need, as it went into Syria to prevent what it said was a terrorist threat from ISIS.

This is why an increasingly authoritarian Erdoğan has oriented Turkey away from the EU and NATO and sought to go it alone. The relationship with the EU had been under strain for some time. In the 2000s, Turkey's denial of the Armenian genocide was a source of concern for many EU leaders and other governments, including Germany, Canada, France, Italy, Poland, and Russia, as well as the Vatican and the US Congress. This is a charge that infuriates Turkey and often hovers in the background of diplomatic and trade negotiations. It is probably the issue most guaranteed to spark fury in a Turk. A few years ago, President Erdoğan said the Armenian diaspora were trying to instill hatred against Turkey, and that "if we examine what our nation had to go through over the past 100 to 150 years, we would find far more suffering than what the Armenians went through." That's not a position many outside Turkey would agree with.

Turkey's isolation from NATO has increased since the 2016 violent coup attempt against Erdoğan, when small groups of the military seized bridges and TV stations in Istanbul. About three hundred people were killed during confrontations before loyalists regained control. In the aftermath, Erdoğan jailed tens of thousands of people and purged the military, media, police, civil service, and education system of anyone suspected of having pro-coup sympathies. Despite a lack of evidence, Erdoğan hinted at what many of his supporters openly said— that the coup was a vast conspiracy backed by the Americans.

Within Turkish military circles, supporters of the concept of Mavi Vatan— the Blue Homeland—are usually skeptical of their country's membership of NATO and believe it to be an American plot (helped by Greece) to prevent Turkey from rising to its rightful place in the world. President Erdoğan may well agree. The Blue Homeland idea encompasses a worldview in which Turkey will dominate the three seas around it—the Black Sea, the Aegean, and the eastern Mediterranean. That is openly stated but behind it appears to be a long-term strategy to tear up the Treaty of Lausanne (1923), in which the Ottoman Empire lost territory and became Turkey. The idea has been popularized by former Turkish rear admiral Cem Gürdeniz.

The Turkish concept of the Blue Homeland would see it control large parts of its surrounding seas.

This worldview is the wider concept, but in popular parlance the Blue Homeland has come to mean Ankara's policy in the Aegean and eastern Mediterranean, specifically vis-à-vis Greece. We saw in chapter 5 how the discovery of underwater gas fields has exacerbated long-running tensions in the eastern Mediterranean, an area contested by Greece and Turkey following the Turkish invasion of Cyprus in 1974. Gürdeniz has seized upon the issue to push the Blue Homeland concept, which, if maps bearing its name are to be believed, include many of the Greek islands coming under Turkish control. His influence can be found in the title of the Turkish Naval War College's journal, *Mavi Vatan*; a large military exercise undertaken in 2019 was also given the name. The admiral's position is clear and widely shared; among numerous provocative statements, he has written, "In the absence of military strength, Greece instead relies upon the United States and Europe to act on its behalf. . . . They should know their place." Erdoğan is only slightly more measured. He too has criticized the Treaty of Lausanne as leaving Turkey too small, and has stated that "Turkey cannot disregard its kinsmen in Western Thrace [Greece], Cyprus, Crimea, and anywhere else." Ankara's position is that Greece has violated the treaty by sending troops to islands that are supposed to be neutral.

When it comes to Crimea, formerly an Ottoman territory, Ankara is not in a position to do very much. It has only a modest fleet in the Black Sea, whereas Russia has spent the years since it annexed Crimea in 2014 building up a major force. So Turkey's navy concentrates on the Aegean and eastern Mediterranean, which has become one of the world's most complicated chessboards, and where it is coming up against significant opposition from its neighbors. It is also being challenged in another region where it traditionally has influence: Azerbaijan. The 2020 conflict between Azerbaijan and Armenia was brought to an uneasy close by Russian diplomatic intervention, followed by the entry of Russian peacekeepers on patrol; meanwhile, Turkish troops were allowed access only to the peacekeeping observation center. The fighting had centered on the ethnically Armenian region of Nagorno-Karabakh, which did not want to be part of Azerbaijan. Turkey sided with the Azeris, who are ethnically Turkic, and Azerbaijan came out on top (partly due to Turkish-supplied weapons, especially drones), but it was Russia that muscled in to bring the conflict to a halt. Much has been made of a bromance between Putin and Erdoğan, but it doesn't really exist beyond a cold-eyed understanding of geopolitics and a mutual respect for the other's ruthlessness. The two sides know each other well, and while they can avoid bumping into each other they will, but both know there will be times when it will be blink first or bump later.

By 2020 Turkey had fallen out with Syria, Egypt, Saudi Arabia, the UAE, Kuwait, Israel, Iran, Armenia, Greece, Cyprus, and France and had irritated all its NATO allies by buying the S-400 missile defense system from NATO's great rival—Russia. The Americans were so angry about what they regarded as a breach of trust that in December 2020 they imposed sanctions on the Turkish defense industry and pointed out that the S-400 had been designed to shoot down the US F-35 stealth fighter. Erdoğan's top adviser responded with a warning that American troops based in Turkey could face the same treatment the Greeks received in 1922 and that Turks would "teach all the Americans how to swim in Aegean waters." In early 2021 Ankara opened negotiations with Moscow to buy a second S-400 system. A few weeks later President Biden made his displeasure clear by recognizing the "Armenian Genocide" to the absolute fury of the Turks.

Ankara's relations with its immediate neighbors are also affected by the two major challenges it has faced on the domestic front: the development of Anatolia, and its "forever war" against the Kurds.

More than 50 percent of Turkey's 85 million people live in the greater Istanbul area or along the narrow coastal plains of the Black Sea and Mediterranean.

The rest are spread out across the high, rugged interior, where many of the mountain ranges surpass 10,000 feet. The highest point is Mount Ararat (16,945 feet), the site where Noah's Ark is said to have come to rest. The challenge has been to integrate this mostly rural, poorer region with the core area around the Sea of Marmara. Given the difficulty of the terrain it remains a work in progress; however, what Anatolia has going for it, especially in the east, is water—lots of it.

Around 90 percent of the waters of the Euphrates River and 45 percent of the Tigris originate in the Anatolian highlands. The Euphrates flows into Syria and Iraq, and runs almost parallel with the Tigris before they merge in southern Iraq. The fertile land between them gave birth to the name Mesopotamia, or "between two rivers." Both, but particularly the Euphrates, are of critical importance for water, food, and energy for more than 60 million people, and Turkey's hand is on the tap.

Turkey began building dams along the two rivers in the late 1960s, reducing the water flow into both downstream countries and invariably raising tensions, which have continued ever since. Hundreds have now been built, including the Atatürk Dam, one of the world's largest. In 1975 Iraq, Syria, and Turkey came to the brink of war after the building of two dams coincided with a drought. In 1989 Syrian fighter jets shot down a Turkish survey plane, and the following year Iraq threatened to launch a bombing raid after Turkey temporarily cut the flow of the Euphrates. A few years later, responding to criticism, then president Turgut Özal said: "We don't tell the Arabs what to do with their oil, so we don't accept any suggestions from them about what to do with our water." In reality all sides have negotiated treaties allowing Ankara to develop its hydroelectric power projects, and Syria and Iraq to access the water flow, but the danger of a water war remains ever present.

The water agreements are where Turkey's two main domestic challenges coincide. Building dams is part of the Southeastern Anatolia Project, aimed at creating jobs, generating electricity, and improving irrigation to bolster the regional economy. But the headwaters of the rivers are in the parts of Anatolia with major Kurdish populations that have periodically risen up against the Turkish state, which until recently insisted on denying their ethnicity and officially categorized them as "Mountain Turks." So, in negotiating guarantees of the water flow, Ankara has frequently insisted on clauses in which Syria agrees to clamp down on armed Kurdish groups inside its borders.

Some of the dams have also been useful in curbing the ability of armed Kurdish groups to move around inside eastern Anatolia. Valleys, used as transit routes, have been flooded, and the north and south of the Kurdish-dominated regions have been cut in two by the construction work. For its part the main Kurdish guerrilla group, the Leninist Kurdistan Workers' Party (PKK), has conducted numerous attacks on dams, including placing explosives on roads leading to them, setting fire to trucks, and kidnapping construction workers. On some projects, workers have had to be escorted by the Turkish army.

The Turkish Kurds are about 15 million strong—approximately 18 percent of the country's population. Most live in the mountainous areas of eastern Anatolia facing Iran, Iraq, and Syria, where another 15 million or so Kurds live, most in the border regions. However, the Turkish Kurds were among the waves of people who began to move to the cities in the 1960s, and the 2 million Kurds living in Istanbul are now the city's biggest minority group.

It's often said that the Kurds are the largest nation without a state. If we consider the 75 or so million Tamils of India and Sri Lanka, that premise is challenged; but it is fair to say that there has been a movement for an independent Kurdish state for close to two hundred years. During that time the Anatolian Kurds have clashed with the Ottoman rulers, and have been in almost constant revolt against the Republic of Turkey.

The Kurds speak an Indo-European language related to Farsi, but the Kurdish regions in Turkey, Iran, Iraq, and Syria have notably different dialects, to the extent that some Kurds have trouble understanding one another. This is one of many factors that has meant they have always been divided, even though the idea of a Kurdish homeland encompassing them all is a constant. But the prospect of a Kurdistan is why in each country they have always been repressed. All four states in which they live fear not only losing some of their own territory but also that the territory could link with the other three Kurdish regions to form a country that could challenge them in various ways.

The Turkish state sought to forcibly assimilate its Kurds by suppressing language and culture in a campaign to create an "indivisible nation." In the 1920s thousands of people were killed as the republic crushed a rebellion that had connections with Kurdish nationalism. Tensions simmered for decades, with occasional outbreaks of violence, before a full-scale uprising broke out in the 1980s. It was led by the PKK, which at first won many supporters; but the party's own repression of Kurdish opponents and its numerous acts of terrorism have alienated large segments of the Kurdish population. Hundreds of civilians have been killed in PKK bombings and the organization has carried out a series of assassinations against politicians and police officers.

During his first years in power, Erdoğan attempted to resolve the Kurdish question by implementing cultural reforms and investing more in Kurdish areas. He even secured a cease-fire with the PKK, and millions of Kurds, believing that Turkish democracy could achieve their demands for equality, began to vote for Erdoğan's AKP party. However, the collapse of the cease-fire triggered a new wave of violence and, as Syria's Kurds carved out a semiautonomous region along the Turkish border, the PKK was emboldened.

The Turkish army went back on the offensive, imposing curfews in rural areas for months at a time, sweeping through regions and intimidating civilians to prevent them giving shelter to PKK guerrillas. Tank fire, artillery, and drone strikes, along with special-forces operations, have squeezed the PKK's ability to move around, and it has suffered several thousand fatalities, while the Turkish military losses are over a thousand.

The renewed violence cost Erdoğan Kurdish support at the ballot box, and to shore up his vote share he began to court ultranationalist Turks and took a sharply hostile stance toward Kurdish political parties. Cross-border raids into the Qandil Mountains in Iraqi Kurdistan, where the PKK has bases, increased, some going as far as 12 miles into Iraq. In a sign of how divided the Kurds are, the Kurdistan Regional Government in Iraq (which has energy contracts with Ankara) cooperates with the Turkish military.

In a further blow to the PKK Turkey then invaded northern Syria, ostensibly to establish a buffer zone between it and ISIS terrorists, but also to ensure that the nascent semiautonomous region the Syrian Kurds were fighting for could not survive. The spearhead of the invasion pushed in 18 miles, straight across the middle of the region the Kurds refer to as Rojava, splitting it in two and ensuring there was no way the Syrian Kurds could attempt to link Rojava to the Mediterranean, which would have given it a potential port and so access to another trade route. They also cut the route the PKK and its Syrian Kurdish ally, the YPG, used to infiltrate into Turkey's Nur Mountains, where Turkey and Syria meet on the Mediterranean. The Turks took almost three hundred villages, six towns, and a range of strategic vantage points, all in territory the Ottomans had vacated a century earlier. The Turkish *lira* is now the currency used in this territory, the electricity grid is connected to Turkey, Ankara appoints local officials, and Turkish is taught in the schools alongside Arabic. Legally it remains part of Syria, but if President Assad wants to actually control it he'll have to come and get it—and bring the Syrian army with him.

So this is the republic's new vantage point: still bestriding the bridge between Europe and Asia, once again pushing forward and creating outposts as it expands. There's been a break with the past century, a reconnection further back to the days of the Ottomans, and simultaneously a call to arms for the republic to own the future.

In the multipolar world, Turkey is a major player among the numerous actors that have undermined the post–Second World War order. The most symbolic moment underlying Turkey's role in this shift came on July 12, 2020. Erdoğan decreed that the Hagia Sophia Museum would be converted back to a mosque, reversing Atatürk's law of 1934. Built as a church by the Byzantines in 537, Hagia Sophia became a mosque in 1453, but Atatürk saw the soft-power benefits for the republic in making it a museum open to everyone and celebrating its shared religious history. It was a message to the West: "The doors are open to all."

Erdoğan sees a different benefit and his social-media accounts told the story. His Turkish and English Twitter accounts were a paean to inclusivity: the mosque would be "wide open to all, whether they be foreign or local, Muslim or non-Muslim. . . . Hagia Sophia, the shared heritage of humanity, will continue to embrace all in a much more sincere and original way." The Arabic-language version of the website of the Office of the Presidency had a different tone. It said that the move "heralds the liberation of the Al Aqsa Mosque," which sits above the Western Wall in Jerusalem. The president's decision was apparently a new beginning for Muslims worldwide, and "the best response to the loathsome attacks on our values and symbols in every Islamic region. . . . With the help of Allah the Almighty, we will continue traveling on this blessed path, without stopping, without weariness or fatigue, with determination, sacrifice and persistence, until we reach our hoped-for destination." In a speech to mark the occasion, Erdoğan harked back to four key battles in Ottoman/Turkish history: "The resurrection of the Hagia Sophia represents our memory full of heydays in our history from Badr to Manzikert, from Nicopolis to Gallipoli."

Is the die cast? Has Turkey "gone" as a NATO ally and a valued, trusted, modern democracy? Almost.

It has taken twenty years to dismantle most of the foundations of what was a secular democracy and replace them with an authoritarian system with an Islamist tinge. The consolidation of power has involved jailing more journalists than any other country and rooting out dissenting voices from academia and civil society. The senior ranks of the military and judiciary have been packed with supporters of the new establishment.

There's no question that Erdoğan and his AKP party have been hugely popular, but they have lost the support of moderate Kurds. In the urban areas there is disquiet at the erosion of freedoms and Islamification of the republic, and so new challengers are emerging. Until the turn of the century, the educated and merchant liberal classes of the Marmara region dominated political and cultural life. However, the flood of people from religiously and culturally conservative Anatolia into the big cities, along with Anatolia's higher population growth, has delivered power to the AKP. But a generation on, many of the new urbanites are adopting more liberal attitudes, and the battle is still on for the heart and soul of the country and its role in the world.

On the diplomatic front Turkey is increasingly more isolated and less trusted. It believes it has a trump card as the main guardian of NATO's southern flank, the host of the US air base in Incirlik, a NATO land base in Izmir, and an early-warning radar system in Kürecik in the middle of the country. But while that is indeed a strong card, NATO has others, even if it would prefer not to play them. If forced to, NATO could build up its facilities in Greece and Romania to offset the loss of Turkey vis-à-vis the Mediterranean and Black Seas, and sweet-talking the UAE into hosting an air base would soften the blow of losing Incirlik. Turkey also knows that although it might be strong enough to go it alone, things can change, and it lives in a tough neighborhood. In the past few years there have been conflicts in four of the countries it borders: Armenia, Azerbaijan, Iraq, and Syria. Iran has always been an opponent, as has Russia, despite the alleged bromance between Erdoğan and Putin ("frenemies" is possibly a better term for their relationship). Turkey has indeed had some successes in Syria and Libya, but the opposition there is hardly comparable to what it would come up against in the Mediterranean if the Blue Homeland strategy provoked a shooting match with Greece, which could easily drag in Cyprus, France, Egypt, and even the UAE.

Modern Turkey seems to see the post–Cold War and post-9/11 world as a jungle full of competitors in which it is one of the lions. It seeks to be self-sufficient in weapons and has enjoyed success in building a defense industry that it hopes will become a world-leading exporter. Seventy percent of Turkish military equipment is now built domestically, and the country has become the world's fourteenth-largest arms exporter, although it's worth noting that orders from NATO allies are few and far between. Its big-ticket project is the TF-X, intended as a state-of-the-art fighter jet to replace the F-16 by 2030. It might have flown earlier, but after Turkey bought the S-400 missile defense system from Russia the Americans persuaded Rolls-Royce and BAE Systems not to cooperate. However, Turkey is expanding its capacity and now builds tanks, armored vehicles, infantry landing craft, drones, sniper rifles, submarines, and frigates, and in 2020 it launched its first light aircraft carrier, which is capable of transporting helicopter gunships and armed drones. It has opened military bases in Qatar and Somalia, and dispatched troops to Syria and Libya as it tries to become less reliant on the outside world. In this respect Erdoğan has had success. Just as Putin has demanded and gained attention, so Erdoğan has ensured that when it comes to a host of issues, from migration to energy to trade and beyond, Turkey has a voice. President Biden came into office saying his administration would be "values based," which suggested he would want NATO allies to share those values. Realpolitik ensured that Turkey's previous incarnations as military dictatorships were overlooked, due to its value to NATO, so the American president's rhetoric may be challenged if Erdoğan's authoritarian streak intensifies.

Atatürk, aware that the Ottomans had overreached, focused westward and pulled Turkey into the twentieth century. Erdoğan's Turkey spent a decade scanning a 360-degree horizon before slowly focusing more south- and eastward. For now, that remains the direction of travel. But there are still elections, and a change could come; there is still realpolitik, and so Ankara will face barriers; and there is always geography to limit how far Turkey travels.

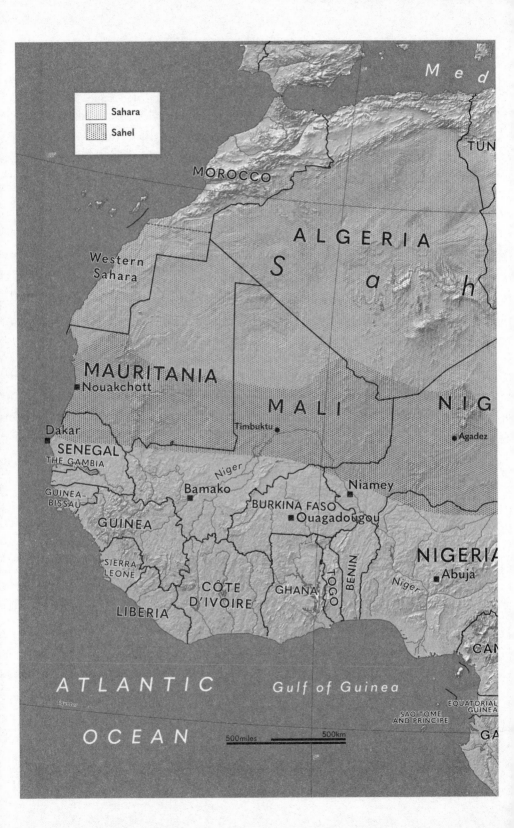

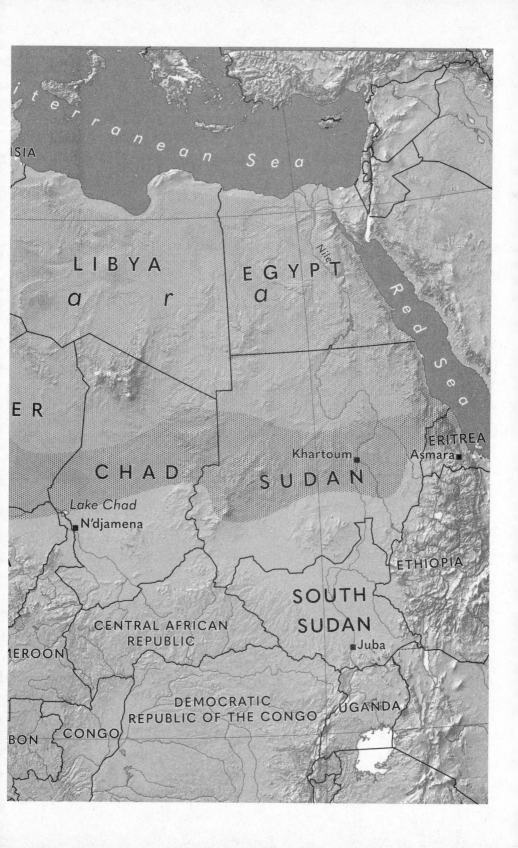

7

THE SAHEL

Where two rivers meet, the waters are never calm.

—Chadian proverb

The Sahel is the shoreline, the Sahara the sea. From this shoreline, growing numbers of people are setting out to cross the sea of sand and reach
another coastline—Europe. They leave behind one of the most troubled, poor,
and environmentally damaged places on the planet, where around 3.8 million
people have been displaced over the past few years, and they head for one of
the richest.

With regional violence and the effects of climate change escalating, things
are only going to get worse. The vultures of Al-Qaeda and ISIS now prey on
the suffering of different groups in a bid to achieve wider aims, even as local
groups borrow their brand names to further their own. The conflicts raging
across several countries have been smoldering for decades. Now they are ablaze
and threatening to spread instability far from the shoreline. António Guterres,
the secretary-general of the UN, warned, "We are losing ground in the face of
violence." In 2020 the Sahel was the site of the world's fastest-growing insurgency; the UN described the levels of terrorist attacks as "unprecedented" and
"devastating."

What happens in the Sahel doesn't stay in the Sahel.

Most Europeans know little about the region and the troubles it faces, or
how much impact those troubles could have on their own countries. Europe has
already struggled with high levels of migration; another large influx of people
would come at a time when European electorates are increasingly wary of allowing in migrants and refugees, with some calling for the construction of "Fortress
Europe." But to stabilize both regions, the real building work needs to be done
not north but south of the Mediterranean.

The word "Sahel" derives from the Arabic for shore, or coast, which is how early travelers thought of the area, having made the voyage across the world's largest dry desert. This shoreline is made up of rocky scrubland, sandy plains of bushes, low-growing grass, and stunted trees. It is a place, in parts, that is always in danger of being blown by hot winds into the desert, or in more recent times blown by the scorching winds of conflict into the abyss. It is a hard land that has shaped its peoples and where the expectation of a comfortable life is rare.

The Sahel has some relative advantages. After 1,000 miles of unforgiving sands and deprivations in the Sahara, there are wells, rivers, and food; there are the yellows, whites, and greens of the acacia trees in the rainy season; and even the pinks, purples, and magenta of the bougainvilleas, and there are a variety of peoples with whom to interact and trade. It also forms a 2,200-mile-long corridor across Africa, connecting the Red Sea to the Atlantic. In it we find places of romantic imagination such as Timbuktu and major cities such as Khartoum, but also small, dusty, flyblown towns in backwaters eking out a living from minerals destined for the international markets. Passing by are nomadic herdsmen, such as the Tuareg and Fulani, using paths forged long before the concept of the nation-state was imposed on Africa, and crossing the recently drawn lines of countries are numerous armed groups whose ideology and violence have again drawn in armies from the outside world.

The corridor is between the sands to the north and the rain forests to the south. In the former, if you stop moving for too long you die from thirst and heatstroke, and in the latter are the kingdoms of the tsetse fly, in which horses, camels, and donkeys cannot survive and in which even today tens of thousands of humans perish each year.

Within the vast spaces of the Sahel are sites of historic and modern interaction among Islamic, Arabic, Christian, nomadic, and sedentary cultures. Given the size of the region, it is no surprise that many people are beyond the reach of governments, some of which seem to care little about providing state services beyond the capital cities. If we add to this the effects of ethnic tensions, poverty, porous borders, and now violent political and religious ideologies, we see how this hard land has fallen into even harder times. Climate change is exacerbating the problem. When the rains fail, so do the crops. When the lakes shrink, so does the food supply. When this happens, people move; and when people move, the places they move to are often not ready for them.

In the Sahel, one of the key factors driving current events and conflicts is the particular way in which geography, history, and the creation of nation-states have collided. And to understand that, we need to start a long way back.

For thousands of years, periods of extreme dry or wet weather have caused the vast spaces of the Sahara to expand and contract, and thus have shaped the Sahel and its peoples—where they live, what they do, and how they behave.

About 10,500 years ago a sudden outbreak of prolonged monsoon rains transformed the Sahara Desert into lush savannah extending down into what is now the Sahel. As the desert shrank, so the expanse in which to hunt and gather expanded. This transition, over perhaps twenty generations, allowed the gradual settlement of the region by people from north and south. Livestock were introduced and rudimentary farming methods learned.

Then came an abrupt reversal. About 5,000 years ago, the rains ended and the desert returned, forcing many inhabitants of what had been the Green Sahara back north toward the liquid coastline of the Mediterranean Sea, or south to the dry coastline of the Sahel and below.

After the return of the desert, it was difficult to journey across the brutal distances. Short routes had been forged, determined by the location of oases, but then, appearing on the horizon, came the camel; it was a revolutionary moment.

From about 2,000 years ago, small, pioneering camel trains allowed longer trading routes to be established. The caravans would grow, some to as many as twelve thousand animals, and become the equivalent of today's supertankers roving very different kinds of seas. "A camel is a horse designed by a committee" is unfair. It may be an ungainly creature but it is superbly designed to do what no other beast of burden can, and in so doing, it changed history. These "ships of the desert" were the only means of mass transport capable of traversing what had been for centuries a land barrier between most of Africa and the Eurasian continent.

The single-humped camel can carry four times the load of a horse and still travel 35 miles in a day. It can do this for more than two weeks without a drop of water, withstanding dehydration of up to 25 percent of its body weight. On sand, the tough skin between its hooves helps it stay on the surface. Should the sand be blowing into its face, it can partly close its nostrils, blink its long eyelashes, and wipe away any particles with a windshield-wiper-like inner eyelid. And food? What have you got? It'll eat it.

I've been on several of these animals in both the Sahara and Negev and have been spat at by many in the sand dunes of Saudi Arabia. Upon mounting one you realize you are dangerously far from the ground, and as you sway along a regular grumbling sound comes from below. For a novice such as myself this was not a comfortable experience, and, given a choice of transport, a 4×4 GMC with a three-liter engine would have been preferable. However, even in the twenty-first century it's possible that your odds of making it across 1,000 miles of Saharan desert without breaking down might be better on a camel than in a car. For the nomads and traders of antiquity, the choice between a horse or a camel for the brutal, weeks-long journey was a no-brainer.

The trading centers along the Mediterranean coastline were soon linked to the regions along the Senegal River, the Lake Chad basin, and the Niger bend, and new routes continued to flourish. The paths used have political consequences even today and now cut across spaces redefined in the twentieth century as sovereign states.

The trade routes increased prosperity, which in turn aided the rise of the Sahelian empires and kingdoms from the eighth century to the nineteenth; their captured ivory, gold, and slaves were taken north from trading "ports" such as Timbuktu by camel trains. Over a period of 1,000 years it's estimated that more than 10 million black African slaves were forced up this route and sold into Arab countries. Coming the other way were all manner of luxury goods from northern cities such as Marrakesh, Tunis, and Cairo, destined for the elite of the southern empires. There were also vast quantities of salt, a rarity in the Sahel, and even today huge slabs of it make this journey, carried on camels by Tuareg tribesmen headed for Mali. Over time some of the starting points and end destinations changed with the shifting sands and fortunes of empires, but the foundations of what we see today in the region were laid.

However, even with the many trading routes, the difficult journeys among these regions still made administration a challenge, and the empires' leaders tended to allow the areas away from their capitals a large degree of autonomy. This trend continues to this day, since the sizes of the modern states are so large and the populations widely scattered. Mali is a good example. The capital, Bamako, is geographically, climatically, and culturally very different from the towns and villages to its north as the Sahel merges into the Sahara.

All empires were limited in southward expansion into the regions of the Yoruba and Ashanti peoples. There the forests began and traders were loath to take their horses and camels into the home of that great killer of pack animals— the tsetse fly.

On the camel trains, the North African and Arab traders didn't just bring goods with them; they brought ideas too, including that there was just one God, that he was known as Allah, and that his messenger on Earth had been called Muhammad. Islam arrived in the Sahel early in the eighth century. Subsequent centuries saw the conversion to Islam of powerful rulers and the gradual blending of the religion with the diverse faiths of the African populations.

In the 1400s European trading ships began sailing down the Atlantic coast, bringing a number of changes to the Sahel. The African slave traders now had a second market and trade route, one that prized men over women. Those involved in the gold industry were well placed to grow their business in what the Europeans quickly described as the Gold Coast. The coastal regions, and parts of the interior, now had direct access to European goods.

At the infamous Berlin Conference of 1884–85 the European powers carved up Africa along arbitrary lines. At the time there were still regions where no Europeans had been, but the great powers knew what they wanted—territory and riches. As British prime minister Lord Salisbury remarked a few years later, "We have been giving away mountains and rivers and lakes to each other, only hindered by the small impediment that we never knew exactly where the mountains and rivers and lakes were."

Much of the Sahel fell under French control—what is now roughly equivalent to Mali, Niger, Burkina Faso, Chad, Mauritania, Senegal, Guinea, Benin, and Côte d'Ivoire, but then going under names such as Upper Volta and French Sudan. What was known collectively as French West Africa extended up to Algeria, which had come under French rule earlier in the century. It wasn't pretty. Perhaps the most shameful episode was the Voulet-Chanoine expedition of 1898–99.

Two army officers, Paul Voulet and Julien Chanoine, set out on an expedition from Senegal toward Lake Chad as part of a strategy to unite French-held territories. The column, at times numbering three thousand soldiers, porters, and captives, found it increasingly difficult to source provisions and took to looting villages and raping and murdering their inhabitants. The French government refused to hold a parliamentary inquiry, and an internal inquiry by the Ministry of Colonies preferred to ignore questions of policy and the numerous previous atrocities carried out in the region. It ended after less than a year by concluding that the two men had been suffering from *soudanite aiguë*, a form of madness caused by the heat. The Voulet-Chanoine expedition is mostly forgotten in France and unheard of in most of the outside world, but it's remembered in the Sahel.

During this period the British, no saints themselves, were consolidating or expanding in Egypt, Sudan, and British Somaliland. The Italians controlled most of Libya, and the Spanish were in the territory now known as Western

Sahara. These new creations cut across trading lines and sometimes disrupted them as the European powers tried to create internal markets. The traditional trade routes were partially eroded by the new rudimentary railway termini and tracks built from the coast, resulting in declining income for people along the old paths.

Over the decades the spheres of influence marked on maps, often governed as administrative regions, became de facto borders. They came to be internationally recognized states after decolonization in the 1950s and 1960s. In 1964 the heads of government in the forerunner to the African Union, the Organization of African Unity, reluctantly decided that they needed to stick with these borders to promote stability. They feared conflicts would break out across the entire continent if they negotiated land swaps with one another based on precolonial ethnic ties. This agreement has mostly held, with the only major adjustment made following Eritrea's withdrawal from Ethiopia, and South Sudan's from Sudan. The former came after prolonged conflict, and the latter preceded a terrible civil war within the newly created state, one that still smolders.

Both the status quo and the renegotiated models carry risks. For example, in the 1960s the Nigerian leadership was so determined to hold the country together that it went to war with the oil-rich, Igbo-dominated region of Biafra. It succeeded, but at the cost of 1 million lives. Even now many Igbo dream of their own state, and across the continent there are similar cases.

Examples exist in today's Sahel, and although at the time of this writing, the borders look like they are holding, this is being challenged as climate change, jihadists, and the precolonial divides within the region combine to create an era of conflict.

Mali is a case in point. In 1960 its borders were created out of French West Africa at almost the same time as the state of Upper Volta, which later became Burkina Faso. They didn't agree on the demarcation, especially in a section in the east thought to hold minerals. Fighting broke out in 1974 and again in 1982, before the International Court of Justice split the zone between them. Both suffered from the structural problems bequeathed by the departed colonial power. They had a name, a flag, a government of sorts, but not a modern infrastructure. There were few highly trained engineers, doctors, or economists and in government many politicians fell back on existing tribal structures to favor their own groups.

Within Mali are two distinct geographical and cultural regions, north and south, roughly separated by the Niger River. Broadly speaking, the north is much drier, especially the areas closest to where the Sahara begins. It is dominated by the Tuareg people, a subdivision of the Berbers of North Africa, and traditionally nomads with ties to Algeria, Niger, and Mauritania. The biggest cities are Gao and Timbuktu, both on the Niger River, and over the past two hundred years each has seen its status and wealth decline as trade via sea routes to Europe grew. The south has more savannah, rain, agriculture, people, and wealth. It also has more political clout. It contains Mali's capital, Bamako, and ethnic groups of the Bambara people, who have ties to the south in Burkina Faso, Côte d'Ivoire, and Guinea.

Decades after independence, many of the elites are still reluctant to accept the "other" as "us." In Mali one of the first things the new leaders in Bamako did, upon freeing themselves from colonial shackles, was to continue the French policy of divide and rule in order to oppress the various lighter-skinned Tuareg tribes of the north, who were regarded as backward, aggressive, and racist. In turn, many of the nomadic Tuareg resented being lumped into a state they didn't recognize, which was now dominated by sedentary people from the south who in previous centuries had feared the warriors from the north. In 1962, just two years after independence, the first Tuareg rebellion occurred. This was followed by periodic outbreaks of violence, and in some ways the current situation is a continuation of that. A Tuareg movement has now grown calling for the creation of an independent state called Azawad.

There are people on all sides working to bridge the gaps and there has even been a Tuareg prime minister. Nevertheless, central government funding for northern regions is significantly lower than for those in the south. If you feel the government doesn't help you, the question arises: What is it for?

In 2012 Tuareg fighters from a group called the National Movement for the Liberation of Azawad launched a campaign against the Malian state that has had widespread repercussions across the entire region. There had been previous Tuareg uprisings, but this was different. Now the Tuareg had support from international terror groups: being allied with Ansar Dine and the Algerian-dominated Movement for Oneness and Jihad in West Africa, both of which were connected to Al-Qaeda in the Islamic Maghreb (AQIM), they were better armed than ever, and for that they could thank the Algerian civil war of the 1990s and the civil war in Libya that had broken out in 2011.

After the Algerian civil war ended in 2002, some of the ultraextremist Islamists, who had been seeking to replace a military junta in Algeria with a theocracy, settled in northern Mali, linking with another group that was funded through drug smuggling and kidnapping. This was the beginning of AQIM as it seized the chance to get inside the local insurgencies. Meanwhile, during the first decade of this century, thousands of Malian Tuareg signed up for military service in Libya, joining the government's Islamic Legion. Colonel Qaddafi had visions of using his oil wealth to control the region and was happy to sow division in Mali by pitting groups against one another and weakening the country, thus allowing him to dominate it. From the Tuareg perspective, if their own state, to which they paid little allegiance, did not help them, they'd take help from elsewhere. To dampen any criticism from the Malian government, Qaddafi paid to set up the Malian TV network and built mosques. When Qaddafi's regime collapsed in 2011, his mercenaries headed home, taking with them heavy weapons looted from Islamic Legion bases. In less than a year Mali was in turmoil; within two so was the Sahel as the violence exploded across borders.

Mali was already one of the world's poorest countries, with weak control over many areas. As such it was ill prepared to repel the waves of well-equipped and highly motivated fighters who fell upon the northern cities, including Timbuktu, and captured territory bigger than France.

In Timbuktu, known as "the city of 333 saints" and a place of pilgrimage and learning, the Islamists set about enforcing strict sharia law on an urban population unused to such practices. Women were forced to cover up and those who refused were flogged. Smoking was banned, musicians had their instruments smashed, and ancient artifacts were destroyed. The Islamists even tore off the gate of the fifteenth-century Sidi Yahya Mosque, claiming that the legend whereby it would stay closed until the end of the world was "un-Islamic idolatry." The fighters offered the imam, Alpha Abdoulahi, about ninety dollars for repairs, but, as he later told the story, "I refused to take the money, saying that what they did is irreparable."

In Bamako, 650 miles southwest, the government issued a strong statement "condemning" the destruction of the country's cultural heritage, but it was powerless to do anything. Its soldiers had fled and its limited government apparatus had been dismantled.

In early January 2013, the Tuareg and jihadist forces overreached themselves militarily and ideologically. Field commanders among AQIM-affiliated groups, and also the Tuaregs, ignored advice from above and advanced south. Senior foreign commanders, who sometimes had a better view of the wider consequences of actions than the local fighters did, appear in this case to have been wary of provoking the main outside power, France.

However, while the Tuareg are often jihadists, fighting in the name of their strict interpretation of Islam, for them, unlike Al-Qaeda, local politics trumps visions of global domination. As a Western intelligence source operating in the region says about many of the local fighters joining outside-led groups, "The caliphate and identification with Al-Qaeda and ISIS, etc., are a red herring. These guys are Muslims, yes, but most aren't fighting for a caliphate, their grievances predate the emergence of ISIS and are far more connected with local and regional issues."

So although Al-Qaeda had often taken a long view, there was no holding back men keen to take their fight to the capital. They crossed the Niger River toward Bamako, and thereby also the Rubicon. Within months, when challenged by a power greater than their own, there was little support for them among the people they sought to rule; the brutal version of sharia they inflicted on the population had turned many against them.

Perhaps the local jihadists were unaware that France would not countenance the possibility of an ISIS-type state on Europe's doorstep. As the leading foreign power in the region, it would not stand by if stability, migration rates, and its economic interests, including nuclear power, were threatened. France has suffered dozens of terror attacks this century, many of them with links to former colonies whose citizens are eligible for dual citizenship, allowing them easy access into France. More than three hundred people have been murdered in attacks in France since 2000 and hundreds more injured. So as the jihadists approached Bamako, French fighter jets took off and special-forces units were scrambled. Colonial history played a part in the decision, but action was taken because of current interests.

The French know that the states of the Sahel are incapable of defeating the myriad threats they face. Left to themselves, it's quite possible that Mali and Burkina Faso could collapse, creating a massive, ungoverned regional vacuum that Al-Qaeda would seek to fill and then expand. The French have thousands of expats in the Sahel states, including in Niger, home to the uranium mines that help fuel the French nuclear industry and keep the lights on in French houses.

As the air strikes went in, the jihadists fled back north pursued by special forces. Following on, at the invitation of the Malian government, was Operation Serval, named after an African wildcat that lives on the savannah.

Twenty-five hundred French troops arrived, along with international approval and support from the Malian army. They routed the opposition in short order—but routed as in killed and scattered, not defeated.

The various militant groups reorganized and reemerged. A sign of things to come was seen in neighboring Niger in May 2013 with a terrorist attack involving a new group called Those Who Sign in Blood, led by a former AQIM commander named Mokhtar Belmokhtar. He later merged his own group with another to create Al-Mourabitoun, whose mission apparently was to "pursue non-Muslims from the Nile to the Atlantic Ocean" and, in a busy schedule, also to fight "the Zionist campaign against Islam and the Muslims."

By 2014 around 4,500 French troops were engaged in Operation Serval, which then morphed into Operation Barkhane, named after the crescent-shaped dunes of the sandy regions of the Sahara. Barkhane is conceived of as a longer-term military intervention and extends to Burkina Faso, Chad, Mauritania, and Niger as well as Mali. These countries make up the G5 Sahel, which contributed 5,000 military personnel, police officers, gendarmerie, and border patrol officers working together against what they realized had become a regional threat to them all. But the G5 personnel and the French were stretched thinly over 1.9 million square miles and were unable to prevent the insurgencies from becoming a network and violence from spreading.

That year, the militants were again operating in northern Mali and by 2015 were seen in parts of central Mali. The following year they spread to western Niger and northern Burkina Faso. By 2018 they were in eastern Burkina Faso amid signs of growing connections with jihadist groups in North Africa and the Horn of Africa as well as with Boko Haram in Nigeria. The fear is that they will increasingly reach into the West African states of Benin, Côte d'Ivoire, Togo, and Ghana. The kidnapping of two French tourists in 2019 in Benin, near the border with Burkina Faso, showed the gradual creep of the jihadists' geographical capabilities.

The militants usually prefer not to engage the local and international forces directly. They are happy to "cede the battleground" and instead use classic guerrilla hit-and-run tactics, including IEDs (improvised explosive devices), before retreating into the vast ungoverned spaces or into the local population. A security expert operating in Mali says, "The militia can create temporary regional dominance. They pour reinforcements into a certain area for, say, twelve hours, then overwhelm a government army outpost, before disappearing again."

One of the worst cases came in December 2019, when an attack on an army base in Niger killed seventy-one soldiers. In January 2020 another eighty-nine were killed, and then in late March, as the world's attention fixated on the coronavirus pandemic, Boko Haram ambushed a military encampment of

Chadian soldiers near Lake Chad. In a seven-hour battle they killed at least ninety-two heavily armed troops, making it the deadliest attack ever suffered by the Chadian military. Questions began to be asked about how that country can hold together. The population of over 16 million is divided into more than two hundred ethnic groups spread over an area twice the size of Texas, with a government that cannot protect its own army, never mind its own people.

Across the region, attacks on military and civilian targets were conducted throughout 2019, and yet to a great extent it was also a forgotten war. This prompted French president Emmanuel Macron to convene a summit in January 2020 and ask for international support. His view was that the region should be part of a new EU defense policy seeking to prevent countries to the south from collapsing and sending millions of people fleeing toward Europe. He said that because French forces had already suffered more than forty fatalities, it was time for other European countries to step up.

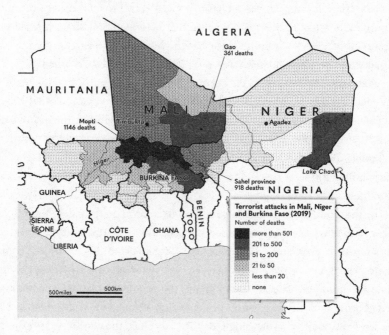

In recent years there has been an escalation of terrorist
attacks in the Sahel region.

Macron had few takers. The UK had been burnt by its experience in Iraq and was busy in Syria, and for decades now other European countries, especially

Germany, have been traditionally reluctant to commit forces. The British had already sent several dozen personnel along with three helicopters to help ferry the French troops around. Denmark had sent a few aircraft and about 70 of its military, and the Czech government weighed in with 60 personnel. Estonia had already deployed an armored infantry platoon from its Scouts Battalion unit consisting of about 50 troops.

It was a limited response, which led Macron to order in another 600 soldiers along with 100 armored vehicles, bringing French troop levels to 5,100. In 2020 Sweden, which already had a few troops in the region under UN command, promised to send a helicopter-borne rapid reaction force and about 150 special-forces personnel. The British then promised a significant reinforcement—a mechanized long-range reconnaissance task group of 250 personnel to "reach parts of Mali that most militaries cannot, to feed on-the-ground intelligence back to the [UN] mission headquarters." In other words, to go where other governments preferred not to send their troops. It was a high-risk decision by Prime Minister Boris Johnson: the UN mission, the Multidimensional Integrated Stabilization Mission in Mali (MINUSMA), set up in 2013, has the highest UN peacekeeping mission casualty rate in the world, with well over 200 UN peacekeepers killed.

President Macron has been keen to persuade Algeria to commit its well-equipped Armée Nationale Populaire to the fray, but, given colonial history, Algiers is not about to put its troops in effect under the command of Paris. The Algerians insist that if they are involved, their troops should be within the umbrella group of the African Union. They're also concerned about further stirring a hornet's nest, as the Tuareg militia conception of an independent Azawad state includes parts of Algeria.

In the summer of 2021 Mali suffered its second coup in less than a year. An exasperated Macron suspended cooperation with the military junta and threatened a "profound transformation of our presence." The reality is more likely to be a modest reduction of troops over two years and an attempt to train more and fight less. ISIS and other groups stepped up their attacks, including in neighboring Burkina Faso, where child soldiers stormed a village and killed 160 people—the country's worst single-day atrocity since the conflict began there in 2015. The French remain stuck, worried that any significant reduction in their presence will lead either to the collapse of governments, or the Russians and Chinese filling the vacuum France creates.

An array of forces and organizations, local and international, are now engaged in a desperate struggle to stabilize the region. The Sahel Alliance was formed in 2017 by France, Germany, the EU, the UN Development Program, the World Bank, and the African Development Bank, and others have since joined, including the UK, Italy, and Spain. In 2018 it committed to funneling more than €6 billion into projects to create jobs and develop infrastructure. The Saudis and the UAE have put money into regional projects, partly to counter the efforts of their rival Iran, which has been trying to enhance its trade and influence in the area, and the US has increased its commitment to aid military budgets, although not all of this has been forthcoming.

The international community has set up shop across the Sahel; there's MINUSMA, the European Union Training Mission in Mali (EUTM MALI), and the G5 Sahel, among others. The pitfalls of creating this alphabet soup were noted by the director of Civilian Crisis Prevention at the German Foreign Office, Heike Thiele, who remarked that coordination was important but "should not only be the exchange of Excel sheets about activities."

It's also been important to keep local people on the government side. The G5 Sahel leaders know that sections of their populations bridle against what some see as a neocolonialist project. In 2020, shortly before the Macron summit, there was an anti-French demonstration by hundreds of Malians in Bamako, during which the French flag was burnt. The French president made it clear he felt that condemnation of these acts by regional leaders did not go far enough.

The governments of the Sahel region walk a difficult line. They must show they are in charge, while often having to defer to the big powers. They also must deal with the ethnic tensions bequeathed them. For example, in Mali self-defense militias were organized within the Bambara and Dogon communities because they felt the government could not, or would not, protect them from the militants. However, this has led to the self-defense militias targeting other groups. There have also been accusations that government security forces in some countries have committed massacres of civilians of particular ethnicities. In states such as Mali and Niger, the army is often dominated by people from the savannah regions in the south, not the desert areas of the north.

The majority of counterterrorism action is undertaken by the French and American militaries. The French mostly focus on Mali and the western Sahel, and the Americans on the Lake Chad basin, but there is close cooperation and intelligence sharing. The American political and military class views the region mostly through the lens of national security and wider strategy. Supporters of US involvement argue that the Americans need to be there to keep failed states from becoming breeding grounds for attacks on US interests. The wider argument is that a US withdrawal will leave China to dominate the region, and also that America needs to be seen to be supporting European allies, especially as massive population movements into Europe would destabilize them. The counterargument is that with a finite budget, the Pentagon ought to focus on the Pacific region and that Europe should be coerced into taking care of its own "near abroad."

Due to the sheer size of the theater of operations and how sparsely populated places are, flooding the region with troops is impracticable, as are numerous large-scale patrols. Instead, both countries make extensive use of drones, special-forces operations, and partnering with local troops to curtail the movements of the militant groups and their ability to ship arms across borders.

The Americans have opened a drone base in the Niger town of Agadez. Previously they had shared an airport with the French in the capital city of Niamey, near the Burkina Faso border, but as the violence spread, the routes used by the militants extended beyond the range of the drones. In Agadez the US has stationed MQ-9 Reaper drones. These have a 1,150-mile range and, in conjunction with a base at Dirkou in northeastern Niger, they now have coverage from western Mali right across to Chad, up to Libya, and down to the Nigerian border.

Niger is of key strategic value to both the US and France. Sitting slap bang in the middle of the Sahel, it offers the potential to keep an eye on troubled North African nations, on Boko Haram in Nigeria, and on the various Islamist groups besetting the seven countries on its borders—Benin, Nigeria, Burkina Faso, Mali, Algeria, Libya, and Chad. Niger has escaped the levels of violence suffered by these neighbors, which along with Niger house the centuries-old trade routes previously discussed. One of these corridors runs north-south through Agadez, another along the Niger-Algeria border, and both of these are now used by people smugglers, who have funneled hundreds of thousands of desperate souls along these corridors during the past decade.

Niger welcomed Western forces and is probably the most active of the G5 Sahel countries in terms of regional cooperation. It funds its army and police well and has made limited efforts to take the issues of minority ethnic groups, including the Fulani, seriously.

Understanding the history and demographics of the Fulani is a key to understanding the current issue, especially since large numbers of Fulani are involved in the insurgencies. Their history, geographical distribution, and cultural practices have had a major impact on the crisis. The Fulani are a nation without a state. There are at least 23 million of them spread across the Sahel, the West African coast, and as far south as the Central African Republic. For example, there are roughly 17 million in Nigeria (about 9 percent of the population), 3 million in Mali (16 percent), 1.6 million in Niger (7.6 percent), 1.2 million in Burkina Faso (6.3 percent), and 600,000 in Chad (4 percent).

In the past there were Fulani empires, even though the people are mostly nomadic herders who have always seen the region as an entity in which they roam, not divided into nation-states requiring pieces of paper to move from one place to another. That they once ruled the area is a fact deeply embedded in their collective memory; the Macina Empire (1818–1862) is considered a golden age.

The empire was centered on parts of what is now Mali and stretched hundreds of miles east and west. Its capital was Hamdullahi (from the Arabic "Praise to God"), which speaks of the strict Sunni Islam religious beliefs of the Fulani. Its leaders banned dancing, music, smoking, and alcohol, and the Fulani were among the first Africans to embrace Islam. Hamdullahi alone garrisoned more than ten thousand soldiers, with thousands more in regional outposts such as Timbuktu.

Prior to Macina, the Fulani had been vassals of other empires, a fact they have not forgotten. Conversely, the collective memory of many of the non-Fulani sedentary communities is that the Fulani are a bellicose people who, when they had power, enslaved huge numbers of them. This was indeed the case, especially among the non-Muslim populations. The current tensions across the Sahel can partly be traced to this history: people equate the rise of jihadism among the Fulani with their seeking to reestablish their empire and forcibly convert Christians.

These fears are reinforced in a variety of ways. After the French-led offensive in Mali in 2013, one of the groups to emerge was the Macina Liberation Front (MLF), named after the nineteenth-century empire and headed by a religious teacher in his fifties named Amadou Koufa. As a younger man he'd espoused conservative religious views, having been influenced by visiting Pakistani preachers; but after trips to Qatar and Afghanistan he had returned brimming with jihadist *takfiri* ideology. A *takfiri* is a Muslim who declares that another Muslim does not believe in the true tenets of Islam and is therefore no longer a Muslim. From a jihadist perspective, this means that as a nonbeliever they can be killed. The ideas have become embedded in the Middle East among those Sunni Muslims who consider themselves *salafists*, or followers of the "purest" version of Islam, but until recently it was a foreign concept to African Muslims, most of whom observe the more moderate Sufi traditions.

Koufa appears to have fallen right into AQIM's lap. Documents found after the French intervention showed that the AQIM leadership told some of its franchise groups to avoid being labeled as Al-Qaeda-related, and instead pretend to be a domestic movement. The Fulani were perfect for this: they had a preexisting national cause for a homeland and could create a front right across the Sahel due to their geographical spread. The MLF appears to be mostly contained within Mali and the border regions. It has carried out numerous atrocities, raiding villages, murdering hundreds of civilians and Malian troops, attacking the Radisson Blu Hotel in Bamako and killing at least twenty people, blowing up religious shrines and playing the "liberation" card to justify its actions, claiming that it would free its supporters from rule by the Malian state. The aim appears to be to take and hold a large area of central Mali and establish an Islamic Macina Republic. In late 2018 the Malian authorities claimed that Koufa had been killed in a French air strike. In March 2019 he appeared in a video, saying reports of his death were greatly exaggerated.

The weakness of the state and perceptions of injustice act as recruitment officers among the Fulani populations. The militant groups may have treated many people badly in the brief time they occupied Timbuktu and other areas in 2012, but the return of government officials did not mean a return to the rule of law. The pattern of shakedowns by civil servants resumed and the military came back, exacting collective punishment in some places. Against this backdrop, in one of the poorest regions in one of the world's poorest countries, Koufa and his senior commanders were pushing at an open door. The MLF offered free religious education, its version of justice, an end to bribes, and, to recruits, over $1,000 if they would be suicide bombers.

In recent years the conflict has spread across borders to the Fulani populations in other countries in the Sahel, including Burkina Faso, Niger, and Nigeria. Similar themes emerge in each outbreak of violence: as drought makes the land increasingly arid and unfit for grazing cattle and sheep, these nomadic people move into new urban and rural areas, where they're seen as outsiders and their interests clash with others such as farmers, leading to violence on all sides. One of the major driving factors here is climate change, and, just like terrorism, it has no regard for borders.

We've seen how the changing climate has shaped the region for thousands of years, sometimes altering it dramatically. But from about 1950 the human factor kicked in. The growing populations resulted in land being stripped of trees for firewood. Simultaneously, an increase in the number of cattle meant that more grass cover was eaten. This led to soil erosion and desertification; the topsoil in the resulting barren landscape was increasingly carried away by wind erosion, which created vast dust storms, and the lack of topsoil made growing crops on a large scale nigh on impossible in a region where it is routine for temperatures in summer to be above 100°F.

In these conditions, the next drought was catastrophic—probably the worst experienced anywhere in the world in the second half of the twentieth century. Beginning in 1968, it came close to wiping out all crops across a huge area. In 1972 there was virtually no rain and by the end of 1973 it's estimated that 100,000 people had died, along with huge numbers of cattle as the Sahara advanced south 60 miles into the Sahel. The mid-1980s brought another drought, another famine, and more of the Sahara. Lake Chad is also a victim. In the last four decades of the twentieth century, it shrank by 90 percent, causing a huge loss of fish, jobs, and income among the millions of people in Chad and neighboring countries who rely on its waters. Across the region 30 million people face "food insecurity," of whom, according to the UN's Food and Agriculture Organization (FAO), about 10 million are at extreme risk of hunger.

The majority of climate scientists agree that since the beginning of the Industrial Revolution global temperatures have risen by an average of 2°F. The average rise in the Sahel is 50 percent higher. Scientists disagree as to whether rainfall is higher or lower than before but do agree that its pattern has changed. This is yet another problem, as the rains now often fall as torrential downpours, which can erode what little topsoil there is; and, given the warming of the atmosphere, the water on the ground then evaporates more quickly.

Such is the picture in a region where over 40 percent of collective GDP depends on agriculture, but in which the FAO says more than 80 percent of the land is degraded. Add to this the projection that temperatures are expected to rise still higher and it's obvious that drastic action is required.

A group of seventeen countries in the region plan to invest $400 billion to fight climate change over the next decade, but most of this comes from foreign aid, and given the economic difficulties faced by the developed world it's uncertain how much of the money will materialize. There is also a huge tree-planting operation in progress, called the Great Green Wall. This began in 2007 as an attempt to create a 5,000-mile-long, 10-mile-wide barrier along the Sahel's shoreline with the Sahara. Spearheaded by the African Union and funded by the UN, the World Bank, and the EU, it involves countries from Senegal in the west to Djibouti in the east.

But the Great Green Wall soon ran into problems. Not all the funding was forthcoming, and, given that most of the proposed wall was in uninhabited land, there was no one around to care for the saplings planted. Most of the trees died. Still the project evolved; the bigger problem was not the Sahara moving south, but the decades of misuse of land within the Sahel. So the Great Green Wall idea is now of greening the whole region. The fightback was renewed with some success by using cheap and effective methods of water harvesting, trying to let grass grow and tending to newly planted saplings.

But again there was a problem. The nomads, whose herds die without fodder, cannot always wait for grassland and trees to mature, and in places the cycle begins anew in terms of both desertification and violence.

Time is not on anyone's side. Africa has the fastest demographic rate of growth in the world. Between now and 2050, the population of the continent is expected to double, from about 1.2 billion to 2.4 billion, and the Sahel is no different. In some regions the figures are even more striking: in Niger, for example, the population is predicted to rise from 23.3 million to 65.5 million during this period.

Education would help to reduce the rate but it is expensive, and boys are often prioritized over girls. Across the region many women have little or no access to contraception and most are subjected to genital mutilation. Health and sex education could change this, but the need bumps up against limited government health budgets. And yet there is money around: not as much as in developed countries, but it could be distributed more equitably and openly.

The poorest region in the world is actually rich in terms of natural resources. There's uranium, oil, and phosphate in Niger, iron ore and copper in Mauritania, oil and uranium in Chad, and gold in Burkina Faso and Mali. In all, there are concerns about governance, corruption, transparency with money, and the economic models of the industries. The Sahel countries mostly don't process their own raw materials, so income comes from taxing the multinationals involved in mining. The problem here is that attracting the multinationals often means giving them tax breaks, which results in less revenue for government coffers.

Niger is the world's fourth-largest producer of uranium, but the government is locked into an unequal relationship with the French state-owned company Areva. Areva owns two mines near the town of Arlit, close to the Algerian border, via its subsidiaries SOMAIR and COMINAK. Documents obtained by several NGOs suggest that the original deal between the Niger government and Areva gave generous discounts to Areva on both customs and revenue taxes. In 2014 the government tried to renegotiate the deal. Areva said the terms would make them unprofitable and closed the mines for maintenance. Eventually a new agreement was signed, but the NGOs still believe the terms favor the company. As the *Times* of London journalist Danny Fortson wrote when visiting Arlit: "In the West you need a bookshelf full of permissions and certificates. In Niger, you give someone a spade and two dollars a day, and you're mining uranium."

The mines have brought jobs and problems. Arlit is in the Agadez region, home to most of Niger's 5 million cattle. Herders complain that they are unable to take traditional grazing routes because of heavy vehicle traffic and dumping of toxic waste. The town itself is on the edge of the Sahara. I've been in the world's most famous desert, including the parts of popular imagination where pristine rolling sand dunes stretch as far as the eye can see. It has a simple but majestic silent beauty, especially at dawn and dusk. And then there's Arlit.

This town of 120,000 people is a dirt-poor, scruffy, jumbled ragtag of run-down houses and corrugated shacks. Fresh running water is scarce, but the nearby mines consume millions of liters a day. During sandstorms the wind blows particles from the debris around the mines into town. The industry is Arlit's biggest employer, and despite health concerns a job there is valued. Greenpeace and other groups have done studies suggesting high levels of radiation in the area due to the spread of radioactive dust, leading to related illnesses. Areva denies such claims, saying they are based on "disinformation." Hospitals in the town are owned by the company, and the population—whether employees or not—get free health care. The staff at the hospitals are also employed by the company, and senior management say there have been no cases of diseases linked to radiation at the mines. The French government points out that it has contributed $10 million to a fund aimed at helping African countries negotiate deals in the extractive industries.

One of the two mines was the target of the 2013 terrorist attack mentioned previously. Security was then tightened, and although the mines are still at risk, at least they are in government-controlled areas and have fixed defensive positions. This is not always the case with the gold-mining industry in Burkina Faso.

In 2009 gold became Burkina Faso's main export, overtaking cotton and making the country Africa's fourth-biggest producer of this metal, which has caught the attention of Islamist groups. The mines are a treasure trove for terrorists. They contain explosives and detonators, a workforce that potentially can be intimidated or persuaded into joining their ranks, and a product that can be smelted, smuggled, and used as currency.

There are also many illegal gold mines. The government outlaws them, but the lure of gold in a country as poor as Burkina Faso is too strong. Some of the unlicensed illegal mines are in conservation areas designed to protect elephants, but as the central government is weak and the territory so large, more than two thousand such mines are thought to be in operation.

The workers are easy prey for criminals and jihadists, with robberies and kidnapping commonplace. In some cases the jihadists simply take over the running of the mines. This happened a few miles outside the town of Pama in 2018. Seemingly out of nowhere jihadists in 4×4 pickup trucks arrived at the mine saying that they were now in charge, that the mining could continue, but that they would be "taxing" it. There wasn't much of a choice; as the old adage goes, there are only two certainties in life, death and taxes.

There are hundreds of such examples, which together amount to a fortune. In 2018 government officials managed to visit twenty-four sites in areas where the jihadists operate. They estimated that the gold mined each year was worth about $34 million. The jihadists' "tax" on this small proportion of mines surveyed is easily enough to purchase large quantities of weapons and pay recruits. As profiteering can be considered *haram*, or unlawful, in Islam, some groups pretend the money is for *zakat*, charity, or that they are being paid to protect the mines.

Gold mining, licensed and unlicensed, has been a boom industry since the 2012 discovery of a rich vein of the metal stretching across Burkina Faso, Mali, and Niger. A 2019 Crisis Group report estimates that "more than 2 million individuals in these three countries are directly involved in artisanal gold-mining: 1 million in Burkina Faso, 700,000 in Mali and 300,000 in Niger. The number of people employed indirectly could be three times higher."

In stable industrialized nations, the authorities would control the industry and more of the revenues would go to the government's coffers. But in the Sahel they are fighting on so many fronts, against such an array of problems, that this is absolutely beyond them. Not only can they not control the illegal industry, but corrupt officials help to smuggle huge quantities of gold across the porous borders and out of airports. Governments will even tolerate local groups taking control and becoming unofficial police forces, as long as they don't challenge the state, but accusations of bribery, confession by torture, and imprisonment are common.

Another resource that could complicate the situation is rare-earth materials. These are a group of seventeen metals under the Earth's surface that are difficult to find and extract but valuable because they have unique heat-resistant, magnetic, and phosphorescent properties. They have names with which most of us are unfamiliar, such as neodymium and ytterbium, but we all use some of the devices containing them—laptops, hard drives, and lasers, but also mobile phones, flat-screen TVs, night-vision goggles, and missiles, products that are crucial to the tech and defense industries in every major country in the world.

The Sahel is not yet known to abound in these metals, but it is thought to have that potential. Niger and Chad have uranium, from which traces of rare-earth materials can be extracted, and Mali has some lithium, which, although not a rare-earth metal, is increasingly of value in technology as it powers the batteries in hybrid and electric cars and in cordless power tools. Mali also has deposits of manganese and bauxite, which are used in electronics. Africa in general is thought to contain more than half of the world's carbonatites, a rock formation anyone seeking rare-earth materials looks at first, and so the region may contain new riches.

Wherever they are found will be a front in a geopolitical battle fought over resources. China will attempt to maintain its control of a majority of the deposits and everyone else will seek to break that control. China contains just over 30 percent of the world's rare-earth deposits and buys extra supplies from abroad. It has more processing facilities than anyone else and can use the material to make and sell products to other countries. The Americans, lacking sufficient processing plants, are reliant on supply from China. They'd prefer not to be, especially after China threatened to reduce distribution as the low-level trade war between the two countries rumbled on in 2019. If, as predicted, China's demand outpaces its domestic supply, it will seek to buy even more and be less keen to sell to others, including the US, whose high-tech weaponry is reliant on the product.

This potential is not the only reason the Chinese are now major players in Africa. The decades of their "hiding our capabilities" and "biding our time" policy have given way to a steady march to restore great-power status.

Beijing's expanding military footprint in the Sahel is part of that process. In 2015 China passed a law allowing the overseas deployment of the People's Liberation Army and other security forces. Chinese special forces are involved in the UN peacekeeping operation in Mali, and Beijing, having persuaded Burkina Faso to end its recognition of Taiwan, is now developing military ties in Ouagadougou. In 2017 it opened its first foreign naval base—in Djibouti.

This activity dovetails with the economic policies of China's Belt and Road Initiative, which seeks to build or update global trade links and thus ensure a smooth flow of goods from and to China. In Africa most of this is below the Sahel, but the naval port in Djibouti is next to the commercial one; China has funded an electric railway line from Djibouti to Ethiopia; and Chinese companies are busy building rail links connecting ports in Guinea and Senegal to landlocked Mali. Several hundred thousand Chinese workers are said to be involved in African Belt and Road activities.

There are numerous examples of anti-Chinese sentiment in the Sahel, including complaints that Chinese companies hire Chinese workers ahead of locals and that private Chinese security firms mistreat people. The *Wall Street Journal's* David Feith says that Chinese state-owned firms have "little regard for trifles such as financial transparency, environmental degradation or human rights," arguing that "Beijing's approach has helped boost African economic growth . . . but it has also helped entrench some of the world's most oppressive governments." He's right, but the track record of the Western countries is also flawed, although in recent years more attention has been paid to transparency and pollution issues.

If the Sahel becomes a source of rare earths, will it be a resource curse or a resource blessing? The evidence to date is not good. The riches of the Democratic Republic of the Congo—copper, diamonds, zinc, and coltan—have helped to bring misery and war to that country, and we've already seen how the gold industries in Mali and Burkina Faso attract corruption and violence.

Without good governance, security, and outside help, the Sahel will not overcome its myriad problems. Colonialism, postcolonial economics, and corrupt governance have allowed domestic and foreign extremists to exploit the weaknesses, poverty, and social fissures rampant throughout the region. In Afghanistan, the Taliban had a saying about the foreign forces they took on:

"You have the watches—we have the time." And so it came to pass: they waited out the foreigners, and most of the foreigners went home. How much time, blood, and treasure are the foreign forces prepared to expend in the Sahel?

The Americans want out—a view that keeps the officials in French military and diplomatic circles awake at night. The US provides logistics, reconnaissance, and intelligence at levels the French would struggle to replicate. Paris quietly reminds Washington that French forces help out in the Middle East and the Horn of Africa, but everyone knows the Americans are preoccupied and shifting their attention toward great-power competition—not what they regard as firefighting in a regional capacity. They have already lost special-forces personnel on operations there and have little appetite to risk more.

If the Americans reduce their forces, France and other European countries will have a difficult choice: reinforce, maintain current abilities, or go home. These are all poor options. Leaving is the least likely option in view of the chaos that would almost certainly ensue. Few experts believe the regional governments have the means to hold their countries together given the centrifugal forces pulling them apart, and if they collapse the ungoverned spaces will be the fiefdoms of local and international terror groups. That would lead to an explosion of violence, sending shock waves southward into Central Africa and northward into North Africa and Europe along with, at minimum, hundreds of thousands of people. Another option is to maintain current levels of support, but if that is tried without American help, there would be a risk of losing ground. The third option—reinforcement—means increased costs in both money and casualties.

The G5 Sahel countries want the French and other troops to stay, as do the West African coastal states, which have seen the violence spread toward them. Côte d'Ivoire, for example, has a robust economy partially dependent on tourism, making it a tempting target. In 2016 nineteen people were gunned down on a beach in Grand-Bassam, with AQIM taking responsibility. If the jihadists were to arrive in force, then the tourists would vacation elsewhere and thousands of French expat workers would leave.

A prolonged uptick in violence and/or a spread into the coastal states will require a response by France and the other Europeans. If not, countries across the Sahel will be increasingly tempted to seek help from other sources; China and Russia are already looking for such opportunities. Countries such as Mali and Chad are not wedded ideologically to the Europeans and Americans. During the Cold War, most African nations struggling to achieve independence took help wherever they could get it. If the Sahel states believe that military and economic assistance from Western countries might dry up, they will not wait for the vacuum to be created, nor will Beijing and Moscow, both of whom are seeking to challenge Western power where they can in economic, diplomatic, and military terms. In the past few years we've seen how Russia used the chaos in Syria to reestablish itself in the Middle East, with President Putin capitalizing on European nervousness and American indifference. A region in flux such as the Sahel could offer new opportunities. The Saudis and other Gulf states still have deep pockets and could fill many funding gaps, but their armed forces are in no position to head across the Red Sea and replace French and American firepower.

At the regional level the European powers—notably, Spain, Italy, and France—all know that their domestic politics will be affected by what happens in the Sahel. The years after 2015, when 1 million refugees and migrants arrived, saw an increased polarization in politics and extremist parties gaining ground.

Whatever the response to the situation, anyone unwilling to tackle the underlying issues driving the conflict is doomed to failure. The phrase "There's no military solution to this conflict" is usually a platitude. There is often a military solution to a conflict. When the Russians were at the gates of Berlin, Stalin didn't ring Hitler and say, "Adolf, there's no military solution to this conflict." However, in the Sahel it is true. Here the American whack-a-mole concept applies. If an insurgency group is crushed in one country, it, and others, will pop up in another. Even if a country is stabilized, the porous borders of its neighbors will allow it to be destabilized again.

To date, the governments of the Sahel countries have been unable or, less charitably, unwilling to address the grievances of their populations as a whole or deal equitably with different ethnic groups. Given this, and the rampant corruption in government circles, no amount of outside military assistance will turn the situation around and build stable nation-states. The ruling elites in government and big business concentrate too much on their own wealth and power and on making sure their own ethnic groups reap the benefits. The geography of ethnicity appears to be stronger than that of state borders.

In Mali the jihadists and Tuareg rebels, who sometimes overlap, tell the people that their government has failed them, arguing that only independence or an Islamic state can resolve their problems. They are warned not to put faith in the foreign powers. AQIM argues that it has prevented France from achieving any of its objectives. It's not wrong.

The French are concerned that they may be trapped in a conflict they cannot win and from which they cannot escape—it risks becoming their "forever war." The British and others worry that a point may come when they have to become even more involved. All the while, millions of civilians across thousands of miles from the Atlantic to the Red Sea watch, and they experience wave upon wave of violence washing up on their shores.

As the conflicts bleed across the borders, the people themselves bleed, and all sides appear locked in. The foreign and regional powers cannot disengage from the conflict, and as long as their forces are there, jihadists will struggle to break the states. Dialogue is not in fashion; many things have changed the Sahel over the years, but it remains a place without compromise.

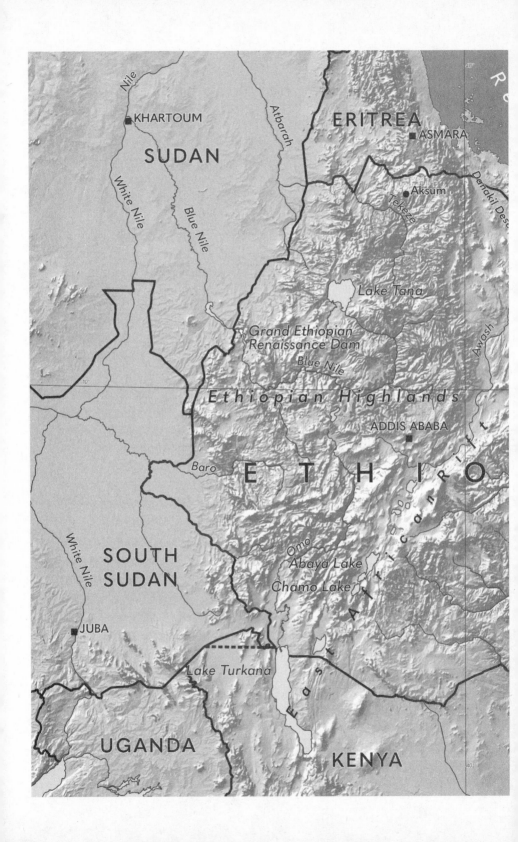

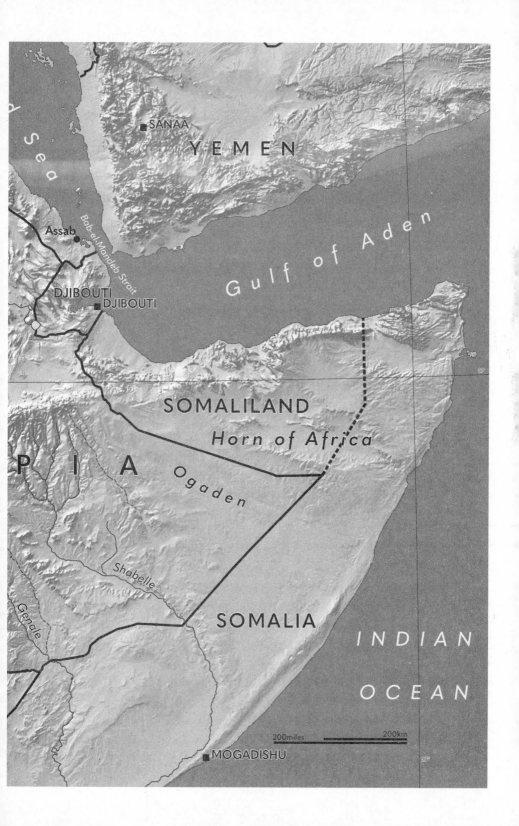

8

ETHIOPIA

Lucy Welcomes You Home

—National Museum of Ethiopia poster

Many things come from Ethiopia—for example, humans. A long time ago, in the Awash Valley, a humanlike ape hominin lived. She could walk on two legs but also hung out in trees; indeed, a fall from one may have caused her demise. Some 3.2 million years later, in 1974, one of her descendants, the paleoanthropologist Donald Johanson, came across her skeleton, and subsequent research suggested that this may be the region from where we all originated. Our ancestor was named Lucy due to the Beatles song "Lucy in the Sky with Diamonds," which played at Johanson's campsite that night. It certainly catches our imagination better than her scientific name: AL 288-1.

The National Museum of Ethiopia's poster "Lucy Welcomes You Home" is a clever piece of marketing, as is the national tourism slogan "Land of Origins," which has helped boost visitor numbers in a country putting itself on the map in many ways. Tourism accounts for almost 10 percent of Ethiopia's GDP, with close to 1 million people a year venturing into an epic landscape of high mountains, tropical forests, burning deserts, nine World Heritage sites, including thousand-year-old churches hewn out of solid rock, and breathtaking waterfalls.

Water defines Ethiopia's geopolitical position and importance. Freshwater is its main strength, and salt water one of its weaknesses. It has twelve large lakes and nine major rivers, most of which supply its neighbors, giving Ethiopia enormous political leverage over them. What it lacks, though, is a coast and direct access to the sea. Nevertheless, its freshwater and its growing influence over and proximity to the Middle East and the Red Sea make Ethiopia the key local player in the Horn of Africa, one of the regions of the world most afflicted by conflict—civil wars, border disputes, extremism, and piracy. Despite this, it has attracted the attention of Turkey, China, the Gulf states, and the US, who see the potential advantages for trade, as well as military and economic strategies. And as the "water tower of Africa" Ethiopia could, if it uses its technology and resources wisely, transform not only its own fortunes but those of the entire region.

After water, perhaps the most defining geographical element about Ethiopia is that a rift runs through it—the East African Rift system. The mountains and valleys it created have long divided the country, and its leaders have always struggled to build the bridges, both literal and symbolic, necessary to bring it together. It's part of what used to be called the Great Rift Valley, which astronauts say is the most significant physical detail they can see from space. The East African Rift system's valleys average about 30 miles in width. They begin in Syria and stretch southward down to Mozambique, 4,000 miles away. As it crosses central Ethiopia, the Rift splits the country's highlands in half, with lakes occupying the valleys between them, making travel and communication difficult.

Seen from above, with the Rift in the middle, the mountainous highlands resemble the shape of human lungs, with the left, or western, lung the dominant of the two. Together they are indeed what allows the Ethiopian people to live and breathe. They are the most populated region of the country and the main agricultural area. Most of the coffee plantations, which are the biggest foreign-exchange earner, are situated there. From the often forested mountains spring the country's rivers, which tumble down to the fertile plains circling the high ground. Most are not navigable for long stretches due to steep gorges and waterfalls, another feature that has held back development. This high ground, which includes the capital, Addis Ababa, is the core of the country and, combined with the surrounding lowlands buffer, makes it very difficult to invade and occupy.

The western highlands contain mountains reaching to 14,872 feet and host the sources of three rivers, including the Blue Nile, before they flow down to the lowlands heading into Sudan in the northwest and South Sudan in the west. Due south is Kenya. On the other side of the divide, the eastern highlands drop quite rapidly, but then roll gently for hundreds of miles eastward to the border with Somalia, which sits between Ethiopia and the Gulf of Aden in the northeast. This is Ethiopia's longest border at 1,000 miles, and of its six neighbors Somalia is the most unstable. It has been embroiled in a civil war for three decades, with the region of Somaliland declaring itself independent in 1991. To the north are Eritrea and Djibouti, which block direct access to the Red Sea. The Eritrean border region contains the country's lowest geographical point—the Danakil Depression. This vast desert plain is more than 300 feet below sea level and is one of the hottest places on the planet, with temperatures recorded at 124°F. Magma flows not too far from the surface, and there is a lava lake that sits in the active volcano of Erta Ale. Small wonder the region is sometimes called "the gateway to hell."

Ethiopia is already the leading military power in the wider Horn of Africa area. With a population of 110 million, projected to rise to 130 million by 2030, it is the second most populous African country and by far the most heavily settled in the region. Kenya has approximately 52 million people, Uganda 45 million, Sudan 43 million, Somalia 15 million, South Sudan 11 million, Eritrea 3 million, and Djibouti 1 million. Together they make up about one-fifth of Africa's population. Regional leadership brings a place at the top table of African politics.

The country sits at the center of one of the most troubled regions in the world. In this century Sudan, South Sudan, Somalia, Ethiopia, and Eritrea have all experienced civil wars, while Kenya has been rocked by wide-scale ethnic clashes and has suffered numerous terrorist attacks by the Somali-based Al-Shabab group. Djibouti has escaped such horrors but, as do all the countries mentioned above, it does have to deal with the inflow of refugees escaping the regional conflicts. This in turn has exacerbated ethnic tensions in what is virtually a port city-state. There are strained relations between states too: for example, Somalia and Kenya are in a maritime dispute over a 40,000-square-mile area rich in tuna and thought to contain large deposits of gas and oil. There is also a long history between the Horn of Africa and the Middle East, linked through ancient cultural heritage and trade routes; indeed, a case can be made for viewing the two sides of the Red Sea as a geographical whole.

The Horn of Africa encompasses the countries of northeast Africa, but it is also closely linked with Middle Eastern countries on the other side of the Red Sea.

Ethiopia could be the center of regional stability, helping its neighbors with economic projects and working to solve disputes, but to do that it needs strong borders and internal peace. It has neither. In 2020–21 a major conflict broke out between the Ethiopian state and the Tigray region in the north of the country, threatening to escalate into a full-blown civil war. To bolster its forces on the Tigray front Addis Ababa withdrew hundreds of its experienced troops from the border with Somalia, where they patrol to deter attacks from Al-Shabab. The fighting also caused tens of thousands of refugees to flee from the Tigray region into Sudan.

Despite being the regional power, Ethiopia has many issues. It has the potential to be self-sufficient in both energy and food; agriculture makes up almost half of Ethiopia's GDP. However, periodic drought, deforestation, overgrazing, military dictatorship, and poor infrastructure have held it back; and only one river, the Baro, is properly navigable, another factor that impedes internal trade. The terrible famine of 1984–85 showed how bad things can be and still influences the view of the country held by some outsiders. Even now, despite abundant water, fertile land, and ample livestock, millions of Ethiopians require humanitarian assistance.

But things are changing. The water flow is increasingly used to generate hydroelectricity using dams and power stations along the Blue Nile, Awash, Omo, Shebele, and other rivers. These projects, together with the Grand Ethiopian Renaissance Dam (on which more later), are expected to feed most of the country's energy needs, as well as supplying power to its neighbors. In turn this should reduce rural people's reliance on firewood and charcoal, which has depleted forests and led to soil erosion.

This technology may also allow a more equitable sharing of the country's riches and help overcome the competition among regions that has marked Ethiopian history. Many African countries have to deal with ethnic tensions between communities encompassed by borders created by the European colonial powers. Ethiopia was, famously, never colonized but, having built its own empire, it has similar problems within its borders. Ethiopia has nine major ethnic groups among its population. There are nine administrative areas and two self-governing cities, all based on ethnicity. More than eighty languages are spoken, which spring from four major groupings, and all enjoy official state recognition. The Oromo are the biggest group with about 35 percent of the population, followed by the Amhara with 27 percent, and then the Somali with about 3 percent and Tigray with 7 percent.

Amharic is the working language of the national government to help the state communicate across federal lines and bind the regional administrations to the capital. However, many people in the frontier regions share ethnic and linguistic ties with their neighbors across the borders. For example, the 6 percent of the population that are Somali inhabit the eastern administrative region of the same name and, linguistically and culturally, have far more in common with people across the Somalian border than with the Tigray people to the far north of Ethiopia. This diversity, along with the geography of the center of the country, has always hindered government efforts to unite the disparate communities.

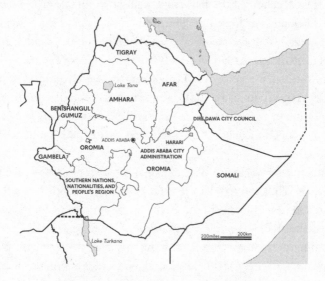

The administrative regions of Ethiopia.

One particular story has long been used as a basis for a shared heritage and national unity. This cultural exchange across the Red Sea is woven into Ethiopian folklore in the tale of the union between the Queen of Sheba and Israel's King Solomon. Known in Ethiopia as Makeda, she is the mother figure in the foundation story of the country.

There are different versions of the tale, one including hairy legs and glass ceilings, which we need not look into. In the fourteenth-century Ethiopian national epic *Kebra Nagast* (*Glory of Kings*), the queen, fascinated by Solomon's wisdom, pays him a visit. He takes quite a shine to her and on the last night tricks her into his bed. The result—a son! He was named Menilek and became the founder of the royal Solomonic dynasty of Ethiopia and its Judeo-Christian tradition. Years later Menilek went to see Dad and brought back a souvenir—

the Ark of the Covenant—containing the Ten Commandments, which had been made some time previously by Moses. If this story is to be believed, then the Ark now resides just up the road from the town of Aksum, in the Church of Our Lady Mary of Zion. You might be able to get a peek of it, but if you do try then the virgin orthodox monks who guard it will have to kill you. This complicates any efforts at authenticating the veracity of its presence.

Either way, every subsequent emperor from Menilek down to Haile Selassie in the 1970s claimed direct descendancy from that last night in Jerusalem.

As a de facto country, Ethiopia's story begins in about 200 BCE, when a small city-state kingdom was forged on the northern high plateau of Tigray, about 100 miles inland from the Red Sea coast. Centered on the capital, Aksum, it expanded in all directions and by 100 CE was the dominant commercial force in the Red Sea region, a position it held for several centuries. At its most powerful, during the Aksum Empire era (100–940), Ethiopia controlled territory stretching up to southern Egypt and across the Red Sea to Yemen. It had a navy and army strong enough to guard its maritime trade routes and dominate the Horn of Africa.

Christianity arrived in the 300s and quickly took root. In 451 the Ethiopian Orthodox Church began to follow the traditions of the Coptic Church in Egypt and broke with the bishops of both Rome and Constantinople. It wasn't until the mid-twentieth century that ecclesiastical relations were resumed.

According to tradition, the relationship between Ethiopia and Islam goes all the way back to the founding of the religion and is another example of the links between the Horn of Africa and the Middle East. In 615 the Prophet Muhammad advised an early group of followers to seek refuge at the court of the Ethiopian king to escape persecution in Mecca. Islamic communities on the periphery of the country grew through conversion and settlement, aided by trade routes along the Red Sea. In the thirteenth century the Muslim leaders expanded their territory into the interior, sparking a series of wars with Christian rulers. Next came the Ottomans, who in the 1500s advanced into the central highlands, destroying churches and monasteries, before eventually being pushed back after the Portuguese helped train and arm Ethiopian forces.

About one-third of Ethiopians are now Muslim, with the majority living in the outlying regions, particularly the eastern lowlands; but there are local concentrations in many parts of the country. Relations between the two main religious communities are mostly peaceful, but in recent years the spread of fundamentalism from the Middle East has influenced some Ethiopian Muslims to question their Sufi Islamic traditions and embrace more radical ideas, and this has raised tensions. There is a tendency for the Christian highlanders to view the country as "an island of Christianity in a sea of Islam."

Modern Ethiopia emerged in 1855, when Emperor Tewodros II forcibly reunified various kingdoms, and then attempted to bring his country up-to-date. The army was reorganized and equipped with modern weapons, and craftsmen from Europe arrived bringing new technologies to revitalize commerce. The country repelled two imperial forces, who quickly realized they had bitten off more than they could chew: the Egyptian army was beaten twice in the Egyptian-Ethiopian War (1874–1876), and then in 1896 the Italians suffered a crushing defeat, losing six thousand men and were forced to abandon designs on Ethiopia while occupying Eritrea.

A period of relative calm ensued, during which the capital was moved to Addis Ababa and the country expanded to its present size. The early 1900s saw an effort to knit its sparse infrastructure together with the building of bridges across numerous rivers and a railway line connecting Addis Ababa to the port of Djibouti, then a French colony, on the Red Sea. These were relatively small steps and the country remained desperately poor, but by the 1920s the capital had a population of well over 100,000 and Ethiopia was emerging as an independent power in a region of European colonies. Nevertheless, it was still subject to pressure from the competing Europeans, and later, during the Cold War, from farther afield.

In 1930, Ras Tafari (Prince, or Duke, Tafari) become Emperor Haile Selassie I, Might of the Trinity, Field Marshal of the Imperial Ethiopian Army, Marshal of the Imperial Ethiopian Air Force, Admiral of the Imperial Ethiopian Navy. Despite being weighed down by these and many other majestic titles, for his time he was a serious progressive. Selassie may have been only slightly over five feet in stature, but he stood tall in African politics and was wise to the ways of the world in leveraging Ethiopia's history and geography to its benefit. He oversaw the modernization of the economy, ensuring that foreign companies had to go into partnership with local ones. He also accomplished a considerable diplomatic success with Ethiopia's entry into the League of Nations, the pre–Second World War version of the UN. One of the conditions of entry was the abolition of slavery, which was still prevalent in Ethiopia; it's thought that there were at least 2 million slaves there in the 1920s and 1930s.

Ethiopia's independence and growing economic base put it back in the Italians' sights and they used its slavery practices as propaganda to justify war. It was the only part of the Horn of Africa that Mussolini's Italy, looking for an empire of its own, could target without running into the British or French. In October 1935 the Italians invaded and by May the following year had occupied Addis Ababa, causing the emperor to flee to London. Mussolini's generals described the opposition as "savages," but there was only one side using poison gas and it wasn't the Ethiopians.

However, despite losing battles, Ethiopian resistance continued until 1941 when, with local help, the British army defeated the Italian forces and brought with them Emperor Haile Selassie.

In 1945 Haile Selassie persuaded US president Franklin D. Roosevelt that Eritrea, now also free of the Italian colonialists, could not sustain itself as an independent country, and so should come back under the control of Addis Ababa. His primary motive was to ensure Ethiopia's access to the sea. It took until 1952 to achieve this via UN approval, but when it happened it was no surprise that the Americans were granted a Cold War listening post in the Eritrean capital of Asmara and a naval base on the coast. Ethiopia then played a key role in US efforts to counter the Soviet Union in the region and Washington invested heavily in infrastructure and military aid.

As leader of the African country that had not been colonized, Selassie was a major influence throughout the continent and one of the architects in establishing the Organization of African Unity in 1963, which was headquartered in Addis Ababa. The organization evolved into the African Union in 2002 but maintained its HQ in the Ethiopian capital. However, although its history made it a symbol of resistance to colonialism, Ethiopia remained poor, underdeveloped, and a fragmented state.

Selassie survived a coup attempt in 1960, but the underlying tensions surrounding his autocratic rule and the ethnic divides of the country worsened. Somalia's independence from the UK encouraged the ethnically Somali Ogaden region of Ethiopia to rebel against central rule. When Somalia came to Ogaden's aid, the Ethiopian forces quickly defeated both, but that led Somalia into the Soviet camp and the two countries found themselves using, and being used by, the two Cold War superpowers. The 1960s also saw insurrection in Eritrea, then still part of Ethiopia. It began as an uprising against the imposition of the Amharic language in schools and quickly turned into a full-blown independence movement.

In September 1974 a military coup d'état was staged by the Coordinating Committee of the Armed Forces, Police, and Territorial Army, which became known as the Derg, meaning "the Committee," led by Major Mengistu Haile Mariam. One of the first ports of call by the soldiers was the imperial palace. There they confronted the eighty-two-year-old emperor, who was in a confused state and appeared unaware of the magnitude of the situation. As he shouted angrily at the troops for their impertinence in manhandling the "Elect of God," they bundled him into the back seat of a Volkswagen and drove him out of the palace gates. On his way through the streets the man whose titles included "His Imperial Majesty the Conquering Lion of the Tribe of Judah" was jeered by crowds shouting "Thief!"

A year later he was dead. Officially he had suffered "respiratory failure following complications from a prostate operation." Only the first part of the explanation was believed. For years the rumor was that he had been suffocated by an army officer using a pillow, and in 2006 a court hearing on charges of mass murder against the Derg was presented with evidence that he had been strangled in his bed. After the Derg was deposed in 1991, the emperor's body was found buried vertically under a toilet in the palace grounds; it was eventually laid to rest at the Holy Trinity Cathedral in Addis Ababa.

In 1977 Major Mengistu "promoted" himself to lieutenant colonel and brought in a Marxist-Leninist regime, overseeing years of economic mismanagement and a campaign of terror. In the time-honored fashion of such governments, it redistributed wealth to itself and took the principle that property was theft to mean it could thieve property. Up to 100,000 people were murdered in the "red terror" of Mengistu's seventeen years in power, with thousands more imprisoned and tortured. Relations with Washington were broken, and Ethiopia realigned itself with the Soviet Union, which poured in arms and military advisers. When conflict again broke out with Somalia, Moscow switched support from Somalia and facilitated the arrival of thousands of Cuban troops, allowing another Ethiopian victory.

Marxist economic policies nationalized the means of production and tried to force subsistence farmers to grow extra crops and sell produce at prices below market rates to feed the cities and the military. Most farmers concluded there was little in this for them, and the policy was a disaster. In the early 1980s the lowland rains failed completely and famine ensued. It was one of the worst humanitarian events of the twentieth century and resulted in an estimated 1 million deaths. At the same time, the Eritrean independence forces were gaining the upper hand against the Ethiopian military and discontent was growing throughout the country.

By the end of the 1980s, the walls were closing in on the Derg. Eritrean forces repeatedly defeated the Ethiopian army and formed an alliance with militia from the Tigray region, which was calling for autonomy from Addis Ababa. With Mikhail Gorbachev in charge in the Kremlin, Soviet military assistance was significantly reduced and the Cubans were heading home. Gorbachev explained glasnost and perestroika ("openness" and "restructuring") to Mengistu, but the idea of an open political and economic system was as much of a foreign language to him as was Russian. The end of the Cold War meant that the game was up for the leaders of the client states that had depended on the USSR. In May 1991, Mengistu fled to Zimbabwe, taking with him as much of the country's wealth as he could steal.

The new government was led by a Tigrayan—Meles Zenawi—causing anxiety to the Amhara, who were used to being in charge. Under Zenawi the constitution was rewritten to make Ethiopia a federation with powers devolved to ethnically defined regional states, although in reality the government held on to as much control as it could get away with. The regions were given the right to seek independence, which in 1993 led to legal recognition of Eritrea as a separate country. At the stroke of a pen, Ethiopia lost its entire coastline along the Red Sea and became the most populous landlocked country in the world.

However, despite these political changes, on the domestic front the regional tensions continued, and yet again war broke out with Eritrea. The recognition of the new state in 1993 had left border issues unresolved, and in 1998 a series of incidents in the disputed village of Badme resulted in a full-scale war. During two years of fighting, each side suffered tens of thousands of casualties before the conflict ended with no territory lost or gained, a peace treaty that wasn't fully honored, and a UN-monitored buffer zone to keep them apart. Ethiopia also sent its troops back into Somalia to try to influence the outcome of the civil war there. The 2000s saw years of steady economic growth, but internal repression continued, with thousands of activists and journalists jailed, often on flimsy pretexts.

The year 2018 witnessed a change—enter Abiy Ahmed. The forty-two-year-old former lieutenant colonel was elected prime minister. What was new was that Abiy was from Oromia—his father was an Oromo Muslim and his mother an Amhara Christian—and despite being the largest ethnic group, an Oromo had never led the country. It was far from the only change, though.

His first six months in charge were a whirlwind. Thousands of political prisoners, including journalists and opposition figures, were released. Abiy then appointed ten women in a twenty-person cabinet, whereas the previous iteration had four women and twenty-four men. This gender-balanced cabinet was another first. He also signed a peace agreement with an armed group fighting in the Ethiopian Somali region and in 2019 dissolved the ethnically based national coalition government, merging most of it into a single national party—a move that sowed the seeds of the civil war with Tigray the following year. Most of the Tigray elite refused to join.

The most surprising change came so quickly it caused amazement. Within weeks of taking office, he announced that Ethiopia would honor the terms of the 2000 agreement with Eritrea that had ended the two-year-long war, in which he himself had fought. A month later he was in the Eritrean capital, where he embraced President Isaias Afwerki on the tarmac at Asmara International Airport. A peace treaty followed, officially ending the twenty-year state of war and declaring a new era of peace and cooperation in trade and diplomacy. His efforts earned him the Nobel Peace Prize, the country's first; however, a genuine warming between the two states remains a work in progress.

Securing peace within Ethiopia's borders proved even more challenging. There were many enemies, some angry at being purged, others hoping to enrich themselves through politics, and, most dangerously, powerful ethno-nationalists seeking to dominate what Abiy was trying to turn into a genuinely pluralistic country. In the first few weeks of his rule, ethnic clashes broke out in several border regions of the nine federal states. Within months hundreds of people had been killed and almost 3 million people had fled their homes.

Abiy had purged some of the political old guard in the military, notably ethnic Tigrayans who had dominated the country. Now many critics were arguing that lifting the oppressive authoritarian apparatus of the previous governments was allowing tensions to boil over and threaten the territorial integrity of Ethiopia. The relaxing of media restrictions led to a sharp rise in people venting their prejudices against different ethnicities on social media and radio. There had been numerous warnings that Ethiopia's federation could easily go the way of Yugoslavia and disintegrate in an ethnic bloodbath; the outpouring of ethnically based hate, followed by the war in Tigray, sharpened concerns. The conflict there again showed the weakness of central control. By the summer of 2021 Tigrayan forces had recaptured the regional capital, Mekelle, from government troops and paraded captured Ethiopian soldiers through the streets.

Abiy has tried to head off the possibility of other regions following Tigray's example by addressing the issue that has plagued the country for centuries. Power has usually been dominated by a particular ethnic group, and others have been left out of the decision-making process. Strong leadership from the center is not trusted, and powerful regions are feared by the center. Abiy has sought to reassure the different power bases that they would all benefit from his reforms and has urged them to buy into the political process. In a speech he gave a year before he came to power, he said, "We have only one option and that is to be united. . . . The other option is to kill each other."

The disparate regions within Ethiopia's borders have always required a degree of force to control. The challenge is to ensure that the ethnic groups buy into the idea of Ethiopian nationhood so that those who join its armed forces will be motivated to defend it. This reduces the support within communities for hostile armies that may cross the border—for example, Ethiopian Somalis who might be tempted to support Somalia.

To create an atmosphere in which people feel Ethiopian first and their ethnic identity second, the state supports a policy known as Ethiopiawinet, or "Ethiopianness," projecting the message that there is an identity common to all Ethiopians. Religious leaders are encouraged to emphasize the unity of humanity and shared values of Christianity and Islam. However, there's an inherent tension between Ethiopiawinet and regional autonomy. Dividing the country up into its ethnic groups silently underlines the sense of mutual suspicion and fear those groups have of one another, and thus weakens the nation-state. But without the divisions there are inevitably insurgencies against the state by those who would fight for autonomy—thus weakening the nation-state. Squaring this circle requires a delicate balance and a fair distribution of wealth.

Despite all these differences there is a sense of Ethiopiawinet, as shown by solidarity on issues such as resistance to invaders, the Grand Ethiopian Renaissance Dam on the Blue Nile, and in sporting achievements by the likes of Olympic gold medalists Haile Gebrselassie, Tirunesh Dibaba, and Tiki Gelana. Its strength waxes and wanes according to time and location, and it is always at risk of falling apart—as shown by the events on the evening of Monday, June 29, 2020.

One of the country's best-known singers, thirty-four-year-old Hachalu Hundessa, was getting out of his car in a suburb of Addis Ababa. A man approached and shot him once in the chest; he was rushed to the hospital but died shortly afterward. Within a few days hundreds of people would be killed as a result of the shooting.

Hundessa was a superstar among the country's largest ethnic group, the Oromo, who are sometimes referred to as the marginalized majority. He was a symbol for them, someone who sang, and spoke, about the political and economic discrimination they feel they have always suffered within the Ethiopian state. That made him many enemies among other groups, but he also angered some Oromo leaders as he fiercely criticized their infighting. Within hours of the shooting, accusations began to fly back and forth amid calls for revenge by some Oromos, and exhortations from some in the dominant Amhara community for the Oromos to be attacked. The government responded by shutting down the internet and trying to contain protests and mob rule.

On Thursday, July 2, his coffin began a televised road journey from the capital to his hometown of Ambo, 60 miles west in Oromia state. The way was blocked by Oromos insisting he be buried in Addis Ababa, which they claim as their capital city—an emotional issue that has been argued about for more than a century. Amid violent scenes, the hearse was forced to turn around and the body was eventually flown to Ambo by helicopter. Dozens of people had already been killed by the security forces during protests or in mob attacks, but now the violence exploded.

The killings were mostly along ethnic Amhara-Oromo lines, but religious identity played a role. The Amhara are majority Christian, while the Oromo are mostly Muslim. Crowds of young Oromo men carrying machetes and knives stormed into Amhara and Christian Oromo neighborhoods chanting "This is the land of the Oromo." Some carried lists of the names and ethnicities of inhabitants. Stabbings, lynchings, and beheadings followed, and numerous buildings were destroyed. The worst-hit place was the ethnically mixed city of Shashamene in Oromia, where the Amhara are a minority. Munir Ahmed, the manager of one of the most popular restaurants there, watched as his premises were destroyed by rioters targeting non-Oromo businesses. "We cried, we begged them to stop," he said. "To them, we were the enemy." His staff fled the city.

Those terrible early July days showed the depths not only of depravity but of the cultural, political, and economic challenges facing Ethiopia. Among all the groups there remain many people who still work only toward power for their own ethnicity. The Oromo continue to seethe about never having held most of the power, despite being the largest ethnic group; the Amhara remember that they ruled the roost for the longest period in the country's history; and the Tigrayans wonder if they can return to the position of the recent past when, despite being just 7 percent of the population, they were in charge. The minorities—the Gurage, the Afar, the Sidama, and others—remain anxious about being dominated by the larger groups.

Keeping the internal borders calm, and the external borders secure, to provide a safe environment for economic growth is the primary challenge. However, all Ethiopian leaders since 1993 have faced the same geographical problem: lack of access to the sea. Modern Ethiopia has no designs on a return to the empire of the Aksum era, but knows that to survive and prosper it must be able to secure reliable trade routes. Ethiopia's imports and exports mostly pass through its neighbors' territory.

The most important trade route is via the Red Sea, a maritime bottleneck that includes the narrow Bab-el-Mandeb strait and passes along the coastlines of six countries. Approximately 90 percent of Ethiopia's imports and exports travel by sea, and almost all cargo goes via the deep-water port of Djibouti. The danger of relying on a single route was amplified in 2019, when Addis Ababa almost ran out of fuel after the Djibouti-Ethiopia highway was blocked by protesters. To hedge against this weakness, Ethiopia has been maneuvering to buy a share of the Djibouti port, has acquired a 19 percent stake in the Berbera port in the breakaway Somalia region of Somaliland, and has holdings in Port Sudan and Kenya's Lamu port. It has also reopened roads leading to the ports in Eritrea.

But Djibouti—and the entire Horn of Africa coastline—has become a geopolitical battleground, leaving Addis Ababa partially dependent on the whims of greater powers.

China is a major player. Roughly 33 percent of Ethiopia's imports and 8 percent of exports involve China. The Chinese are also funding large infrastructure projects: they have built a 450-mile-long, fully electrified railway linking Djibouti to Addis Ababa, replacing a century-old line that had fallen into disrepair.

When Beijing secured its military base in Djibouti it attracted attention, but China is just one of many countries involved in the scramble for the Red Sea's coastline. The US, China, Japan, France, and Italy all have military bases there and other countries are interested in moving in—Russia, Qatar, the UAE, and Turkey have also taken stakes in competing ports.

When the Saudi-UAE coalition entered the war in Yemen in 2015, the UAE rented part of the Eritrean port city of Assab and turned it into an air base from which to launch attacks across the Red Sea. It is also involved in the construction of a pipeline connecting Assab to Addis Ababa. The UAE is hoping not only to influence the politics of the Horn of Africa but to invest and capitalize on the growing consumer market in Africa, where it sells fuel, plastics, and animal products. But for the Middle Eastern countries, the Red Sea and Horn of Africa are part of a regional struggle—it is a place that draws in disputes and rivalries from farther away.

In 2017 Saudi Arabia and the UAE cut ties with Qatar after accusing it of supporting terrorism and destabilizing the region. Turkey, a rival of the Saudis and Emirates, came in on the side of Qatar, and the feud then jumped across the Red Sea, as the rivalries played out in the Horn of Africa and drew in the bitter disputes between Turkey and the UAE and Turkey and Egypt. Some hawks in President Erdoğan's government believe the UAE financed the 2013 coup d'état against Egyptian president Mohamed Morsi (an ally of Erdoğan) and then supported the attempted coup against Erdoğan himself in 2016.

The UAE had good relations with the government in the Somali capital of Mogadishu but, after concluding it was in league with Qatar and Turkey, switched its funding to the autonomous regions of Somaliland and Puntland, where it has established a military base and two ports. Other countries have seen the benefit of having a presence on Somalia's coastline, the longest on the African continent. Turkey had been investing there for years before the Gulf states showed an interest, and it now has a controlling interest in all of the major air- and seaports under the authority of the Somali government. When Turkey added a major military base in Mogadishu, it heightened Arab fears that it intends to reestablish itself in the territory of the former Ottoman Empire. That's a charge Ankara denies, describing its foreign policy as one that is "enterprising and humanitarian." But the Arab world doesn't see it that way and any escalation of tensions between Turkey and the Arab states could spill over into the Horn as well.

Geographically, Ethiopia is part of this Qatar/Turkey–Saudi/UAE clash, but it has tried to remain neutral. Instead it attempts to cooperate with all the region's players while taking care not to be seen as a client state of any of them.

The Saudis and Emiratis have invested in Ethiopia's energy, tourism, and manufacturing sectors and boosted funding for its agriculture in a bid to protect their own food security. Turkey has also been busy in Ethiopia after it was frozen out of Eritrea by the Gulf states; Ethiopia's studied neutrality has allowed Turkey to maintain a significant economic presence there. On the soft-power front, Turkey has been busy building schools and mosques while expanding its economic footprint, and is now the second-biggest investor in the country behind China. This is part of an Open to Africa policy that Ankara embarked on in 2005. It is a predominantly economic strategy, but in Ethiopia it comes with added potential diplomatic benefits because Ethiopia and Turkey both have very tense relations with Egypt. This shared suspicion comes in handy for the Ethiopians when they need allies to support them on their biggest bone of contention with Cairo, which is also their biggest construction program: the Grand Ethiopian Renaissance Dam (GERD). It is Africa's largest hydroelectric power plant.

When the Blue Nile reaches Khartoum, the capital of Sudan, it merges with the White Nile and becomes the Nile, which then flows on to Egypt. The dam and reservoir begin a couple of miles in from the border with Sudan. At some point in the 2020s the reservoir is expected to be full; it will then stretch back about 150 miles toward the Ethiopian highlands and the source of its water. In the summer of 2020, nine years after construction began, satellite images from high above the East African Rift showed that water levels in the reservoir behind the dam were very slowly rising despite the lack of an agreement between Addis Ababa and Cairo to do so. The Ethiopians were using the rainy season to lift levels to a point where they could test the turbines destined to bring electricity to most of the country.

For the Egyptians, the building of this dam is an existential matter—and one of the clearest examples of a country being a prisoner of its geography. The Nile is the very lifeblood of the country and its people; no Nile, no Egypt. Eighty-five percent of the Nile's flow into Egypt originates from the Blue Nile, and now the Ethiopians have their hands on the tap. It's not that Ethiopia intends to cut the flow completely, it's just that it will have the power to do so.

The passions on each side are understandable. Egypt is mostly desert, and so 95 percent of its 104-million-strong population live along the river's banks and delta. Cairo fears that holding back even 10 percent of the Nile's water will, over just a few years, put 5 million farmers out of work, cut agricultural production by half, and further destabilize a country fighting against an Islamist insurgency. Even with the usual amount of water from the Nile, the northern delta areas, already hit by saltwater intrusion from the Mediterranean, are at risk of greater salination. Cairo's starting points in the dispute are colonial-era agreements and a 1929 Anglo-Egyptian treaty that gave Egypt an annual allocation of water, plus a veto over any attempt by an upstream state to construct dams along the river.

Ethiopia sees things differently, arguing that it is not bound by agreements it didn't sign, and that as the upstream nation it has geography on its side. The whole project has for years been a source of national pride and sits at the heart of Ethiopia's future. The dam will create so much energy that Ethiopia will be able to supply the surplus to Sudan. Addis Ababa says that too many of its upstream regions have to rely on rain-fed agriculture, which, given periodic droughts, leaves millions of Ethiopians vulnerable to food shortages. Ethiopians have lit-tle time for Cairo's stance; they view Egypt as a colonial power that assisted the slave trade with its large slave markets, attempted to invade them, and is trying to prevent their bid to escape poverty.

Egypt's President Sisi said he would use "all available means" to defend his nation's interests. That's fighting talk and has led many analysts to speculate that a major "water war" is in the cards. The possibility has been present for more than fifty years. In 1970 the Ethiopian government approached an Amer-ican company to study the impact of building a dam on the Nile. Egyptian pres-ident Anwar Sadat was so infuriated he threatened war.

However, there are many things constraining the Egyptian military. Here again, geography favors Ethiopia. Because Ethiopia is landlocked, an Egyptian ground force would have to go through Sudan, or, after a journey down the Red Sea, through Eritrea. Neither option would be attractive to any army, never mind one without recent combat logistical experience. Egypt's military history is not positive. Its disastrous attempted invasion of Ethiopia in 1874–1876 is a reminder of the dangers of taking on a country strong enough to see off coloni-zation. In the 1960s, seventy thousand Egyptian soldiers crossed the Red Sea to fight in the Yemeni civil war, but only sixty thousand came back.

The option of an air assault on the dam was considered, but that seems to have been abandoned. Hitting it when the reservoir has water risks flood-ing Sudan and causing international outrage. Besides, the Egyptian F-16s and Rafael jets are thought not to have the refueling capability to get them back home even if they survived the Israeli-supplied modern missile defense sys-tems surrounding the thick GERD reservoir walls. The Ethiopian military is not as well armed as the Egyptian, but it has been buying weaponry from the French, Russians, Israelis, and Americans. It also has combat-experienced troops and would be fighting on home ground. Ethiopia does not have any real military allies other than its geography, but that's quite a friend to have. President Sisi doesn't seem to be much of a gambler, and in his part of the world fighting a war risks not just losing it but then losing your grip on power, and even your life.

Another restraining influence is diplomacy. Saudi Arabia and the UAE have substantial investments in both Egypt and Ethiopia and do not wish to see them undermined by conflict; the Chinese, who support the GERD, feel the same way. Beijing has leverage in Addis Ababa; it may not bother with linking good governance and working conditions to aid and trade, but it does care about stability and urges restraint on both sides. The Ethiopians have attempted to reassure Cairo that they will use the dam in a way that does not have a significant impact on downstream flows, but Egypt is slowly trying to switch some of its agricultural sector to products that are less water-intensive.

The governments of Sudan and South Sudan are watching carefully, but are less concerned. Ethiopia has promised it will keep the water flowing and export surplus electricity to its neighbors. Both could take advantage of favorable terms to export Sudanese and South Sudanese oil in exchange. "Black gold" for "blue gold" would supplement Ethiopia's small oil-producing industry.

Water is a matter of national security for all the countries that rely on the Nile River system. Uganda, Burundi, Congo, Egypt, Kenya, Ethiopia, Eritrea, Rwanda, South Sudan, Sudan, and Tanzania all monitor the flow of the river through their borders, but none is as at risk as Egypt, and none is less at risk than Ethiopia. The Egyptians are having to get used to the idea that, after a century of being the preeminent Nile power, times have changed. The Greek historian Herodotus described Egypt as the gift of the Nile—but what the Nile gives, the Grand Ethiopian Renaissance Dam can take away.

Conversely, the GERD provides Ethiopia with a unique opportunity to break the centuries-long cycle of poverty and ethnic violence. Technology is allowing Ethiopia to bend the bars of its geographical prison. As in many other African countries, only relatively short stretches of its rivers are navigable because they plunge so violently down from the highlands, and these waterways are therefore of limited use for trade. The waters have always given Ethiopia a degree of political power, but now the "water tower" becomes water power in the energy sense.

Used wisely, meaning equitably, cheap and abundant electricity can transform the lives of tens of millions of people, which in turn will reduce tensions among them. Together with good governance, this brings the possibility of Ethiopia becoming a stable country and an acceptance of what is already the reality—that it is the regional power.

Nevertheless, Ethiopia faces numerous challenges. Climate change has exacerbated the frequent droughts that hit the lowlands, and deforestation is causing soil erosion and desertification. The country continues to host hundreds of thousands of refugees from South Sudan, Somalia, and Eritrea, along with well over a million internally displaced people. The Horn of Africa is a hub for extremist groups and piracy, and that does not look likely to change much in the foreseeable future.

Coping with these problems requires stability, and that may be the biggest challenge of all. There's an Ethiopian saying: "When the spider webs unite, they can tie up a lion." The adage did not spring from political thought, but it applies. If the political and business classes can manage the economy successfully and the politicians can work together to unite the country, then the "African success story" is a viable option; if not, the ties that bind may not be strong enough to hold.

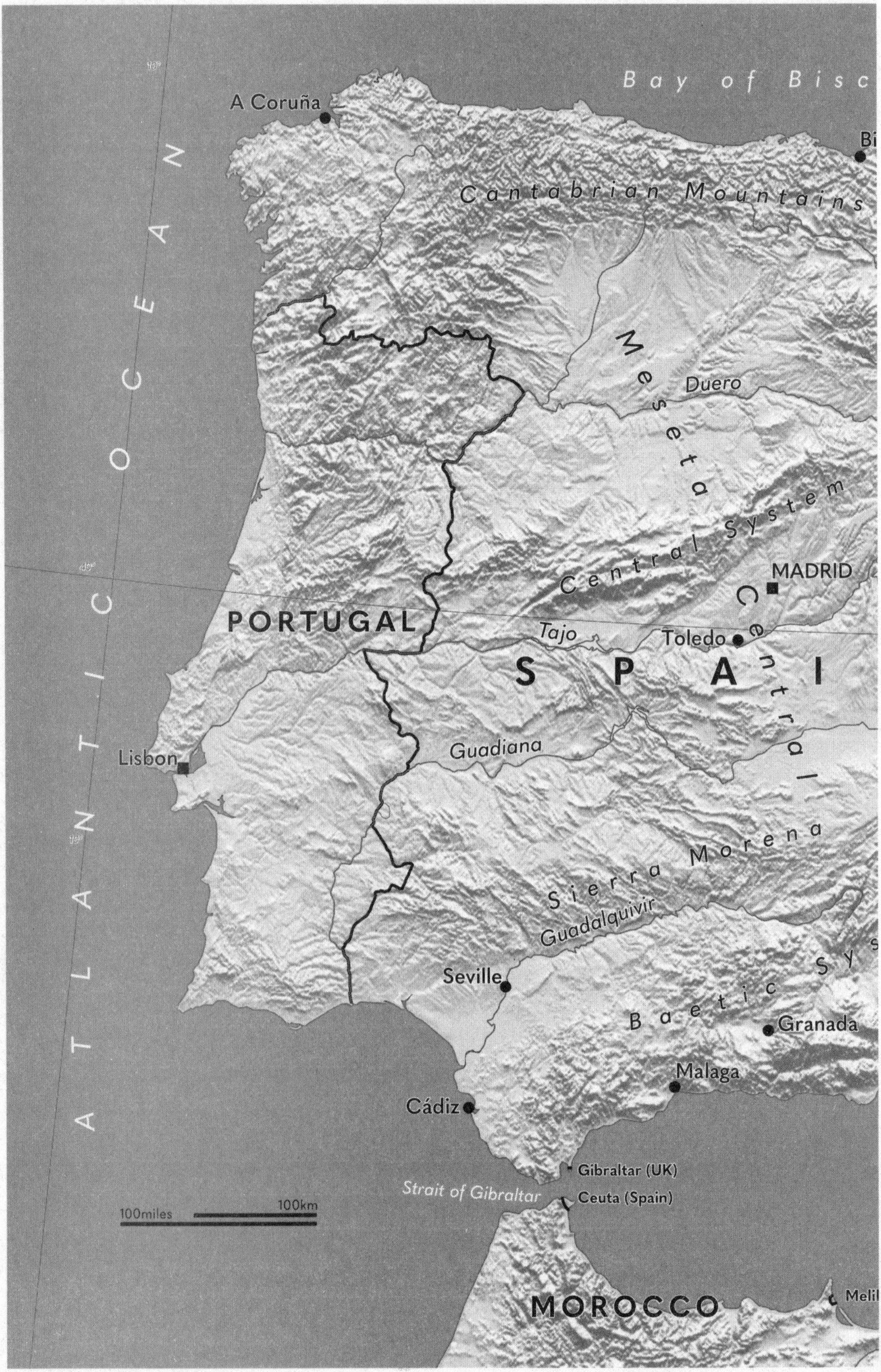

Bay of Bisc
A Coruña
Bi
Cantabrian Mountains
ATLANTIC OCEAN
Meseta
Duero
Central System
MADRID
PORTUGAL
Tajo
Toledo
SPAI
Central
Guadiana
Lisbon
Sierra Morena
Guadalquivir
Seville
Baetic Sys
Granada
Malaga
Cádiz
Gibraltar (UK)
Strait of Gibraltar
Ceuta (Spain)
100miles
100km
MOROCCO
Melil

9

SPAIN

Nature and man are opposed in Spain.

—Gertrude Stein

O ne of the many joys of driving along the small, dusty, winding roads in the mountains of Spain is to round a corner and find yourself heading toward a huge fortress sitting majestically atop a seemingly unassailable mass of rock. Some are crumbling ruins, some beautifully preserved; all are keys to understanding the geography and history of Spain.

In early medieval times these magnificent structures were the defining feature of a large area of the Meseta—the extensive plains of central Spain dotted with mountains—to the extent that the region's name is derived from the Spanish word for "castle," *castillo*: Castile, "Land of the Castles."

It's an apt name for the whole country. Spain is a vast fortress. From the Mediterranean Sea and the Atlantic Ocean, narrow coastal plains quickly bump up against great walls of mountains, and the entire central region is a plateau with its own high ranges and deep valleys. The Meseta makes Spain one of the most mountainous countries of Europe.

At the heart of the Meseta is Madrid. The city was chosen as the capital in the sixteenth century precisely because it is in the middle of Spain; theoretically this meant it could exert a more centralized control over the country, with less distance between it and potential rival centers of power. However, Spain's mountainous terrain and size (it's twice as big as the UK) have always hampered trade links and strong political control, ensuring that its different regions retain strong cultural and linguistic identities. Such are the complexities and passions of these differences that the Spanish national anthem does not have lyrics, because no one can agree on what they should be. These differences remain— in the north to the extent that in modern times there has been a campaign of terror in the Basque Country by extremists willing to use violence to break free from Madrid, and a political movement in Catalonia to achieve the same aim. Outright domination and repression from Madrid are things of the past, but the specter of violent regional nationalism remains.

In many Western countries we often think that our nations, and national identities, are fixed, partly because the idea of the nation-state in its modern form grew up in Europe. We also think that liberal democracy is the norm. However, if we look back at history and across the globe, it is far from normal, and identification with the state is a fragile concept in those countries with several nations, or peoples, inside their boundaries. Spain may be one of the oldest European states—it began to come together in the 1500s—but it has always struggled to get its regions to coalesce around the center. Spain is an enthusiastic member of the EU, but the very fact of the union dilutes the strength of the existing nation-states and encourages regional separatism, as seen in Catalonia, where nationalists envisage a future outside Spain but inside the EU. Spain is also a young democracy. The foundations of that democracy appear solid, and there are few threats to it on the horizon, but there is also a long antidemocratic strain in the country that, given the right conditions, could make a comeback. All these issues are grounded in Spain's geography and history.

The regions of Spain have always maintained strong identities, particularly Catalonia, the Basque Country, and Galicia.

The kingdom of Spain has a lower population density than most Western European countries. With the exception of Madrid, most major cities are along the coastlines—for example, Barcelona, Valencia, and Bilbao; and the interior, especially the Meseta, is sometimes called "*la España vaciada*" (emptied Spain), due to the migration from rural areas to the towns and cities that gathered apace through the twentieth century. The population figures have risen and fallen over the centuries—testament to an explosive and violent history. It now stands at about 47 million but projections suggest it will shrink by about 5 million over the next four decades.

Spain is the fourth-largest country on the continent of Europe, behind Russia, Ukraine, and France, with which it shares a border. Its other borders are with Gibraltar, Andorra, and Portugal, the latter being the longest uninterrupted frontier in the EU. But Spain has another, less-known border—with Morocco. This is due to its coastal enclaves, Ceuta and Melilla. From the Spanish mainland Ceuta can be seen on the North African coastline just 8 miles away across the Strait of Gibraltar. In the Mediterranean are the Balearic Islands—all 151 of them. They form Europe's largest archipelago but only five are inhabited: Majorca, Minorca, Ibiza, Formentera, and Cabrera. Way south are the Canaries, just 70 miles off the coast of northwest Africa but 1,000 miles of Atlantic Ocean from the Spanish mainland; there are eight main islands, the best known of which being Tenerife and Gran Canaria.

All this combines to give Spain a defensive military advantage, potential control of access into and out of the Mediterranean, and ports and bases with which to maintain military and trade links and that helped to build one of the strongest militaries in Europe—and then an empire. Nevertheless, even at the height of Spain's powers, its internal geography limited its wealth creation and political unity.

The Pyrenees act as a barrier for an invader, but they have also been an obstacle to the flow of trade. The narrow coastal plains, close to the mountain range, have limited space for agricultural development, although Spain has done well with what it has and is famous for its olives, oranges, and wine. The flat regions of the Meseta plateau produce huge quantities of food, but here again the mountains on and surrounding it have hindered the ability to move the produce around the country and to the ports.

Unlike France and Germany, Spain does not have large rivers that flow uninterrupted along vast plains. Most are short and carry only small volumes of water, and some run dry in the summer months. In recent years droughts have been so severe that crops withered and whole regions were subjected to water rationing. Spaniards have a dark joke about such times: "Now the trees chase the dogs," such is their desperation to be watered.

Of the five main rivers, four empty into the Atlantic, with only the Ebro flowing into the Mediterranean. Most become unnavigable a short way inland, making them useless for moving goods or, during invasions, troops. The Rio Guadalquivir is the only one that's navigable inland. This means that Seville is the country's only inland river port capable of accommodating oceangoing ships, which is why, on occasions, Seville has been Spain's biggest city. It's also why the Moors, who arrived in the eighth century, established a caliphate, and stayed for eight hundred years, were able to set up their seat of power as far north as Córdoba. Limited though they are, these rivers are vital for irrigation of the agricultural regions, and in modern times as a source of hydroelectric power. But Spain is generally a dry country, to the extent that there is the threat of desertification. The mountain ranges in the south run across the Iberian Peninsula east to west and act as a giant barrier to the moist Atlantic air. Galicia and the Cantabrian Mountains reap the benefit, but this leaves the Meseta plains with little rainfall, thus putting pressure on resources. On the Mediterranean coast excessive pumping of groundwater around porous rock areas has allowed seawater to encroach and salinate the land. This leads to sometimes fractious negotiations about resources among the regions. Many countries have disputes with neighbors over water allocation; Spain's are internal.

The difficulties in moving goods and people, due to the mountains and rivers, are among the factors that have held back the creation of a strong, centralized state and maintained regional identities and languages. Madrid has attempted to overcome these geographical barriers via rail and road. The first train line was built in 1848, linking the 18 miles between the port towns of Barcelona and Mataró. After that, most lines began in Madrid and radiated out in a spoke system. The modern road system was joined up properly only in the second half of the last century; the first short stretch of motorway opened in 1969, again linking Barcelona and Mataró. But while national governments have been determined to create "the Spanish," the Catalans, Basques, Galicians, and others have been determined to remain what they are—and geography has helped to separate them. The Despeñaperros, for example, a stunning, sheer-walled river gorge, is the only major natural route through the 300-mile-long Sierra Morena mountains separating Andalusia from the Meseta.

Spain's position at the far southwest of Europe meant that from antiquity it was peopled from both Europe and North Africa, including the Carthaginians and Romans. Hispania was part of the Roman Empire for six hundred years. Despite building only a handful of settlements for Roman civilians, the Romans left a lasting impression on the country's architecture, religion, and language, laying the broad foundations of an Iberian Peninsula–wide culture. Latin crumbled, but from it emerged Castilian, Catalan, Galician, and Portuguese.

And here come the Visigoths! By contrast with the Romans, the Germanic invaders from the north who took their place left little of themselves behind, despite being part of Spanish history for several centuries. In 710 the Visigoth king Witiza died and Hispania was split between rival claimants. This is usually a recipe for disaster, especially if one side invites a foreign army to invade. A house divided cannot stand, and the Visigoths' house was so weakened that the roof fell in almost overnight. The facts are opaque, but it appears that Witiza's family appealed to Muslim armies in North Africa to help defeat their rival, King Roderick. The response appears to have been "Nice country—we'll take it."

In May 711, Tariq ibn Ziyad landed at Gibraltar with an army of 7,000 men. By mid-July he had routed Roderick's forces and taken the opportunity to kill him. From there Ziyad headed north and occupied the capital, Toledo. An 18,000-strong army arrived as reinforcements and within a couple of years the Muslims controlled a majority of the peninsula, which they called Al-Andalus.

They made repeated raids north of the Pyrenees, but then came the Battle of Tours, which many historians believe preserved Christianity in Europe. In 732 a huge army advancing north to the Loire River was met by the Frankish leader Charles Martel and, against the odds, the Franks triumphed. Martel believed the Muslims had to be kept in Iberia or Christian Europe would fall. A thousand years later, the great British historian Edward Gibbon agreed: "The Rhine is not more impassable than the Nile or Euphrates, and the Arabian fleet might have sailed without a naval combat into the mouth of the Thames."

Had Martel failed, there would have been no Charlemagne (Martel's grandson). He established a buffer zone south of the Pyrenees in part of what is now Catalonia, and the region became the east flank of what would grow to become the *reconquista* (reconquest) of Iberia. After Tours the Muslims eventually fell back, and from 756 to 1031 settled for the establishment of the Andalusian Umayyad dynasty, controlling about two-thirds of Iberia.

The capital, Córdoba, was probably unrivaled anywhere in the world for its civilization. Libraries were set up, literature, science, and architecture flourished, and Muslim scholars brought knowledge and a reawakening of culture to Western Europe. Arabic in particular left its mark on Spain: more Spanish words are taken from Arabic than from any other language apart from Latin. The very name Gibraltar comes from Tariq ibn Ziyad: the rock became known as "Jabal Tariq" (Tariq Mountain).

When the caliphate collapsed in 1031, it shattered into mini-kingdoms. The Christian authorities saw their chance to liberate once Christian lands from Islamic rule, and in the 1060s Pope Alexander II offered forgiveness of sin to any warriors prepared to join the fight. By 1085 Toledo, the key to the Meseta central region, had been retaken—a key moment both in terms of the military outcome and how Spain and Europe would develop.

In 1212 Christian forces broke through the Despeñaperros pass and by 1250 almost all of Iberia was back under Christian rule, the exception being the kingdom of Granada on the southern coastline. Granada, seeing which way the tide was turning, chose to pay tribute to Castile and managed to endure for almost another 250 years—time enough to build many of the palaces of the magnificent Alhambra.

It's easy to think of the *reconquista* as a unified project, but because of Spain's geography the northern Christian kingdoms often acted unilaterally. In the northeast, Aragon might be conducting an offensive aimed at gaining a particular piece of territory, while in the northwest Galicia could be in a period of regrouping and planning its next campaign. The reconquest went south in strips, not as a wave, which meant that even as modern Spain began to be pieced together, it remained in pieces.

Fast-forward to 1469 and we see the beginning of the end of the Muslim presence. Isabella I of Castile married Ferdinand of Aragon, and the crowns of Aragon and Castile were unified. In geographical terms that meant the northeast and west of Spain were united. It was a limited political union with few economic effects, and there were still autonomous regions, but it was a key part of the birth pangs of modern Spain. A great leap forward followed within two decades.

In 1482 the royal couple, known as the Catholic Monarchs, launched a decade-long wave of attacks on Granada. In 1492 the emirate surrendered, Granada was incorporated into Castile, and eight hundred years of Muslim rule in Iberia came to an end. The Muslims had blazed a trail across the land and shone very brightly. By the standards of the time their brutality was no worse than that of others; they advanced knowledge, and for the most part oversaw a period of relative religious freedom. Christians and Jews lived under restrictions, had to pay the non-Muslim *jizya* tax, wear badges denoting their faith, and suffer a host of other indignities, but they were not forced to convert or die, nor to live in ghettos.

Isabella and Ferdinand, on the other hand, had already taken over the Spanish Inquisition from the Catholic Church in a bid to unite Spain under one religion. With the *reconquista* complete, Muslims and Jews were given a choice: convert, be exiled, or die.

The Jews had been on the peninsula for more than one thousand years, but in March 1492 they were given four months to leave and forbidden to take gold, money, horses, or arms with them. Historians differ over the numbers expelled, but forty thousand is a modern estimate. Spain has never had a significant Jewish population since. The expulsion was officially renounced only in 1968.

In 1502 attention turned to the Muslims. There were many conversions, among them some who continued to practice Islam in secret. The converted became known as Little Moors, endured suspicion about an "enemy within," and in 1609 were expelled. Several hundred thousand were forced out; the kingdom of Valencia lost a third of its inhabitants, leaving its agricultural sector in ruins for a generation.

Alas, polls suggest that the depths of Spain's antisemitic roots mean they have been difficult to pull out of its culture. This is reflected in a handful of words still used by Spaniards, often without realizing how offensive they are; for example, *judiada* means "a dirty trick" or "cruel act," and in the city of León a drink called *matar judíos*—"kill Jews"—is still consumed during Holy Week. It took until 2014 for the village of Castrillo Matajudios (Camp Kill Jews) to change its name. A few years ago, I was about to go on assignment to Israel. The woman in the flat above me, a warm, smiling, stout sixty-something from northern Spain, was concerned enough about my well-being to drag me to one side and hiss: "Tim. Be careful of the Jews!"

It's true that many European countries are reexamining their vocabularies in the light of modern sensibilities, but Spain seems to have more offensive terms than most. In the province of Extremadura lies the village of Valle de Matamoros, or Kill the Moors Valley, and Matamoros is also a surname in Spain, albeit a relatively rare one. For centuries, from the Inquisition all the way up to the end of the Franco era, one of the ways in which Spain sought to define itself as a unified country was as being innately Catholic—indeed, a defender of the faith. Minorities such as Jews and Muslims were always useful as examples of "the other."

Spain's monarchs believed they had a religious duty to convert as many people as possible, not just within Spain but also beyond. Sailing into this scenario as the Jews were being expelled in 1492 was a forty-year-old Italian adventurer named Christopher Columbus who'd been badgering the Catholic Monarchs for years to fund an expedition to find a quicker sea route to the Indies. Isabella and Ferdinand came up with enough money for him to get to Hispaniola (now Haiti and the Dominican Republic) and find a small amount of gold, which in a letter to the queen he spun into "vast mines." The reaction of the court was: "Gold! Gold you say? We're going to need a bigger boat." The riches subsequently discovered in Latin America would help Spain become the most powerful country in the world.

Naturally, others wanted to get in on the act. By 1493, Portugal was threatening war to claim land Columbus had stumbled upon. Fortunately for the two countries, if not for the peoples of Latin America, Pope Alexander VI felt that he had "the authority of Almighty God" to create an imaginary line running north to south down the Atlantic. All new land found west of it would be Spain's, anything east Portugal's, and anyone who said otherwise would be thrown out of the Church. And so peace was maintained, apart from the centuries of war, looting, pillaging, slavery, and pestilence that the Treaty of Tordesillas, as it was called, helped to stimulate in the conquered lands.

The Jews had gone, the Muslims were going, and so were Isabella and Ferdinand. By 1516, both were dead even as Spain advanced into its Golden Age— from about 1500 to 1681. It was marked by vast sums of money, coming in from the gold and silver mines of South America, that funded an increased standard of living, an expanding military, and brilliance in architecture, literature, and painting.

But Spain's regions continued to develop with differences in identity, politics, and economics. The internal problems created by Spain's geography, the cracks holding back development, were papered over by a river of gold and silver from 6,000 miles away, one that flowed into the Atlantic and back to the kingdom.

Much of the wealth was spent on European conflicts. This meant there was less money for the Atlantic naval forces required to safeguard the routes funding the whole enterprise. By the mid-1600s the Spanish were losing control of the sea routes. Spanish merchant ships in the Caribbean would take on board

Chinese goods hauled across land from Central American ports on the Pacific. They would join vessels loaded with silver and gold, and, guarded by military galleons, head out to Cuba and onward to Spain. But the pirates of the Caribbean learned how to pick them off. Word spread that Europe's most powerful nation was becoming vulnerable. In earlier decades England's Elizabethan "sea dogs," Walter Raleigh and Francis Drake, never ones to miss a bit of looting and murder, had joined in with gusto, further undermining Spain's revenue flow and setting the scene for what was to follow.

To stem the losses, in 1588 King Philip II of Spain came up with a cunning plan, but failed to know which way the wind would blow. The big idea was to sail 130 warships into the English Channel and smash the English fleet, ending its ability to support the Dutch in their battles with Spain and steal Spain's treasure. As a bonus, Spain could invade England, overthrow the Protestant queen, then cross back to finally quell the Dutch rebellion. They had by far the heavier ships and ferocious firepower. What, other than everything, could possibly go wrong?

Having an admiral in charge who had sailed the open sea might have helped. Appointed four months before this armada sailed, the Duke of Medina Sidonia had told his king: "I know by the small experience I have had afloat that I soon become seasick." The drain on funds had also left the Spanish navy in poor shape. And when they reached Calais, Medina Sidonia was left waiting for essential equipment without a deep-water port in which to shelter. The English seized their chance.

During the following battle the armada suffered serious losses and its formation was scattered. It sailed up toward the North Sea to regroup. It was time to abandon the mission and head home, but the Spanish have a saying: "*La geographia manda*"—Geography controls everything. Geography was against them.

The Spanish needed to return south, but the winds blew in the wrong direction and the English were situated between them and the route back. They headed farther north, but as they rounded the tip of northern Scotland they ran into an unusually early North Atlantic storm. Many ships were driven onto the rocks of the Irish coast in freezing-cold weather. When the remnants of the fleet made it home in October, only about sixty ships docked. As many as fifteen thousand men had been lost, and with them Spain's reputation as the world's greatest navy. A new century was on the horizon and the balance of power was shifting.

Spain simply wasn't ready to give up its perception of being the dominant power and unsuccessfully continued to wage war in the Netherlands to hold on to territory. During many of these years, the Spanish crown couldn't even control Spain.

The Basque uprising of the 1630s was triggered when Madrid, seeking funds for the wars, imposed a tax on Bilbao's cloth industry and requisitioned its huge salt stores. It didn't go down well. The rebellion lasted three years and it took the intervention of the army to crush it. The Basques never forgot.

In 1640 it was the turn of the Catalans. Spain launched a military campaign from Catalonia into France, the purpose of which appears to have been to ensure that Catalonia would have to be involved in the war. If the Catalans were fighting for their country, the logic went, they'd support the Spanish army. Somehow the Catalans, not known for their enthusiastic support for Madrid, failed to follow this line of thought.

Catalan leaders joined with the French, whose troops crossed the border, and together they defeated the Spanish forces. However, in 1648 France withdrew, and by 1652, after starving the city of Barcelona into submission, Madrid was back in charge.

The Catalans call the conflict la Guerra dels Segadors—the Reapers' War— in homage to the peasantry. The anthem of Catalonia, officially adopted in 1994, is called "The Reapers." The song can be traced back to 1640, the words to 1899, and it still causes consternation in Castile:

> Catalonia triumphant
> shall again be rich and bountiful.
> Drive away these people,
> Who are so conceited and so arrogant.

Chorus: Strike with your sickle!

> . . .
> May the enemy tremble,
> upon seeing our symbol.
> Just as we cut golden ears of wheat,
> when the time calls we cut off chains.

Spain's reputation, economy, and population were in decline, and it was racked with instability and violence. Over the course of the seventeenth century, the country's population fell from about 8.5 million to only 6.6 million in 1700. Military fatalities averaged 10,000 or so a year, emigration to the colonies another 5,000, and extreme poverty and recurrent plagues also held back growth. As it headed into the 1700s, Spain remained a major power with territories around the globe, but it was in poor shape to hang on to what it had, fighting numerous wars and losing many of its European lands, including Naples, Sicily, Milan, and Gibraltar, which the British seized in 1704.

Conflict plagued the eighteenth century. Spain both fought and allied with France before seeing their joint fleet defeated by the British at Trafalgar in 1805. Two years later, French troops crossed into the Iberian Peninsula, sparking what the Spanish call the War of Independence, but known as the Peninsular War in English-speaking countries. The word "guerrilla" comes from this conflict, being derived from the Spanish word for "war"—*guerra*. It began to be used to describe groups of Spanish irregulars who took a fearsome toll on the French.

Latin Americans were asking what legitimacy the mother country now had over them. Rebellions began in the north and south, led by Simón Bolívar and José de San Martín. After taking control over their regions, they converged on the center and met on the Pacific coast. Bolívar then mopped up the remnants of loyalist resistance in Upper Peru, which was renamed Bolivia in his honor. With Mexico taking a similar path, Latin America was free of Spanish control by 1826.

Spain, however, was not free of violence. On and on it went through the 1800s, urban against rural, liberals against traditionalists, region against region, Spaniard against Spaniard. The civil wars helped the military to embed themselves into the political machinery of the country. Staunch Catholics were pitted against liberals attempting to reduce Church power. During the various rebellions, attempted coups d'état, and outright war, both sides committed atrocities that contributed to a lasting bitterness that would spill into the twentieth century.

In the second half of the nineteenth century, Madrid attempted to catch up with the Industrial Revolution it saw rapidly developing in Britain, Germany, and France, three rivals who all developed a greater sense of unity than Spain did. However, the slow growth of the rail and road network struggled to knit the economy together and it continued to trail those of countries farther north. The population remained divided, with many still more loyal to region than country.

The last of the old empire had broken free in 1898, with the loss of Puerto Rico, Cuba, and the Philippines. Although the Ottoman Empire had been dubbed the sick man of Europe, Spain was not in the best of health either. And if it was no longer a great power, there was even less reason for its regions to identify as Spanish.

Despite managing to stay out of the First World War, Spain was not immune to the clash of right- and left-wing politics that was increasingly being felt across Europe with the rise of fascism and communism. It was what passed for a democracy in that age, but the roots were weak. A military coup brought the dictator Miguel Primo de Rivera to power in 1923, but his rule lasted only six and a half years. When elections were held in 1931, the Republicans won, and the new government declared Spain a republic. It set about removing senior army officers, attacking the privileges of the Church, nationalizing landed estates, and giving large wage increases to industrial workers. In short, it guaranteed opposition from the four most powerful forces in the land: the Church, the military, the landed gentry, and the industrialists.

It was less than a year before the next coup. It failed, but the chaos around it forced another election in 1933. In came a right-wing government, which immediately overturned the policies of its predecessor, including those granting Catalonia greater freedom. In 1936, amid a wave of strikes, brutal suppression, and an economy in tatters, another election was held. This time the left came back to power in the shape of the united Popular Front, but the differing factions were now gravitating toward the extremes and Spain was sliding toward the abyss of civil war.

On July 12, José Castillo, a Republican loyalist and a lieutenant in the Popular Front government's paramilitary Assault Guards, was assassinated. Revenge was swift, and equally brutal. The same night police officers and left-wing gunmen raided the home of José Calvo Sotelo, a leading right-wing politician. As he was driven away in a police van, he was shot in the back of the neck.

Thousands of right-wing supporters attended Sotelo's funeral before marching into the city center to be confronted by the Assault Guards, who shot dead several protesters. The murder of Sotelo was regarded by the right wing as the final outrage. Three days after the funeral, the army uprising began when the Army of Africa, based in Melilla, mutinied under the command of four generals, including Francisco Franco, triggering the Spanish Civil War.

Over the next two years, the conflict raged bitterly. With Hitler and Mussolini supplying a trained army, it was only a matter of time before the Nationalists, as the right-wing forces were known, would grind down resistance, despite Soviet attempts to arm the Republicans.

By the winter of 1938–39 the Republican forces were exhausted, their food stocks depleted by blockades and the 3 million refugees who had fled the savage repression of Franco's forces in conquered territory. That January, a half million civilians and soldiers left Barcelona in freezing conditions, heading for the French border. Some, in what became known as La Retirada (the Retreat), had to walk 100 miles even as German and Italian planes strafed the columns.

Franco's forces entered Barcelona, and at the end of February Britain and France recognized Franco as head of the government. The following month, 200,000 troops entered Madrid unopposed. Many citizens lined the streets to celebrate their victory; many others spent a sleepless night fearing the inevitable revenge Franco would wreak.

April saw Franco accept an unconditional surrender. Historians differ as to the number of those killed; estimates range from half a million to a million if hunger and lack of health care are factored in. Tens of thousands of men and women were executed by both sides and the postwar period saw thousands more Republicans murdered as Franco's version of fascism tightened its grip on every aspect of life. Early in the war one of Franco's generals, Emilio Mola, had said, "It is necessary to spread terror. We have to create the impression of mastery, eliminating without scruples or hesitation all those who do not think as we do."

A cult of personality emerged around the general who became known as El Caudillo—the leader. The liberal laws of the Republicans were swept away. In their stead came a wave of legislation by which women were banned from being university lecturers, and not only could they not serve as judges, they couldn't even testify in trials. The Church did not demur at the concept that divine providence had sent Franco to save the nation, and the junta promoted the idea that the nation was a single, unitary entity. That meant regional identities such as Basque and Catalan would have to be quashed. The languages of both provinces were banned from the public sphere, backed by a government slogan that said, "*Si eres Español, habla Español!*" ("If you are Spanish, speak Spanish!") Catalan and Basque retreated into the private sphere, spoken at home, but every syllable was a form of rejection of Madrid's authority.

Franco ruled until 1975. He intended to create a homogeneous Spain but, like many before him, was defeated by geography, which kept alive the regional languages and identities for so long. One of the fortresses he ran up against was the Camp de Les Corts stadium—home to Barcelona Football Club (a soccer team). Franco was known to support Real Madrid, not so much as a fan but to create a symbol of Spanish success. He could hardly promote a club from a region that wanted autonomy. The regime had changed Barcelona FC's name into Castilian and altered the club badge so that the Catalan flag on it resembled the Spanish flag. But it couldn't alter the spirit of the fans. Thousands would sing in Catalan—after all, the police could hardly arrest them all. The tradition survived the move to Camp Nou in the late 1950s. Across in the Basque Country, supporters of Athletic Bilbao showed their view of Madrid in a similar manner. Many in both cities still do.

The *sardana*, a Catalan folk dance, was also banned. It involves people linking hands in a circle that widens and shrinks as they join or leave. Naturally, the Catalans performed it wherever and whenever they could as an act of defiance, the circle symbolizing unity.

Others were more direct in their opposition. Throughout the 1940s Franco's Civil Guard forces were harassed by what they termed "bandits" but were actually guerrilla fighters. Some operated from across the border in France, others from mountainous regions inside Spain, sometimes surfacing in the cities. However, the regime's grip on power was never seriously threatened. Details are scarce, but studies suggest that several thousand guerrillas were killed, along with several hundred Civil Guards. The last rebel to die is thought to have been José Castro Veiga, shot in Galicia in 1965.

The state-run media was silent about most of these events and the public knew little of the situation; they were trying to make ends meet in an economy battered by war and which had fallen to levels last previously seen in 1900. Franco imposed an economic system known as autarky—self-sufficiency, state control of prices, and limited trade with other countries. It had a devastating effect. The 1940s became known as Los Años de Hambre—the Years of Hunger.

Despite this, the regime found the money and (forced) labor to fortify the French border with several thousand bunkers, forming the Pyrenees Line. The military knew that throughout the long, violent past many attackers had entered the peninsula by going through the low-lying corridors on each side of the mountain range, into the Basque Country and Catalonia. Many of these bunkers can still be found today, abandoned and overgrown with weeds; they are a physical reminder of the partially self-imposed isolation of the Franco years. The regime felt that foreign influences weakened the purity and strength of Spain; as one of its top generals said, "Spain is not Europe, it never was."

Franco did have friends; the problem was they were called Adolf and Benito. With Hitler's Germany and Mussolini's Italy destroyed, Franco's Spain was alone, stewing in its fascist juices. The Western powers would have nothing to do with a man who had sent fifty thousand troops in the División Azul to fight alongside the Nazis on the Eastern Front. After the war Spain was a pariah state, shut out of the United Nations, the Marshall Plan, and NATO.

Franco bided his time. He knew the British prized stability on the peninsula due to their ownership of Gibraltar and would be unlikely to support a violent overthrow of his regime. More important, the realpolitik forced upon the Western powers by the Cold War could be turned to Spain's advantage. The new threat in Europe was not fascism but Soviet communism.

The Americans in particular were concerned that if the Soviets invaded Western Europe, some of Stalin's forces might swing southwest into Spain. They also thought of Spain in terms of their own "strategic depth"—a space in which they could build defenses and fall back if they failed to stop the Red Army at the Rhine. A 1947 study by the US Joint War Plans Committee suggested that within three months of attacking Western Europe the Soviets could arrive at the Pyrenees. They would then take twenty days to cross the mountains, before splitting and advancing along the Mediterranean coast to Barcelona and the Atlantic coast to Lisbon. Within forty days they would be in Gibraltar, controlling access to the Mediterranean and the Atlantic. Tentative negotiations were opened with Franco to gain military basing rights. They took years, but in 1951 President Harry Truman made it clear that policy toward Spain was changing, saying, "I don't like Franco and I never will, but I won't let my personal feelings override the convictions of you military men."

The Pact of Madrid was signed two years later, granting the US Army, Air Force, and Navy bases in return for $2 billion worth of military and economic aid over twenty years. The French were opposed, nervous that the Americans might abandon the defense of France in the case of war. In this scenario, democratic Europe's last stand would be made in fascist Spain.

Truman did not have to meet Franco; that dubious honor went to his successor, Dwight D. Eisenhower, in 1959, on the first-ever visit to Spain by a serving American president. Fewer than twenty years earlier, Franco had been filmed walking in step with Hitler while giving the fascist salute to a Nazi guard of honor. Now he paraded around the streets of Madrid with an American president as a Spanish band played "The Yellow Rose of Texas." It was a bitter blow to those sections of society that yearned for a democratic Spain.

Nevertheless, everyday life became a little easier. The agreement meant that Spain had to relax trading restrictions and allow foreign investment. The quiet abandonment of autarky contributed to inflation, but by the 1960s Spain experienced an economic boom and Spaniards rushed to buy consumer goods such as washing machines and TV sets, items that had become the norm in Western Europe.

In the 1960s the dictator looked ahead to a post-Franco era. By 1969, at the age of seventy-six, his health had declined, and he signed a law of succession naming Prince Juan Carlos to succeed him as head of state and king. Franco believed Carlos would acquiesce in maintaining the political structures, the regime believed he could be their puppet, and the public believed he neither would nor could change their lives. He proved everyone wrong.

Francisco Franco died at eighty-two in November 1975, after thirty-six years of totalitarian rule. The junta hoped to rule as kingmaker, but they hadn't counted on the king playing state maker.

The president of the Cortes, the Spanish parliament, Alejandro Rodríguez de Valcárcel, said, "It was the prince's task to succeed Franco only in his ceremonial functions." But in his speech the new king contradicted regime philosophy: "Spain must be part of Europe, and Spaniards are Europeans." It wasn't spelled out, but to be truly a part of political, as well as geographical, Europe, Spain would have to become a democracy.

He had to tread a fine line, but Juan Carlos set about dismantling the political machine. He knew he must speak to all sides in Spain's many divides. He'd already said he would be "king of all the Spaniards," a tacit recognition that the centuries-long project to create one people had failed; one of his next moves was to visit Catalonia and Galicia, giving speeches recognizing each region's individuality. At one point in Galicia, where Franco was from, he even spoke briefly in Gallego, the Galician language, which is closer to Portuguese than Spanish, and ended with a rousing "*viva Galicia!*" New times had arrived.

Political parties were reintroduced and restrictions on the media further loosened. The old guard attempted to block reforms, and there was constant fear of another military coup, which might trigger a bloodbath. Nevertheless, the king navigated his way along the road to democracy. In 1976 a referendum was held. In a turnout of 77.7 percent of voters, 97.4 percent supported proposed reforms for Spain to become a parliamentary monarchy, with all political parties legalized including the Communists, who were most feared by the Francoist remnants.

The next year Spain held its first democratic election since 1936. Of 350 seats, the center-right party won 165 and formed the government. The Social Democrats came second with 118 seats, and the Communist party third with 20. As important as the winner was the loser. The AP party, founded by former Franco loyalists, won just 16 seats. One, Manuel Fraga, managed to hold the right wing together as a political force but might be best remembered for accidentally shooting Franco's daughter in the buttocks while on a hunting trip. Either way, the Spanish people had overwhelmingly and categorically rejected Francoism.

However, Francoism refused to die. In 1981, two hundred members of the Civil Guard led by Lieutenant Colonel Antonio Tejero entered the parliament building in an attempted coup d'état. It's easy to think of Tejero as a pantomime villain, with his magnificent moustache and pistol-waving antics. At one point he tried to wrestle Deputy Prime Minister General Manuel Gutiérrez Mellado to the ground, giving up when the sixty-eight-year-old general refused to lie down. But this was deadly serious stuff. Tejero, who was only one of the military ringleaders, fired shots into the air, as did some of the guards, using submachine guns. He pointed his weapon at the prime minister, Adolfo Suárez, who calmly faced him down. All this was captured on live TV.

At 1:00 a.m. King Juan Carlos appeared on television wearing full military uniform to say: "The Crown, the symbol of the permanence and unity of the nation, cannot tolerate, in any form, actions or attitudes of people attempting by force to interrupt the democratic process." And with that it was over. As arrests were being made elsewhere, a dejected Tejero emerged from the Cortes at midday to be taken into custody. He and other ringleaders were sentenced to thirty years in prison, decades in which Spanish democracy took root.

The victory of the Socialist party in the 1982 elections marked the first government in which no members had served the Franco regime. Spain joined NATO in 1982, became a member of the EU in 1986, and adopted the euro in 1999. Its new constitution, which divided the country into seventeen regional administrations (now nineteen), recognizes historic and geographical differences. But the oldest tensions still remain. That is true for Galicia, Catalonia, the Basque Country, and, to a lesser extent, Andalusia.

In a dictatorship the "solution" to regions seeking degrees of autonomy or independence is usually outright repression, but in a democracy, with its adherence to "the will of the people," it is much more complicated. Joining the EU was supposed to be the answer to the questions about Spain's regionalism, relative backwardness, and authoritarian tendencies. As long ago as 1910 the philosopher José Ortega y Gasset wrote: "Spain is the problem and Europe the solution." Perhaps it was; many Spanish people were content to relinquish degrees of sovereignty in order to gain from not just the economic benefits of the EU but also its requirements for good governance. Within the EU, Spaniards are second only to Romanians in mistrust of their own government. However, the existence of the EU, and Spain's membership in it, has also opened up the possibility of regions being European but not Spanish. The same is true in the UK, Belgium, Italy, and elsewhere.

In recent years the most violent opposition to rule from Madrid came in the Basque Country. The region consists of seven historic provinces that were split between Spain and France in 1512. The Spanish side is about half the size of Northern Ireland and contains 2.2 million people. It begins as the western Pyrenees slope down toward the Bay of Biscay, then continues for about 110 miles along the coastline, where a majority of the population live and which houses heavy industries. The interior is mostly mountainous, a feature common among peoples who retain a distinct difference from near neighbors, and is marked in the south by the Ebro River. The geographical area may span two states, but many Basques consider it still to be one nation, which they call Euskal Herria. Its language, Euskara, spoken by about a quarter of the population, predates the Indo-European tongues of the rest of Europe and is unrelated to any of them. For example, "I live in Bilbao" translates as *"Ni Bilbon bizi naiz"* and is constructed as "I Bilbao in to live am." Its roots remain a mystery, but they were strong enough to see off Latin, Arabic, and Spanish.

This sense of nationhood has always driven calls for degrees of autonomy or even outright secession. Its most modern form came in the shape of ETA, a group founded in 1959. The initials stand for Euzkadi ta Askatasuna (Basque Homeland and Freedom). In the Franco years Euskara was banned from being spoken in public, at risk of imprisonment. Birth and marriage certificates that featured Basque names were erased in civil registries and replaced with ones in Spanish. The regime had stripped the Basque territory of any autonomous status; however, ETA was formed not to regain that status but to create a Basque state straddling the Spanish-French border.

Its first victim was a police officer who was murdered in 1968. ETA went on to kill more than 850 people in a series of shootings and bombings targeting politicians, judges, and ordinary civilians. The state responded by hunting down ETA units but was accused of hundreds of cases of brutality against members of the public, which continued for years after the fall of the dictatorship.

In 1989 ETA bombed a Barcelona supermarket, killing twenty-one men, women, and children—the worst incident in four decades of murder and mayhem. However, the atrocity that did them the most damage was the murder of a single man, Miguel Ángel Blanco. In 1997 ETA kidnapped the twenty-nine-year-old Basque councillor and demanded that its members, in jails across the country, be transferred to Basque prisons within forty-eight hours. The event shocked the country; everyone knew that the government would not give in, and 6 million people came out on the streets to demand Blanco's release by ETA. Two days after his abduction, he was taken to a forest, forced to his knees, and shot in the back of the head.

This was too much, even for many ardent supporters of independence. What public support ETA had began to seep away. The 1978 Spanish constitution had reinstated autonomy, and the region controls its own police force, taxation, and media, enough to satisfy a majority of the population. After several broken cease-fires, ETA finally agreed to a "complete cessation of violence" in 2011, and in 2018 announced it was disbanding. The Basques retain their sense of difference, and all recent opinion polls suggest they accept that they can exist as an autonomous nation within the modern Spanish state. The situation was beautifully expressed by the president of the Basque Nationalist Party, Andoni Ortuzar, in an interview with the *Financial Times*'s David Gardner: "The average Basque need meet the Spanish state on three occasions: to get a driving licence, a passport or a pension. The rest is what we, the Basque institutions, give them."

Many Catalans wanted more—full independence—and their fight to get it has led to the biggest crisis since the 1981 putsch. Since the seventeenth century there have been numerous attempts to break free from Madrid, but this latest bid caught many people by surprise as the Catalans too had been granted a large degree of autonomy after Franco's death.

Catalonia is the wealthiest region in the country, a fact that has played a role in the recent upheavals. It is about four times larger than the Basque Country, approximately the same size as Belgium, and has a population of 7.5 million, most of whom speak Catalan. It is wedged into a triangular shape in the most northeastern corner of Spain. The region is framed by the Mediterranean Sea to its east and the Pyrenees to its north; to the west the Ebro River marks the border with Aragon, and to the south is Valencia. As with the Basques, the majority of the population now live near the coastline.

Catalonia became wealthy through its textile industry, but these days has a diversified economy including heavy industry and tourism. This century, supporters of independence have been quick to tell the rest of Spain that Catalonia pays more into the national coffers than it receives in services. But the system of paying in, and receiving, is complex and the percentages can be argued in different ways. Nevertheless, it is clear that despite having only 16 percent of the population, Catalonia accounts for almost 20 percent of Spain's GDP and a quarter of its exports.

This meant that when the 2008 economic crisis hit, the independence movement was able to stir up old grievances about the "injustice" of Catalan taxes being used by Madrid. By 2014 an "informal" independence referendum was held, followed in 2017 by one approved by Catalonia's parliament, but declared illegal by Spain's Supreme Court. Both resulted in majorities for independence, but on very low turnouts. The run-up to the 2017 vote revealed the depths of the bitter split between Barcelona and Madrid. A few days before polls opened, Spanish police seized millions of ballot papers from a warehouse, arrested officials, and moved to assert control of the Catalan police. The day of the vote saw riot police using batons to prevent people from entering polling stations. The chaos meant that claims of a 42 percent turnout and a 90 percent yes vote were difficult to prove. What was clear was that most Catalans who were against independence boycotted the vote.

Despite this, the Catalan parliament declared independence, leading Madrid to dismiss the Catalan cabinet, suspend autonomy, and impose direct rule, citing Article 155 of the Spanish constitution, which allows the national government to intervene if it decides that a regional government has not complied with the obligations of the constitution. Some Catalan leaders were thrown in jail, others fled abroad.

Spain was not going to lose Catalonia without a fight. There are many reasons for this, including national pride and economics, but one sometimes overlooked is geographical. Throughout Spain's history, armed forces from the north have moved into the country by using the narrow belts of flatter land on each side of the Pyrenees—the Basque Country in the west and Catalonia in the east. The most efficient way of defending Spain in the north is to block these corridors; therefore, the idea of an independent Catalonia or Basque state controlling them is anathema to Madrid. If either were hostile to Spain, it would become a nightmare. There are now road tunnels through the Pyrenees, but from a military perspective these can be easily blocked. The corridors also lead into Spain's major land-based supply routes from the rest of Europe, and the two regions are home to some of Spain's biggest ports, including Barcelona and Bilbao.

Many other countries are taking a keen interest in this recent example of Spain's long struggle with insurrection. If an independent Catalonia was frozen out of the EU, China and Russia would attempt to make new friends and influence people. Russia has spent two decades trying to get a foothold in Greece; it would dearly love to achieve the same in the western Mediterranean. However, more plausible would be Beijing's purchasing power, barreling into the ports of Barcelona, offering investment and trade as part of its global Belt and Road Initiative. China has been blocked in the EU due to the union's economic clout and rules against individual trade deals, so instead China has been knocking on the door of Europe's non-EU countries and is a serious player in the Balkans, especially Serbia. During the Covid-19 crisis, Serbia's politicians openly spoke of how the EU failed to help them but praised Beijing's efforts. If Catalonia was a state, and Spain used its veto to prevent EU membership, the Catalans would be open to the Chinese strategy.

This is partly why the EU has been lukewarm about Catalonia's right of self-determination. When the Spanish police drove would-be independence voters out of polling stations and off the streets it looked terrible, but the national government argued that Catalonia did not have the right unilaterally to decide to hold the vote—and Brussels was notably restrained in its response. The day after the referendum the EU statement looked as if it could have been drafted in Madrid: "Under the Spanish constitution, yesterday's vote in Catalonia was not legal . . . this is an internal matter for Spain that has to be dealt with in line with the constitutional order of Spain . . . these are times for unity and stability, not divisiveness and fragmentation."

The EU and leaders of its member states would like the Catalonia problem to go away and so were further troubled in February 2021, when elections in Catalonia saw independence-supporting parties win a small majority in the regional parliament for the first time. An independent Catalonia would embolden those campaigning for an independent Corsica, Scotland, Flanders, Sicily, Bavaria, etc. Every secessionist movement in Europe would learn lessons. There's a paradox here. True believers in the EU "project" still want to move toward ever closer union, eventually establishing a single entity with one currency and fiscal policy. At the same time, Brussels promotes strong regional governance through its cohesion policy, which divides the EU into more than 250 regions. But endorsing stronger regional governance risks encouraging separatism, and therefore the EU risks breaking up nation-states but with no guarantee that a separatist region would gain access to the EU.

Conversely, in the event of independence, the EU would be tempted to grant Catalonia membership in order to prevent China moving in, even though this would further encourage other regional nationalists. Brussels would also be nervous that if it did not allow Catalonia in, an alternative to the EU could be the European Free Trade Association (EFTA), which has access to EU markets. This brings us to the UK.

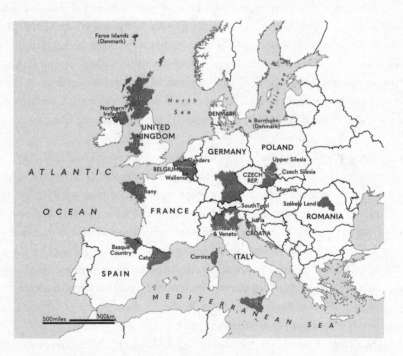

There are numerous separatist movements in Europe that could take encouragement from a successful independence movement in Catalonia.

Catalonian membership in EFTA alone would not unduly worry Brussels, but Catalonian membership in a UK-dominated EFTA would. If, in the future, the UK joined EFTA, it would create a much stronger organization, comprising Norway, Iceland, Lichtenstein, Switzerland, Catalonia, and the UK. This might tempt other EU nations to leave the union and join EFTA. This is indeed all "mights" and "coulds," and some EFTA countries are nervous about UK membership, but the EU has to factor in these scenarios and act accordingly—in the first instance, by supporting Spain's territorial integrity and, if that fails, by keeping its options open both to block China and prevent a stronger EFTA.

The UK is in a difficult position on Catalonia. It needs to support self-determination due to its position on the Falkland Islands and Gibraltar, but simultaneously cannot endorse Catalonian self-determination because it opposes Scottish independence. It backed Spain after the referendum, but sits uncomfortably between two stools.

Spain has wanted Gibraltar back ever since it was lost to the UK at the beginning of the eighteenth century. It's a prime piece of real estate guarding the exit and entrance to the Atlantic, and the Royal Navy has made good use of it down the centuries. The UK says it will abide by the wishes of the Gibraltarians. In 2002, when they were asked if they wanted to share sovereignty with Spain, 99 percent said, "No thank you."

If Gibraltar were under Madrid's control, it would form a key part of Spain's modern defense posture. The country has more than 5,000 miles of coastline to defend, and four-fifths of its imports come in by sea. It has the largest fishing fleet in the EU, part of which ventures as far as the Indian Ocean, and more than sixty islands, some of which, as we noted earlier, are a very long way indeed from the mainland. To protect this requires a large navy, and a large navy needs ports.

Fortunately for Spain it has many, including deepwater harbors. On the northwest tip of Galicia, the harbors at A Coruña and El Ferrol look out into the Atlantic and guard the approaches to France and the English Channel. The main base for the Mediterranean is in the southeast at Cartagena, which houses submarines as well as surface ships. This is also the headquarters of the Maritime Surveillance and Action Operations Center. It monitors the Mediterranean and the Atlantic up past the Canary Islands, and sends the information to a huge bunker in Madrid for action. In the south, Cádiz looks after the Straits Maritime Zone and protects the deepwater port of Seville 50 miles inland. The Spanish territories of Ceuta and Melilla on the Moroccan coast each house several thousand troops and limited naval assets.

The region between Morocco and Gibraltar is a crossroads for people and drug smuggling. Large quantities of both enter Europe via Spain having crossed the strait, which is the second-busiest shipping lane in the world. Every year thousands of migrants attempt to scale the fences separating Morocco and Spain, knowing they are the EU's border with Africa, but, despite the short distance, far fewer people cross into Europe via this route than they do from Libya to Italy. This is mostly because Libya is a failed state whereas Morocco has a functioning administration which cooperates with Spain. Both countries are acutely aware of the situation in the Sahel and fear that if the Sahel countries fall apart it will destabilize Morocco, with a knock-on effect on Ceuta, Melilla, and mainland Spain. Hence Spain is involved in training government forces in Mali and elsewhere.

The other main navy base is in the Canary Islands, which also hosts army and air force installations. The Canaries are up from the Gulf of Guinea, where Spain has economic interests and which is crucial for its trading routes and modern communications system via underwater cables that connect eighteen countries.

To achieve the defense of trade routes, shipping, and fishing fleets, the navy has about 130 ships, 20,000 personnel, and can call on 11,500 troops in the Infantería de Marina—the marines. They are backed by the army and air force, and the Americans and NATO. The US retains two bases in Spain, Naval Station Rota near Gibraltar and Morón Air Base located about 30 miles south of Seville. Spain is involved in Operation Atalanta, the EU's antipiracy naval mission off the Horn of Africa. When the UK withdrew from the EU, the mission's HQ was transferred to the part of the Rota naval base used by Spain.

For all its faults and problems, modern Spain is a success story. It survived the 2008–2009 financial crash, recovering to become one of Europe's largest economies. It has an excellent infrastructure and vibrant cities populated by people with the highest life expectancy in Europe.

It wrestles, as do its peers, with the issues of climate change, population movement, economic problems, and splintering politics, but it is in reasonable shape to take them on. Its coal has gone, it never had much oil or gas, but one-sixth of its energy needs now comes from hydropower and it has sunshine in abundance. Spain is one of Europe's leaders in renewable energy, especially solar and wind.

Spain will continue to face external pressures, but its main challenges come from within and are based on its geography. For the foreseeable future, the kingdom brought together in the 1500s will still have to balance the tensions of being a nation-state comprised of nations. Despite all this, though, the sentiment of Franco's general—"Spain is not Europe, it never was"—has never seemed less true.

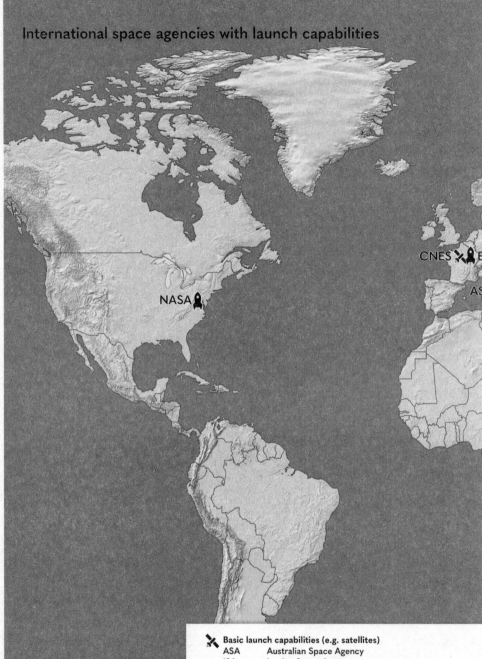

International space agencies with launch capabilities

CNES ✗🚀 E

AS

✗🚀 Basic launch capabilities (e.g. satellites)
ASA — Australian Space Agency
ISA — Iranian Space Agency
ISA — Israeli Space Agency
KCST — National Aerospace Development Administration
KARI — Korea Aerospace Research Institute
CNES — Centre National d'Études Spatiales
SSAU — State Space Agency of Ukraine
ASI — Italian Space Agency

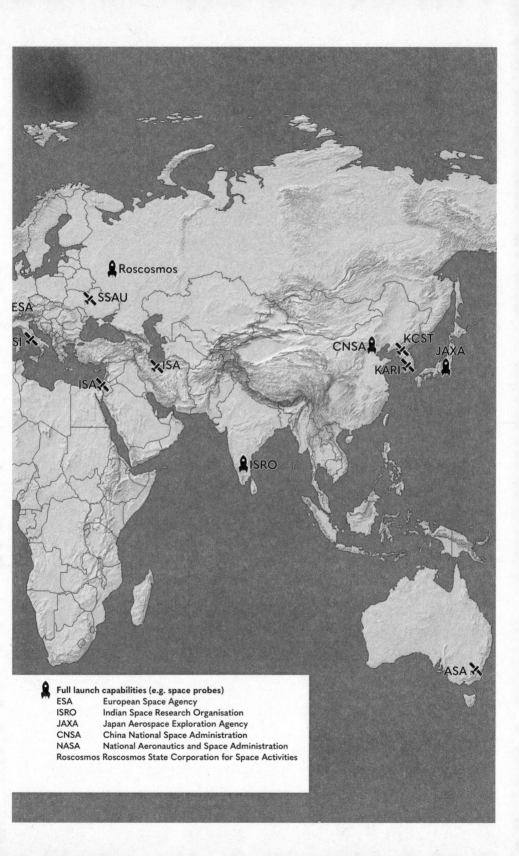

Roscosmos

SSAU

ESA

SI

ISA

ISA

CNSA

KCST

KARI

JAXA

ISRO

ASA

Full launch capabilities (e.g. space probes)
ESA   European Space Agency
ISRO   Indian Space Research Organisation
JAXA   Japan Aerospace Exploration Agency
CNSA   China National Space Administration
NASA   National Aeronautics and Space Administration
Roscosmos Roscosmos State Corporation for Space Activities

10

═══

SPACE

Once you're in Earth orbit, you're halfway to anywhere.

—Robert A. Heinlein, science fiction author and engineer

I f you establish a sovereign colony on the Moon, are you a colonialist? The Russians and Chinese think so, and they may have a point.

Ever since we pushed through Earth's atmosphere and out, edging a millimeter into infinity, space has become a political battleground. At the heart of this issue is not just the physical territory countries might try to claim—on the Moon or Mars, for example—but, as in previous centuries on Earth, the fueling stations required to get there, and the bottleneck points along the way. If we can't agree on a legal framework governing their use and the territories they lead to, it follows that we may end up fighting over them just as we have done on Earth for most of human history.

Alas, it appears almost written in the stars that we will compete for them. The "space race" now looks to be accelerating, bringing with it the temptation to go it alone, or at least with allies, to ensure "we" beat "them." In October 2020, the US, Japan, the UAE, Italy, the UK, Canada, Luxembourg, and Australia were the first space-faring nations to sign the Artemis Accords governing the exploration of the Moon and extraction of its resources. Signatories must inform one another of their activities during the operation to land the first woman, and thirteenth man, on the Moon by 2024. That is planned as the next giant step for mankind before creating Moon bases for mining purposes by 2028. In turn, these bases could be the launchpad to "enable human expansion across the solar system."

However, neither Russia nor China signed the accords. Both were lukewarm about the idea, but even if they had wanted to participate, they would have been excluded. Russia may be a NASA partner on the International Space Station, but it was frozen out after the newly formed US Space Force accused it of tracking US spy satellites in a dangerous and "unusual and disturbing manner." China cannot be part of the agreement because Congress has banned NASA from working with Beijing. Both Russia and China have their own plans for lunar bases, though, and are not about to allow rivals to establish a set of "rules" that do not involve them.

Going ahead without everyone agreeing is, according to the head of the Russian space agency, Dmitry Rogozin, an "invasion" of the Moon, which could turn it into "another Afghanistan or Iraq." That's fighting talk.

To prevent space from becoming a theater of war will require a shift in thinking away from state competition and toward peaceful cooperation. The first few pages of our space history have already been written and have shown us examples of both competition and cooperation.

There's always been a military dimension to the space race. One of its pioneers, Wernher von Braun, was so obsessed with space flight that he allowed himself to be co-opted by Nazi Germany in the 1930s. The Treaty of Versailles, signed after the First World War, prohibited German rearmament but there was nothing in it about rockets. The Nazis funded von Braun's research, resulting in the V-2 rockets that fell on London during the Second World War. In 1944 a V-2 became the first object fired into space, reaching a height of 110 miles following a vertical takeoff. After the war von Braun and 120 other scientists were brought to the US, along with captured V-2s, to begin work on the American space project, and twenty-four years later he was at the Kennedy Space Center watching as Apollo 11 set off for the first Moon landing.

The Russians were busy too, and at times led the space race. In the early twentieth century a self-educated and reclusive scientist named Konstantin Tsiolkovsky was working on theories of space flight and was the first to work out that the escape velocity required to get into space was 5 miles a second and could be achieved using liquid fuel and multistage rockets. He also configured blueprints for space stations, air locks, and oxygen systems. Many of his papers were published before the first airplane flew, which is partly why he is sometimes called the Father of Space Travel. In a 1911 letter, he wrote: "Earth is the cradle of humanity, but one cannot live in the cradle for ever." His memory lives on, not least in a crater named after him on the far side of the Moon.

The Soviets built on Tsiolkovsky's work. By 1957 they'd launched their first intercontinental ballistic missile (which leaves the atmosphere) and put the Sputnik satellite into space. The same year saw Sputnik 2—this time with added dog! It's quite right that the names Yuri Gagarin and Neil Armstrong are up there with the great explorers such as Marco Polo, Ibn Battuta, and Columbus, but history should spare a thought for the first animal to go into orbit. She was a placid little dog named Laika (Barker) after the public heard her barking on the radio in the run-up to the mission. Attached to sensors, and in a tiny space suit, she made at least one orbit around Earth before succumbing to heat and stress. A popular Soviet children's book at the time told her story with a happy ending. In reality, her death aboard Sputnik 2 helped prove that humans could live in space.

The Americans responded a few months later with the launch of a satellite, but back came the Russians. On April 12, 1961, the cosmonaut Yuri Gagarin became the first man to slip the surly bonds of Earth and break into the highest echelons of what the poet and fighter pilot John Gillespie Magee described as "the high untrespassed sanctity of space." It was a phenomenal moment in human history, surely comparable with Armstrong walking on the Moon in the magnitude of what it represented, and yet outside Russia Gagarin is almost an afterthought. It is a sad reflection on human nature that the name of one of his contemporaries, Mikhail Kalashnikov, is far better known around the world.

America responded again. Just six weeks after Gagarin's mission, President John Kennedy declared that the US "should commit itself to achieving the goal, before this decade is out, of landing a man on the Moon and returning him safely to the Earth."

The Americans made it with just over five months to spare. By then a crewed Apollo mission had circled the Moon and the astronaut William Anders had taken the awe-inspiring 1968 *Earthrise* photograph from Apollo 8 showing the surface of the Moon with the Earth in the background. It may be the most famous photograph ever taken and is credited with massive influence on the environmental movement. From space the crew read out verses from Genesis, "In the beginning God created the heaven and the earth," capturing the spirit of the times, the sense of wonder about how far humanity had come and how much further it could go.

The following year, on July 20, 1969, Neil Armstrong set foot on the Moon and uttered an eight-second-long sentence that will be known for as long as humans exist: "That's one small step for man, one giant leap for mankind." Since then twelve astronauts, including Armstrong, all American, have walked on the Moon, but the territory covered so far would fit into a small town, so claiming that we have explored it would be akin to aliens landing in Roswell, New Mexico, and saying they'd explored Earth.

Nevertheless, what the US had done was to make the definitive Cold War statement of geopolitical power. The Stars and Stripes was planted on the surface of the Moon and set against a backdrop of the Earth and cosmic infinity. And then, race won, the Americans lost interest.

Expensive stuff, this space-travel business. The Americans packed up their lunar-landing modules and went home, leaving behind some flags, footprints, and ninety-six bags of human waste. They lowered their sights to what they thought would cost less—space stations to conduct experiments and the Space Shuttle to help build them and position satellites in orbit. President Nixon canceled the final three Apollo missions and NASA refocused. Using bits and pieces left over from the Apollo years, they put together a two-story laboratory and launched it into orbit. Skylab failed to capture the world's attention, but it did advance human knowledge, conducting experiments and proving that humans could live in space for prolonged periods.

Next up was the symbolic docking of the Soviet Union's Soyuz module with an Apollo craft in 1975—an event that reflected the détente between the great rivals of the Cold War. The two spacecraft began to maneuver when almost 600 miles from each other. Two hours later, Thomas P. Stafford fired Apollo's engines for just one second to line up with Soyuz and reported that he could see the Russian craft as "just a speck right now." At 125 miles out Soyuz turned on its radar and Apollo locked on; with 21 miles to go there were two more quick bursts from its engines to adjust the trajectory, before Stafford slowed Apollo down and they met. "Contact!" shouted Stafford, while in the Soyuz Alexei Leonov replied, "Contact!" The air locks were opened and Leonov and Stafford shook hands. Konstantin Tsiolkovsky had worked out the theory; six decades later the two superpowers had made it a reality.

The event drew headlines and underlined that the ideal of cooperation in space could be achieved. Numerous countries had already done so with the agreements setting up the multination communications organizations Inmarsat and Intelsat. Countries have also shared information on climate change and helped one another to identify pollution hot spots—indeed, it was satellite technology that confirmed the discovery of the ozone hole over Antarctica. These are some of the day-to-day advantages of us being able to work together at the highest level, and the Soyuz-Apollo mission was a highly visual public demonstration of what could be. It was also a floating stepping-stone to the International Space Station (ISS).

The first piece of the ISS was launched by the Russians in November 1998;

two weeks later the American space shuttle *Endeavour* went up carrying the next piece and attached it to the first. It was a bit like building an Erector set in space but using rocket science. Within two years there was enough room for the first occupants to move in, and by 2011, when construction was finished, it had about the same volume as a five-bedroom house, with fantastic views but limited transport links.

The ISS is so big it can be seen in the night sky with the naked eye. At 360 feet long and 245 feet wide, it is about the same size as a football field and within it are three laboratories and living quarters for up to six astronauts. It's a little cramped, so helmets off to the American Peggy Whitson, who holds the record for the most time spent in space—665 days. She is one of more than 240 men and women from nineteen countries who have enjoyed the limited comforts of the station. These include a sleeping bag tied to a wall to prevent "sleep floating" and a water-recovery system (WRS). The latter is a fascinating piece of equipment that will help when humans begin long-haul journeys to planets in the next few decades. The WRS recovers about 93 percent of the moisture in the space station, whether it is from the astronaut's breath, sweat, or urine. It is distilled and processed before being mixed with treated wastewater and goes back into the system for drinking and washing. Again and again. This hugely reduces the amount of water the station requires on resupply missions, but while the technology will help long-distance travel, the diminishing return of 93 percent recycling means more work is required.

The work that is carried out both on and for the ISS provides dozens of examples of how rocket science benefits humanity. Technology developed for the WRS has been used to advance water-filtration systems in regions back on Earth where people lack access to clean water; the space station's microgravity environment is the best place to grow the complicated crystal structures of human proteins that are used to develop medical treatments; and its robotic-arm technology has been adapted for numerous uses on Earth, including surgery. The ISS is a floating lily pad, one of many that will be built as we hop farther from home. The lessons learned there are part of the journey.

Space travel is no longer only the domain of powerful states. Getting out there is becoming cheaper and within reach of private companies, so we can expect competition for the Moon's resources. Elon Musk, a cofounder of PayPal and the entrepreneur behind Tesla cars, is fanatical about getting humans to Mars within his lifetime (possibly in this decade). His company SpaceX has been carrying cargo to the ISS for years and in 2020 took two NASA astronauts there. Musk figured out how to reduce costs by introducing reusable rockets. As he said, "Six million dollars is falling through the sky. Would we try to catch it?" He is an example of how private enterprise is out ahead of governments but is also partnered with NASA. There's usually a link between commercial outfits and the state—the East India Company comes to mind, which aligned its trading interests with those of the British Empire from the sixteenth century onward, and at times acted almost as a governing body in some territories controlled by the British.

Musk is leading the pack in commercial space companies but Jeff Bezos, the man behind Amazon, is trying to chase Musk down with his Blue Origin company. Its vision is "a future where millions of people are living and working in space. In order to preserve Earth, our home, for our grandchildren's grandchildren, we must go to space to tap its unlimited resources and energy." The key word here is "unlimited." As we'll see later, the untapped minerals expected to be found on the Moon and meteorites, such as titanium and precious metals, would not only feed our appetite on Earth but allow us to build as many space stations and lunar bases as we like. At the state level, an unmanned Chinese craft landed on the far side of the Moon in December 2020, planted the Chinese flag on the surface, and began digging for rocks. However, when it comes to private enterprise, the Americans are leading the way.

Going farther afield, we've already launched unmanned missions to Mars, Venus, and Jupiter; there's even been a landing craft sent out to one of Saturn's moons (Titan) and a flyby of Pluto. We're on our way, but before we go back to the future, it's back down to Earth.

The Artemis Accords are an example of the legal, political, and military difficulties space exploration is facing up. When it comes to Artemis, Moscow and Beijing are particularly concerned about the articles allowing the signatories to establish "safety zones" on the Moon to protect the area in which a country is working. Nations are asked to "respect" the zones in order to "prevent harmful interference." This throws up the scenario of a Russian spaceship landing within a zone, setting up shop next door to a Japanese or American base, and the new arrivals getting their drills out. By what law could the Japanese or Americans object, and in the absence of law, what would they do about it?

They could hardly turn to the now horribly outdated 1967 document popularly known as the Outer Space Treaty upon which most of the rules governing the use of space are based. It says, "Outer space is not subject to national appropriation by claim of sovereignty, by means of use or occupation, or by any other means." A safety zone looks an awful lot like national appropriation, and the more zones there are and the bigger they are, the more crowded the Moon will be—especially with private companies increasing competition for its resources.

The Outer Space Treaty says the Moon shall be used only for peaceful purposes. It doesn't define peaceful, and once you've put "facts on the Moon" it would be easy to argue that you need defensive weapons, not for aggressive purposes but to ensure the peace.

The treaty needs rewriting to reflect today's technology while keeping to the spirit of the text and its promise that exploration "shall be carried out for the benefit and in the interests of all countries and shall be the province of all mankind." So far, though, we can't even agree where the Earth ends and space starts.

Our atmosphere doesn't just suddenly vanish, it becomes thinner over hundreds of miles. NASA and other US organizations define space as beginning 50 miles up from sea level, whereas the Swiss-based Fédération Aéronautique Internationale, which ratifies astronautical records, says it is 60 miles. Other definitions are available, but none can pinpoint an exact distance. Some countries have resisted an international legal definition on the grounds that it is not necessary; but while that may have been true one hundred years ago, it isn't now. Let's say country A defines it as 60 miles up, but country B says it's 50. It follows that if country B flies a satellite 55 miles above country A, country B risks having its satellite shot down.

Happily, to work out these issues we have the United Nations Office for Outer Space Affairs. Based in Vienna, it has a Committee on the Peaceful Uses of Outer Space (COPUOS), and reports to the Fourth Committee of the UN General Assembly, which then adopts an "annual resolution on international co-operation in the peaceful uses of outer space." So, you see, we can all sleep easily in our beds.

There is a slight flaw, though. Take the 1979 Moon Treaty, for example. Developed by COPUOS, it was built on the Outer Space Treaty and was adopted by the UN General Assembly. However, only a handful of countries have ratified it, while Russia, the US, and China have neither signed nor ratified it. When a country signs a treaty, it signals it is willing to support it provisionally; ratification is the agreement to be legally bound by it. Given that most of the space-faring countries have done neither makes the Moon Treaty barely worth the paper it hasn't been written on.

On the plus side, the Moon Treaty, if ever fully ratified, would close a loophole in the Outer Space Treaty, which spoke only of "national appropriation" regarding celestial bodies; it didn't say anything about individuals. The Moon Treaty addressed that oversight and specified that the Moon, and its natural resources, could not be owned by any organization or private person. However, until the Moon Treaty is ratified, the Outer Space Treaty stands, and an enterprising chap in America named Dennis Hope spotted the loophole. In 1980 he filed a declaration of claim with the UN, took its lack of response as acquiescence, and started selling plots of land on the Moon for twenty-five dollars an acre. For this you received a fancy certificate of ownership. Hope claims he has sold more than 611 million acres. If you bought one for any reason other than as a novelty gift, then it was the triumph of Hope over sense. And I have a bridge to sell you.

The Outer Space Treaty was drawn up at a time when our ability to explore outer space was limited and people thought of it as a featureless void where the politics on Earth did not apply. It's true that the Soviet-American space race took place within the context of the Cold War, but it was mostly about prestige—which political model could prove itself superior. Since then, along with advances in technology, a new way of thinking has arisen and with it new "astropolitical" theories.

There is a view that assumes the great powers will seek to dominate space to achieve commercial and military dominance. This is realpolitik for space—astropolitik. It starts from an understanding that space is not featureless, but is, in the words of the astropolitik theorist Everett Dolman, "a rich vista of gravitational mountains and valleys, oceans and rivers of resources and energy."

Professor Dolman, of the US Air Force's Air Command and Staff College, builds on the writings of the great twentieth-century geopolitical theorists Halford Mackinder and Alfred Mahan. Both helped shape strategic thinking by drawing on geographical realities, territories, and ways in which new technologies could impact them. Students of geopolitics are familiar with how the corridors of trade, and who controls them, have played a major role in history. Astropolitics takes a similar approach and applies it to the cosmos, looking at place, distance, fuel supplies, and a lot of science.

Military astro-strategists tend to divide the geography of the issue into four parts. They use different descriptions, but Dolman's categorizations are useful for a broad-brush view. First there is Terra—the Earth and its immediate airspace, up to the limit after which a craft could go into orbit around the Earth without being powered. Above this is Earth Space—the region from lowest-possible orbit up to geosynchronous orbit, which aligns with the Earth's rotation. After this is Lunar Space—from geosynchronous orbit to the Moon's orbit. From there you enter Solar Space—everything in the solar system beyond the Moon's orbit.

For the next few decades, the most important of these for the future of space exploration is Earth Space, particularly low Earth orbit. This is where our communications—and increasingly our military—satellites are placed. Control of this belt will give countries a huge military advantage across the Earth's surface. Dolman created a maxim that echoes Halford Mackinder's famous 1904 "Heartland" geopolitical theory about control of the world beginning, "Who rules East Europe commands the Heartland." Dolman's version is: "Who controls low Earth orbit controls near-Earth space. Who controls near-Earth space dominates Terra. Who dominates Terra determines the destiny of humankind."

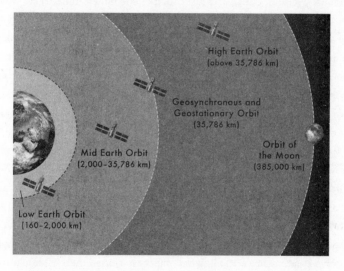

The categories of orbits surrounding the Earth (not to scale).

In previous centuries, dominance of Terra relied on placing land and sea forces in strategic positions, jealously guarding sea routes and entry and exits of choke points such as the Straits of Gibraltar or Malacca Strait. The twentieth century saw airpower added to the requirements. In the twenty-first century, positioning assets in Earth Space is a necessity unless a state is prepared to fall far behind its rivals (and allies).

Low orbit is also the area where spacecraft seeking to travel beyond the Moon could be refueled. Mars is millions of miles farther away from Earth than the Moon, but because of the incredible effort required to slip the bounds of Earth's gravity, more energy is required to get from the Earth's surface to the Moon than from low orbit to Mars. If one powerful state gained full control of this corridor it would become the gatekeeper and could prevent rivals from refueling within it and thus hamper their ability to travel farther.

Again, the situation on Earth provides useful analogies. Currently, if a Black Sea state wishes to sail a military ship through the Bosporus to get out into the Mediterranean and then the Atlantic, it must ask Turkey for permission. At a time of great tension, that permission might be refused. Control of Earth Space would give similar power and, in the absence of any meaningful treaties, the law of the "space jungle" would apply.

There are commercial considerations as well: if technology is developed allowing massive solar panels to reflect solar energy down to Earth for power generation, that technology will probably be placed in low orbit. Given that this is also the area in which refueling for long journeys will take place, if you want to get up to a meteorite for mining purposes you may have to pay the gatekeeper a cut.

The more we learn about the geographical regions of outer space, the more our navigational space maps will have to be updated and the more scope for competition. For example, the Van Allen radiation belts are two areas extending out from Earth up to around 36,000 miles in which high-energy particles are trapped by the Earth's magnetic field. They have such a high concentration of radiation that crewed spaceships are better off avoiding them. Spend too long there and the craft's electronics may begin to fail, as might the crew. There are also particular pathways that crafts can follow to use the planet's gravitational force to "slingshot" them on a long-distance route. And there are five "libration" points near the Earth. These are places where the gravitational effects of the Earth and Moon cancel each other out, allowing objects stationed there to remain in position without having to use fuel. These points may become areas of competition. Two in particular are in locations allowing a commanding "view" down to the belt containing satellites. Another, known as L2, is on the far side of the Moon. China has stationed a satellite there, allowing it to see what is happening on the "dark side" which, by no coincidence, is where they are considering establishing a base.

These are the types of geographical realities we may become more accustomed to hearing about as astropolitics comes of age and the great powers integrate space warfare into their military budgets. It is clear that, without binding treaties limiting the militarization of space, low Earth orbit is a probable battlefield for military weapons aimed firstly at rivals within the belt, and then below it.

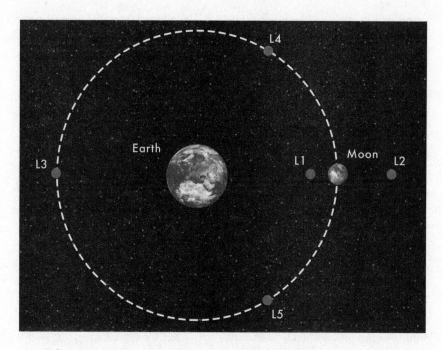

Libration points in the Earth–Moon system (L1–L5) are key positions for placing satellites, which could lead to competition between nations.

Russia and China have both made organizational changes to their military, as has America with the formation of the US Space Force in 2019. There are concerns that this activity violates the Outer Space Treaty, but that agreement states only that weapons of mass destruction such as nuclear missiles should not be placed "in orbit or on celestial bodies or [stationed] in outer space in any other manner." There's nothing in international law to prevent the stationing of laser-armed satellites. And every page of history suggests that if one country does it, so will another, and then another.

This is why in June 2021 NATO's Article 5, which states that an attack on one member is considered an attack on all of them, was extended to include a collective response to attacks in space, and why the US Department of Defense has a mantra: "Space is a war-fighting domain." In the previous century the possibility of nuclear war threatened to destroy our way of life; now the weaponization of space looks as if it will pose a similar danger. War in space could be earth-shattering.

Hence Space Force. At its inauguration President Trump said, "American superiority in space is absolutely vital. . . . The Space Force will help us deter aggression and control the ultimate high ground." The Chinese and Russians view space in the same way, as do a range of less powerful nations. However, it's the Big Three who are at the cutting edge of both space travel and its military dimensions.

All three accept that the military concept of "full-spectrum dominance" now includes space, from low orbit to the Moon, and eventually beyond. We saw an early and limited attempt to gain this advantage with the American Strategic Defense Initiative in the 1980s, an attempt to develop a missile defense system that could protect the US from nuclear attack. One of the options it investigated was a range of space-based weaponry, earning it the name "Star Wars" and heralding the militarization of space.

Now the development of hypersonic missiles, which can fly at more than twenty times the speed of sound, is also focusing attention on this area. Unlike conventional intercontinental ballistic missiles, hypersonic missiles do not fly in an arc and can change direction and altitude. Therefore, at launch the potentially targeted country cannot work out where they are heading and coordinate its antimissile defenses. Hitting a missile with a missile is hard enough; hypersonic missiles make it much more difficult. To meet the challenge, governments are examining the possibility of positioning anti-hypersonic laser systems in space to fire downward. If deployed, it follows that machines capable of firing on the laser systems would be developed, and then defensive systems for them. Add an "etc." and we are well into the space arms race.

The situation will become only more complicated as we continue to turn science fiction into reality. An example of that came in July 2020. Russia's Kosmos 2542 military satellite had been "stalking" an American satellite, USA 245, at times coming within 95 miles of it, a distance regarded as close. It then released a mini-satellite from within itself—Kosmos 2543. The US military calls these "Russian dolls." This "baby" Kosmos also shadowed the American spacecraft before maneuvering toward a third Russian satellite. It then appeared to fire a high-speed projectile traveling at about 435 miles an hour. The Kremlin says it was simply inspecting the condition of its satellites, but the British Ministry of Defence and the US Department of Defense both believe it was a form of weapons test.

Naturally, the US also shadows foreign satellites and is researching its own space weapons, but it was furious about what it believes was a breach of conventional behavior—the actual firing of a weapon in space. Again comes the legal problem: such protocols and understandings are not codified in ratified law. But the threat to satellites is one that all countries must take seriously.

Satellites no longer just relay TV pictures and phone calls; they are vital for both daily life and modern warfare. Knocking out or blinding a satellite could mean your car's GPS system goes blank and your bank cards stop working. When you switch on the TV to find out what's happening, you may find just a blank screen. After a few days the supermarkets' delivery systems, both to their stores and your house, would be in chaos. Without GPS ships and planes would struggle to navigate, and in an extreme scenario the electricity grid could go down. As for getting a weather forecast—forget it.

At the military level, all advanced countries rely on satellites for intelligence and surveillance. If a series of military satellites was hit, the high command would immediately worry that this was a precursor to being attacked on the ground. Early-warning systems of a nuclear launch might go down, triggering a decision on whether to launch first. Even if a conflict remained conventional, the other side would have the advantage of precision-targeting its enemy and moving its own forces without being "seen," even as its opponent's ability to send encrypted communications would be limited.

This is all a very real threat. Already Russia, China, the US, India, and Israel have developed "satellite-killer" systems—specialist space weapons that destroy satellites. Techniques are being invented to shoot down satellites with lasers, to "dazzle" them so they cannot communicate, to spray them with chemicals, and even ram them. And with no laws about who can be where, how close they can be, and what activity is allowed, there is the growing danger of an exercise, or even faulty navigating, being mistaken for an impending attack.

The US government is working with Lockheed Martin to develop "Space Fence." This is a surveillance system using ground-based radar to track satellites and orbital debris. The Department of Defense can currently track more than 20,000 of these; it expects to increase this figure to 100,000, and to be able to identify the exact source of a laser fired at a satellite.

Conflict in Earth Space creates another problem: a huge amount of debris that would hurtle around in orbit, smashing into the satellite infrastructure of all countries and devastating the global economy. This is something that is already a risk, given that there are currently 3,000 dead satellites and 34,000 pieces of space junk at least 4 inches in size, and many smaller, orbiting the planet. Some countries are trying to address the problem. If you've been to Japan you will have noticed the absence of something—litter. Japan's SKY Perfect Corporation and the Japanese government have been working on a satellite to remove space debris with lasers that will push bits of debris into the Earth's atmosphere, where they will burn up. The British, dreadful litterers, are researching something similar.

Perhaps war in space will never become a reality, but, just as on Earth, the plans are for "what if," not "what won't" happen.

It doesn't have to be this way; although our past has often consisted of intense competition at the state level, there have also been many examples of cooperation. As well as conflict, the twentieth century witnessed the flowering of internationalism and world-governing bodies. It also saw, even during the Cold War, systems developed to avoid conflict, such as the installation of a hotline between Moscow and Washington so the two leaders could communicate directly with each other if either suspected a launch had been ordered. The leaders of the two superpowers saw clearly that nuclear war meant that everyone loses, and we may come to see space war in the same terms. There's always the danger that one state might risk limited strikes to gain an advantage, but it's more likely that countries will focus on deterrence based on "mutual assured destruction." This doctrine is as logically "mad" as it was during the Cold War, but it held then and may apply in the future. Just as there were kinetic wars inside the Cold War, so we may see limited forms of warfare in space, stopping short of action endangering our entire existence. The diplomatic channels necessary to achieve standard operating procedures can build trust and reduce tensions.

Perhaps our leaders should suit up and take a trip. As the NASA astronaut Karen Nyberg said, "If I could get every Earthling to do one circle of the Earth, I think things would run a little differently." She was talking about environmentalism, but it is an equally effective call for better diplomacy.

If all countries could live up to the spirit of the US National Space Policy and its "commitment to enhance the welfare of humankind by co-operating with others to maintain the freedom of space," we could imagine a future very different from the one we are currently heading toward. In this future, Congress overturns its hostility to NASA working with the fastest-growing space power, China. Japan and South Korea also overcome their differences, forge a regional partnership, and tie in with the Americans, Chinese, Indians, and others to create a global initiative in which each nation pools its resources and contributes its particular expertise.

In ten years' time the International Space Station becomes the "International Musk Spacetel"—a billon-star twenty-room hotel where guests can take in the sights and eat the finest gastronomical freeze-dried food. The $10 million-per-week cost includes a free spacewalk and an excursion to the World Space

Lab, the international laboratory situated a convenient 30 miles away, where, in 2028, the discovery of the cure for Alzheimer's disease was made. Video calls to the fledgling moon base are also offered, although with only twelve people working there this may not always be possible, even if your call is very important to them. Some things never change.

In twenty years' time spaceships are refueling in low Earth orbit, en route on long journeys across the vast reaches of space. Others land on the Moon, where 3D printers are producing huge solar panels for both the expanding "Gateway" multinational bases there and also to fit onto visiting craft to allow them to venture to Mars. Some of the crews still grumble at the six-month journey time but are reminded that it is almost 56 million miles away, and that it used to take ships two months just to get from the UK to America. As they lift off again, still grumbling, they pass the Chinese and UAE space stations positioned on the far side of the Moon. Other craft are crewed by robots designed to conduct experiments as their vehicles head into deep space. Closer to home, large meteorites are being mined, providing huge quantities of what are no longer "rare-earth" minerals. The price of gold has collapsed after 12 percent of the huge "Midas" meteorite was found to be made of the previously precious metal.

By 2060, serious "terra-forming" is under way by the hundred-strong multinational team on Mars. Back in 2054 scientists finally worked out a formula whereby heating and releasing the planet's greenhouse gases and mixing them with massive payloads of the Earth's remaining CFCs would trap enough heat from the sun to spark a chain reaction, transforming the atmosphere. It's projected that by 2075 it may be possible to walk on the planet's surface without a space suit.

So far, so theoretically within our grasp. The farther out we go, the more like science fiction it gets. By 2080, thank goodness, the perennial idea of dropping nuclear bombs behind spaceships to achieve the sort of propulsion required for deep-space travel has been superseded. Instead, mini hydrogen bombs are exploded, at a safe distance, in front of the craft, followed by "gravity waves" temporarily warping space and allowing a short burst of the ship's thrusters to massively accelerate the craft for several hundred thousand miles. We still haven't cracked light speed, though: the crew who made it to Pluto in just two years were still twenty thousand years from our nearest star (apart from the sun)—Proxima Centauri. So the talk of "freezing" a crew came to nothing, and the plan for embryos to be looked after by robots and AI was equally pointless, and in any case it was thrown out by the Planetary Council on Ethics.

The universe is endless, which means that so are the possibilities, which is what makes science fiction such fun. But for the foreseeable future we are both restrained and yet liberated by our current knowledge. We are liberated because it is what allows us to reach for the stars, something that until very recently in our history was impossible; yet restrained because our knowledge cannot overcome the immensity of space and the constraints of natural law.

Until we can travel at, or close to, the speed of light (and perhaps we never will), then we will struggle to get out of our solar system, because everything we see is so far away. Light from Proxima Centauri takes 4.25 years to reach us—putting it around 25 trillion miles away. When we see the Andromeda constellation in the night sky, we are seeing it as it was 2.5 million years ago. Because of these vast distances, and because we seem to be decades away from achieving propulsion at even a tenth of the speed of light, the problems of deep-space travel can be left to science fiction writers, a few pioneering theorists, and future generations.

There are several other theories as to how to achieve greater speeds, including launching small probes the size of computer chips into space that would unfold sails to be propelled by lasers fired at them from Earth. The private-enterprise Starshot project is already working on this with a view to sending a probe to a potentially Earth-like planet near Proxima Centauri with a journey time of twenty years, instead of the tens of thousands currently required. Among a host of hurdles to overcome is that a laser powerful enough to achieve this has yet to be invented. And when it is, or several are combined, they will need to be able to project short bursts of 100 gigawatts of power, roughly the output of about a hundred nuclear power stations.

Scientists say the theory is sound; indeed, it concurs with what the seventeenth-century astronomer Johannes Kepler wrote to his fellow genius Galileo Galilei: "With ships or sails built for heavenly breezes, some will venture into that great vastness."

My issue with this is that the lasers might miss the computer chip and hit an alien spacecraft 250,000 miles away, whose occupants turn out not to be vegetarians and who say, "Nice planet—we'll take it." Given the size of space, that's unlikely, but then again, given the size of space and the billions of planets in it, it's probable there is intelligent life out there. Science tells us so. Some mathematicians even guess that there are more Earth-like planets than there are grains of sand on all of our beaches!

The claim is based on the latest information from the telescopes on satellites, such as the Kepler, which can see ever more clearly. Extrapolating from that, we find that the chances of the third rock from the sun being the only planet with intelligent life are trillions to one.

If you're wondering why, given these odds, ET hasn't phoned yet, Eric Mack at the CNET tech site has come up with the best analogy I've found so far. Try imagining that all the grains of sand on the world's beaches are on one single beach, but each grain (planet) is separated from its nearest neighbor by several trillion miles. That's the universe, so, as the astrophysicist Neil deGrasse Tyson says about our current extent of exploration, "Claiming there is no other life in the universe is like scooping up some water, looking at the cup, and claiming there are no whales in the ocean."

If there is anyone out there, we already have a present for them—the Pioneer Plaque (PP). The six-by-nine-inch plaque is attached to the Pioneer 10 spacecraft, launched in 1972 and last heard from in January 2003 when the power source finally ran out; but the craft ran on into infinity. On it is a map, which, in effect, says: "We're over here!"

The PP was designed by the great astronomers Carl Sagan and Frank Drake. They began from the premise that intelligent life out there may, or may not, have vocal chords or ears, but does have what we have—the natural laws governing science. So the plaque is inscribed with two hydrogen atoms, each in a different energy state, because when one changes from one state to another, electromagnetic radiation is released in a measurable wavelength and period of time. A man and woman are depicted; the man's arm is raised, displaying an open palm in what is the international symbol of greeting, but for all we know might be the galactically accepted symbol of aggression. In the center is a radial with each line in it tracing back to our sun, and underneath it is a depiction of our solar system's planets. The lines, of different lengths, connect back up to pulsars. Pulsars rotate at specific speeds and if you work out their speed you can figure out when the map was made and triangulate back to the sun, and therefore to Earth.

The map is good for only a few million years, after which our entirely unremarkable sun and entirely unremarkable solar system will have spun around our entirely unremarkable Milky Way a few times and the constellations will have shifted. So PP and ET had better get a move on.

Space exploration is still in its infancy, and we need to decide in which direction we wish to take it. Will we follow the "Westphalian" conception of the universe—a system of states holding sovereign power over mutually recognized territories, which history has repeatedly shown breaks down? Or will we recognize our common humanity and the challenges of space travel, propelling us into acting as one people as we venture beyond our earthly home?

To date, we are following the more familiar pattern. Almost all the great discoveries of land and sea ended up with the same result—competition, a power struggle, and the winner deciding the rules and where the lines were drawn. You could argue that when it comes to space, as far as we know, there is no current owner to be displaced, and that those who venture, and risk, and invest should be able to reap the benefits. However, even if you were to make that case, we have arrived at a time when, despite all the conflicts and injustices on Planet Earth, there is a widespread acceptance of our responsibility to one another at a global level—climate change has shown that. Even if the limitless energy riches and raw materials of the cosmos can be sought out and brought to Earth only by the most powerful states, it is in all of our interests for them to be shared. Raising living standards across the world and simultaneously reducing carbon emissions benefits everyone. Our resources here are finite and competition for them sparks conflict, but above us is an asteroid named 3554 Amun. In it are nickel, cobalt, iron, and other metals with an estimated value of $20 trillion, approximately the same as the GDP of the US. It's one of countless many, more than enough to share.

It would be naïve to believe that the country, or company, whose spacecraft lands on such wealth will simply give it away. However, we should be working on codifying agreements whereby the space-faring nations cooperate on projects, agree to share profits and knowledge, and set binding targets on transferring a percentage of their gains to everyone else. An example could be giant solar reflectors positioned in low orbit, which bounce the sun's energy onto solar farms when they are in darkness to enable them to run twenty-four hours a day. A percentage of the budget to build the reflectors could be committed so that developing nations received free power from this source. There are as many similar ideas as there are imaginations. It's doable. As the science fiction writer Arthur C. Clarke said, every revolutionary idea passes through three phrases characterized by the views of its critics: (1) "It'll never work—it's pure fantasy"; (2) "It might work, but it's not worth doing"; (3) "I said it was a good idea all along."

It is also in all our interests to cooperate on finding and tracking the as yet undiscovered asteroids and other objects that may threaten us, like the Tunguska meteor, which flattened hundreds of square miles of a forest in Siberia in

1908. Much bigger objects may be on the same trajectory. The dinosaurs never saw it coming—we can, and we can do something about it.

Cooperation in space would not necessarily end hostility between states on Earth. American astronauts are given a lift to the International Space Station in a Russian spaceship, but that hasn't prevented the reemergence and growth of tensions between the two countries. However, in previous decades, when the threat of war between them was much higher, technological cooperation was the door they used to achieve détente, resulting in the Soyuz-Apollo docking in 1975.

Looking back at this "pale blue dot" from space, as the cosmonauts and astronauts did together then, is a way to dissolve the "us and them" virus that has infected us from the beginning. Space gives us a chance to stretch our minds to the limitlessness of the universe. Humans have always looked up, deep into the night sky, and dreamed. Now we've actually reached the high ground; it is manifestly our destiny to go higher, and we will get there more quickly if we do it together. The sky is not the limit.

ACKNOWLEDGMENTS

Thank you to everyone who provided expertise, quotes, and support. Dr. Alison Hudson, Mina Al-Oraibi, Dr. Anne-Marie Schleich, Dr. Sajjan Gohel, David Waywell, Ioannis Michaletos, John Saunders, Sarah Williams, Liam Morrissey, Jason Webster, Peter Bellerby. Also my gratitude goes to several embassies and military organizations for their background information, and to the individuals who prefer to remain in the background due to political sensitivities. And thank you, as always, to the wonderful team at Elliott and Thompson: Jennie Condell, Pippa Crane, Marianne Thorndahl, and Lorne Forsyth.

Bibliography

1. Australia

- Attard, Bernard. "The Economic History of Australia from 1788: An Introduction." EH.Net Encyclopedia, March 2006. https://eh.net/encyclopedia/the-economic-history-of-australia-from-1788-an-introduction/.

- "Border Lengths—States and Territories." Geoscience Australia, Australian Government. https://www.ga.gov.au/scientific-topics/national-location-information/dimensions/border-lengths.

- Christie, Nancy J. "'Pioneering for a Civilized World': Griffith Taylor and the Ecology of Geography." *Scientia Canadensis* 17, no. 1–2 (1993): 103–54. https://www.erudit.org/fr/revues/scientia/1993-v17-n1-2-scientia3119/800366ar.pdf.

- "Confluence of the Two Seas" (speech by Prime Minister Shinzo Abe at the Parliament of the Republic of India, Ministry of Foreign Affairs of Japan, August 22, 2007). https://www.mofa.go.jp/region/asia-paci/pmv0708/speech-2.html.

- Curtin, John. "The Task Ahead." *Herald* (Melbourne), December 27, 1941. http://john.curtin.edu.au/pmportal/text/00468.html.

- "Edward Hammond Hargraves." *Sydney Evening News*, October 31, 1891. https://trove.nla.gov.au/newspaper/article/111989656?searchTerm=Edward%20Hargraves&searchLimits=.

- Elkner, Cate. "Immigration and Ethnicity: Overview." Electronic Encyclopedia of Gold in Australia. https://www.egold.net.au/biogs/EG00006b.htm.

- "Geographic Distribution of the Population." Australian Bureau of Statistics, May 24, 2012. https://www.abs.gov.au/ausstats/abs@.nsf/Lookup/by%20 Subject/1301.0~2012~Main%20Features~Geographic%20distribution%20 of%20the%20population~49.

- Hughes, Robert. *The Fatal Shore*. London: Collins Harvill, 1987.

- Macfarlane, Ingereth, ed. *Aboriginal History* 26 (2002). https://press-files .anu.edu.au/downloads/press/p73361/pdf/book.pdf.

- Rudd, Kevin. "The Complacent Country." KevinRudd.com, February 4, 2019. https://kevinrudd.com/2019/02/04/the-complacent-country/.

- Schleich, Anne-Marie. "New Geopolitical Developments in the South Pacific: The Cases of Australia and New Zealand." *ISPSW Strategy Series: Focus on Defense and International Security*, no. 533 (2018). https://css.ethz .ch/content/dam/ethz/special-interest/gess/cis/center-for-securities-studies /resources/docs/ISPSW-533%20Schleich.pdf.

- Ville, Simon. "The Relocation of the International Market for Australian Wool." *Australian Economic History Review* 45, no. 1 (2005): 73–95.

- Worgan, George Bouchier. Letter to his brother Richard Worgan, June 12–18, 1788. https://www.sl.nsw.gov.au/collection-items/collection-10-george-bouchi er-worgan-letter-written-his-brother-richard-worgan-12-1.

2. Iran

- Ansari, Ali M. *Iran: A Very Short Introduction*. Oxford: Oxford University Press, 2014.

- ———. *Iran, Islam and Democracy: The Politics of Managing Change*. London: Gingko Library/Chatham House, 2019.

- Langton, James. "The Day the Oil Came: Sixty Years Ago, the Sea Gave Up Its Secrets and Changed Abu Dhabi Forever." *The National*, March 28, 2018. https://abudhabioil.thenational.ae.

- "Mapping the Global Muslim Population." Pew Research Center, October 7, 2009. https://www.pewforum.org/2009/10/07/mapping-the-global -muslim-population/.

- "Saddam Hussein and His Advisers Discussing Iraq's Decision to Go to War with Iran." History and Public Policy Program Digital Archive, Conflict Records Research Center, National Defense University, September 16, 1980. https://digitalarchive.wilsoncenter.org/document /110099.

- "Their Last Chance?" *The Economist: Special Report*, January 15, 2004. https://www.economist.com/special-report/2004/01/15/their-last-chance.

3. Saudi Arabia

- Acemoglu, Daron, and James A. Robinson. *The Narrow Corridor: How Nations Struggle for Liberty*. New York: Penguin Books, 2020.

- Al-Rasheed, Madawi. *A History of Saudi Arabia*. Cambridge: Cambridge University Press, 2010.

- "Basic Law of Governance." The Embassy of the Kingdom of Saudi Arabia, March 1, 1992. https://www.saudiembassy.net/basic-law-governance.

- "Civilian Gasoline Supply Report." Office of War Information, October 13, 1943. http://plainshumanities.unl.edu/homefront/homefront.docs.0015.

- "Diriyah: The Original Home of the Saudi State." Saudi Press Agency, November 20, 2019. https://www.spa.gov.sa/viewfullstory .php?lang=en&newsid=2001219.

- Husain, Ed. *The House of Islam: A Global History*. New York: Bloomsbury, 2018.

- "Ikhwan." GlobalSecurity. https://www.globalsecurity.org/military/world /gulf/ikhwan.htm.

- "King Abdulaziz Al Saud: Founder of the Kingdom of Saudi Arabia." House of Saud, Saudi Royal Family News and Information. https://houseofsaud .com/king-abdulaziz-al-saud/.

- Riedel, Bruce. *Kings and Presidents: Saudi Arabia and the United States Since FDR*. Washington, D.C.: Brookings Institution Press, 2019.

- "Saudi Arabia." US Department of State Archive. https:/2009-2017.state .gov/documents/organization/171744.pdf.

- "Saudi Arabia: Youth Unemployment Rate from 1999 to 2020." Statista (2020). https://www.statista.com/statistics/812955/youth-unemploy ment-rate-in-saudi-arabia/.

4. The United Kingdom

- Collier, Basil. *The Defence of the United Kingdom: History of the Second World War*. London: Her Majesty's Stationery Office, 1957.

- Crane, Nicholas. *The Making of the British Landscape: From the Ice Age to the Present*. London: Weidenfeld & Nicolson, 2017.

- "The Defence Implications of Possible Scottish Independence." House of Commons Defence Committee, vol. 1, Sixth Report of Session 2013–14 (2013). https://publications.parliament.uk/pa/cm201314/cmselect/cmdfence/198/198.pdf.

- Harvey, Michael. "Perspectives on the UK's Place in the World." Chatham House: Europe Programme Paper 2011/01 (2011). https://www.chatham house.org/sites/default/files/public/Research/Europe/1211pp_harvey.pdf.

- Lipscombe, Nick. "Napoleon's Obsession: The Invasion of England." *British Journal for Military History* 1, no. 3 (2015).

- McKirdy, Alan, and Roger Crofts. *Scotland: The Creation of Its Natural Landscape; A Landscape Fashioned by Geology*. Perth: Scottish Natural Heritage, 1999.

- Parker, Joanne. *Britannia Obscura: Mapping Hidden Britain.* London: Vintage, 2015.

- Simms, Brendan. *Three Victories and a Defeat: The Rise and Fall of the First British Empire, 1714–1783.* London: Allen Lane, 2007.

5. Greece

- Brunwasser, Matthew. "The Greeks Who Worship the Ancient Gods." BBC News, June 20, 2013. https://www.bbc.co.uk/news/magazine-22972610.

- "Greece—Agricultural Sector." International Trade Administration: United States of America, June 4, 2019. https://www.export.gov/apex /article2?id=Greece-Agricultural-Sector.

- "Greece Population 2020." World Population Review. http://world populationreview.com/countries/greece-population/.

- "King of Hellenes Murdered." *The Times* (London), March 19, 1913.

- "Lausanne Peace Treaty VI. Convention Concerning the Exchange of Greek and Turkish Populations Signed at Lausanne, January 30, 1923." Republic of Turkey, Ministry of Foreign Affairs, January 30, 1923. http://www.mfa.gov.tr /lausanne-peace-treaty-vi_-convention-concerning-the-exchange-of-greek -and-turkish-populations-signed-at-lausanne_.en.mfa.

- "Military Expenditure (% of GDP)." The World Bank. https://data.world bank.org/indicator/MS.MIL.XPND.GD.ZS.

- Sienkewicz, Thomas J. "The Hellenic Language Is Immortal: The Grandeur of the Hellenic Language." Monmouth College. https://department.monm .edu/classics/Courses/GREK101-102/HellenicLanguage.Shadowed.htm.

- Weiner, Eric. *The Geography of Genius: A Search for the World's Most Creative Places from Ancient Athens to Silicon Valley.* New York: Simon & Schuster, 2016.

BIBLIOGRAPHY

6. Turkey

- Alkan, Can, et al. "Whole Genome Sequencing of Turkish Genomes Reveals Functional Private Alleles and Impact of Genetic Interactions with Europe, Asia and Africa." *BMC Genomics* 15, no. 1 (2014). https://www.ncbi.nlm.nih.gov/pmc/articles/PMC4236450/.

- Arango, Tim. "A Century After Armenian Genocide, Turkey's Denial Only Deepens." *New York Times*, April 16, 2015. https://www.nytimes.com/2015/04/17/world/europe/turkeys-century-of-denial-about-an-armenian-genocide.html.

- Mandiraci, Berkay. "Assessing the Fatalities in Turkey's PKK Conflict." International Crisis Group, October 22, 2019. https://www.crisisgroup.org/europe-central-asia/western-europemediterranean/turkey/assessing-fatalities-turkeys-pkk-conflict.

- "Mavi Vatan" [Blue Homeland]. Turkish Naval War College, 2019. https://www.msu.edu.tr/mavivatandanacikdenizleredergisi/mavivatan_baski.pdf.

- Murinson, Alexander. "The Strategic Depth Doctrine of Turkish Foreign Policy." *Middle Eastern Studies* 42, no. 6 (2006): 945–64.

- "Targeting Life in Idlib." Human Rights Watch, October 15, 2020. https://www.hrw.org/report/2020/10/15/targeting-life-idlib/syrian-and-russian-strikes-civilian-infrastructure.

- Turkish Presidency [@trpresidency]. "President Erdoğan: 'Hagia Sophia's doors will be, as is the case with all our mosques, wide open to all, whether they be foreign or local, Muslim or non-Muslim,'" July 10, 2020. https://twitter.com/trpresidency/status/1281686820556869632/photo/1.

- Westermann, William Linn. "Kurdish Independence and Russian Expansion [1946]." *Foreign Affairs* 70, no. 3 (1991). https://www.foreignaffairs.com/articles/russia-fsu/1991-06-01/kurdish-independence-and-russian-expansion-1946.

BIBLIOGRAPHY

7. The Sahel

- "Areva and Niger: A Sustainable Partnership." Areva, February 2011. https://inis.iaea.org/collection/NCLCollectionStore/_Public /50/062/50062650.pdf.

- Bassou, Abdelhak. "State, Borders and Territory in the Sahel: The Case of the G5 Sahel." Policy Center for the New South, October 6, 2017. https:// www.policycenter.ma/publications/state-borders-and-territory-sahel-case -g5-sahel.

- Berger, Flore. "West Africa: Shifting Strategies in the Sahel." *The Africa Report*, September 30, 2019. https://www.theafricareport.com/17843 /west-africa-shifting-strategies-in-the-sahel/.

- "Beyond Aid: The UK's Strategic Engagement in Africa" (written evidence from the Foreign and Commonwealth Office on behalf of Her Majesty's Government). House of Commons Foreign Affairs Committee (FAC) Inquiry (2019). http://data.parliament.uk/writtenevidence/committee evidence.svc/evidencedocument/foreign-affairs-committee/beyond-aid-the -uks-strategic-engagement-in-africa/written/105575.html.

- Comolli, Virginia. *Boko Haram: Nigeria's Islamist Insurgency*. London: Hurst, 2015.

- Cooper, Rachel. "Natural Resources Management Strategies in the Sahel." K4D Helpdesk Report, Institute of Development Studies, October 1, 2018. https://assets.publishing.service.gov.uk/media/5c6acc2340f 0b61a196aa83a/453_Sahel_Natural_Resources_Management.pdf.

- Devermont, Judd. "Politics at the Heart of the Crisis in the Sahel." Center for Strategic and International Studies, December 6, 2019. https://www.csis .org/analysis/politics-heart-crisis-sahel.

- Fortson, Danny. "The Great Uranium Stampede: Everybody Wants Supplies as Nuclear Power Comes Roaring Back." *The Sunday Times* (London), February 7, 2010. https://www.thetimes.co.uk/article/the-great-uranium -stampede-c7p3m6h9xxd.

- "General Act of the Berlin Conference on West Africa," February 26, 1885. https://loveman.sdsu.edu/docs/1885GeneralActBerlinConference.pdf.

- "Getting a Grip on Central Sahel's Gold Rush." International Crisis Group, Report no. 282/Africa, November 13, 2019. https://www.crisisgroup.org /africa/sahel/burkina-faso/282-reprendre-en-main-la-ruee-vers-lor-au -sahel-central.

- Grove, A. T. "Geographical Introduction to the Sahel." *The Geographical Journal* 144, no. 3 (1978): 407–15.

- Le Roux, Pauline. "Confronting Central Mali's Extremist Threat." Africa Center for Strategic Studies, February 22, 2019. https://africacenter.org /spotlight/confronting-central-malis-extremist-threat/.

- Lewis, David, and Ryan McNeill. "How Jihadists Struck Gold in Africa's Sahel." Reuters Investigates: A Special Report, November 22, 2019. https:// www.reuters.com/investigates/special-report/gold-africa-islamists/.

- Nicholson, Sharon E. "Climate of the Sahel and West Africa." *Oxford Research Encyclopedia*, September 26, 2018. https://oxfordre .com/view/10.1093/acrefore/9780190228620.001.0001/acrefore -9780190228620-e-510.

- Taithe, Bertrand. *The Killer Trail: A Colonial Scandal in the Heart of Africa.* Oxford: Oxford University Press, 2009.

- Watson, Abigail. "ORG Explains #12: The UK's Pivot to the Sahel." Oxford Research Group, January 27, 2020. https://www.oxfordresearch group.org.uk/org-explains-the-uks-pivot-to-the-sahel.

8. Ethiopia

- "Ethiopia Imports by Country." Trading Economics. https://tradingeconom ics.com/ethiopia/imports-by-country.

- "Ethiopia: The Criminal Code of the Federal Democratic Republic of Ethiopia." The Protection Project, Proclamation no. 414/2004 (2005). http://www.protectionproject.org/wp-content/uploads/2010/09/Ethiopia_Criminal-Code-TIP_2004.pdf.

- "Geopolitical Dynamics in the Horn of Africa and Mechanisms for Collaboration Between NATO and IGAD Countries." NATO Strategic Direction South Hub/Institute for Peace and Security Studies, Addis Ababa University (2019). https://thesouthernhub.org/resources/site1/General/NSD-S%20Hub%20Publications/Geopolitical%20Dynamics%20in%20the%20Horn%20of%20Africa%20and%20Mechanisms%20for%20Collaboration%20between%20NATO%20and%20IGAD%20Countries.pdf.

- Getachew, Samuel, and Geoffrey York. "Ethiopia's Latest Violence Exposes Ethnic Fault Lines, Threatening the Country's Democratic Dreams," *Globe and Mail* (Toronto), July 20, 2020. https://www.theglobeandmail.com/world/article-ethiopias-latest-violence-exposes-ethnic-fault-lines-threatening-the/.

- Kessels, Eelco, Tracey Durner, and Matthew Schwartz. "Violent Extremism and Instability in the Greater Horn of Africa: An Examination of Drivers and Responses." Global Center on Cooperative Security (2016). https://www.globalcenter.org/wp-content/uploads/2016/05/GCCS_VIOLENT-EXTREMISM_low_3.pdf.

- Selassie, Haile. *My Life and Ethiopia's Progress, 1892–1937: The Autobiography of Emperor Haile Selassie I.* Translated by Edward Ullendorff. Oxford: Oxford University Press, 1976.

- Verhoeven, Harry. "Black Gold for Blue Gold? Sudan's Oil, Ethiopia's Water and Regional Integration." Chatham House: Briefing Paper (2011). https://www.chathamhouse.org/sites/default/files/19482_0611bp_verhoeven.pdf.

BIBLIOGRAPHY

9. Spain

- Aróstegui, Julio, and Jorge Marco. *El último Frente: La Resistencia Armada Antifranquista en España, 1939–1952*. Madrid: Libros de la Catarata, 2008.

- Bown, Stephen R. *1494: How a Family Feud in Medieval Spain Divided the World in Half*. New York: Thomas Dunne Books/St. Martin's, 2012.

- Gardner, David. "Why Basques and Catalans See Independence Differently." *Financial Times*, July 12, 2019. https://www.ft.com/content/3ec93f84 -a2a1-11e9-974c-ad1c6ab5efd1.

- Garr, Arnold K. *Christopher Columbus: A Latter-Day Saint Perspective*. Provo, Utah: Religious Studies Center/Brigham Young University, 1992.

- Gorostiza, Santiago. "'There Are the Pyrenees!' Fortifying the Nation in Francoist Spain." *Environmental History* 23, no. 4 (2018): 797–823. https:// academic.oup.com/envhis/article/23/4/797/5091299.

- Latham, Andrew. "Medieval Geopolitics: The Iberian Crusades." Medievalists.net. https://www.medievalists.net/2019/03/iberian-crusades/.

- "Letters of Pope Alexander II Concerning Just Warfare Against the Forces of Muslim Iberia (1063–1064)" (2012). http://www.web.pdx.edu/~ott /hst399/Alexanderletters/index.html.

- Marco, Jorge. "Rethinking the Postwar Period in Spain: Violence and Irregular Civil War, 1939–52." *Journal of Contemporary History* 55, no. 3 (2020): 492–513. https://purehost.bath.ac.uk/ws/portalfiles/portal/190057157 /Rethinking_the_post_war_period.pdf.

- Pimenta, João, et al. "Spatially Explicit Analysis Reveals Complex Human Genetic Gradients in the Iberian Peninsula." *Nature*, May 24, 2019. https:// www.nature.com/articles/s41598-019-44121-6.

- "The President's News Conference," August 23, 1945. Harry S. Truman Library and Museum, National Archives. https://www.trumanlibrary.gov /library/public-papers/107/presidents-news-conference.

BIBLIOGRAPHY

- "Spain: Charles II." Britannica.com. https://www.britannica.com/place /Spain/Charles-II.

- "Spain Population 2020." World Population Review. https://worldpopula tionreview.com/countries/spain-population/.

- "Substantial Minorities in Some Countries Hold Negative Stereotypes About Jews." Pew Research Center. https://www.pewforum.org/2018/05/29 /nationalism-immigration-and-minorities/pf_05-29-18_religion-western -europe-01-20/.

- Webster, Jason. *Violencia: A New History of Spain; Past, Present and the Future of the West.* London: Constable, 2019.

10. Space

- "The Artemis Accords: Principles for Cooperation in the Civil Explora- tion and Use of the Moon, Mars, Comets, and Asteroids for Peaceful Purposes." Gov.uk. https://assets.publishing.service.gov.uk/government /uploads/system/uploads/attachment_data/file/926741/Artemis_Accords _signed_13Oct2020__002_.pdf.

- "Challenges to Security in Space." Defense Intelligence Agency, United States of America (2019). https://www.dia.mil/Portals/27/Documents/News /Military%20Power%20Publications/Space_Threat_V14_020119_sm.pdf.

- "45 Years Ago: Historic Handshake in Space." NASA, July 17, 2020. https://www.nasa.gov/feature/45-years-ago-historic-handshake-in-space.

- Havercroft, Jonathan, and Raymond Duvall. "Critical Astropolitics: The Geopolitics of Space Control and the Transformation of State Sovereignty." In *Securing Outer Space: International Relations Theory and the Politics of Space,* edited by Natalie Bormann and Michael Sheehan, 42–58. New York: Routledge, 2009.

- "International Space Station Facts and Figures." NASA, July 16, 2020. https://www.nasa.gov/feature/facts-and-figures.

BIBLIOGRAPHY

- Pappalardo, Joe. "A 10-Year Odyssey: What Space Stations Will Look Like in 2030." *Popular Mechanics*, June 10, 2019. https://www.popularmechanics.com/space/satellites/a27886809/future-of-iss-space-station/.

- Rader, Andrew. *Beyond the Known: How Exploration Created the Modern World and Will Take Us to the Stars.* New York: Simon & Schuster, 2019.

- Sagan, Carl. *Pale Blue Dot: A Vision of the Human Future in Space.* New York: Ballantine, 2011.

- Slann, Phillip A. "The Security of the European Union's Critical Outer Space Infrastructures." Thesis, Keele University, 2015. https://core.ac.uk/download/pdf/43759498.pdf.

- "Space Fence: How to Keep Space Safe." Lockheed Martin. https://www.lockheedmartin.com/en-us/products/space-fence.html.

Index

Page numbers of illustrations appear in italics.